Canada; the Country, Its People, Religions, Politics, Rulers, and Its Apparent Future, Being a Compendium of Travel From the Atlantic to the Pacific, the Great Lakes, Manitoba, the North-West, and British Columbia, With a Description of Their...

YALE, B.C.

ENLARGED EDITION.

CANADA;

The Country, its People, Religions, Politics, Rulers, and its apparent Future,

BEING A COMPENDIUM OF TRAVEL FROM THE

ATLANTIC TO THE PACIFIC,

The Great Lakes, Manitoba, the North-West, and British Columbia,

WITH A DESCRIPTION OF THEIR

RESOURCES, TRADE, STATISTICS, ETC., VIEWED IN ITS BUSINESS, SOCIAL AND POLITICAL ASPECTS. THE VARIOUS CITIES AND RESORTS, SALMON RIVERS, ETC.,

TOGETHER WITH THE

LEGENDS OF THE OTTAWA, THE LOWER ST. LAWRENCE, AND THE COAST. A VALUABLE AND INTERESTING BOOK FOR BOTH TRAVELLERS AND HOME FOLKS.

WITH 40 ILLUSTRATIONS, RAPIDS OF THE ST. LAWRENCE, &c.

BY CAPTAIN "MAC."

PRICE: PAPER, $1.00; CLOTH, $1.50.

Montreal:

1882.

TO

GEORGE WASHINGTON STEPHENS, M P.P.,

AN ABLE REPRESENTATIVE, A TRUTHFUL ADVOCATE
OF THE PEOPLE, AND AN HONEST MAN,

ONE OF THE FEW AND GALLANT MINORITY WHO HAVE
DEVOTED TIME, ENERGY AND TALENT IN PROTECT-
ING THE RIGHTS OF THE PEOPLE OF
THE PROVINCE OF QUEBEC,

This volume is most respectfully dedicated

BY THE AUTHOR

CANADA AND THE CANADIANS;

FROM THE ATLANTIC TO THE PACIFIC.

REVISED EDITION.

In April, 1880, I laid back in a comfortable chair at the St. Charles Hotel, New Orleans, whilst a negro boy was energetically endeavoring to put " de Crescent City polish on de shoeses," prior to my rambling at the Lake-end and around Spanish Fort. Whilst the boy was thus occupied, I fell into a reverie, and my mind seemed fully occupied in trying to decide upon which route to take during the long summer months now fast approaching. Whilst still mentally cogitating, the porter, an acquaintance with whom I had become tolerably familiar, soon brought me to a decision, for, said he : " Say, Captain, so they say you're goin' away, so you are ; which way are you goin' ? " "Well, Phelim," I answered, " I expect to go north, through Alabama, Georgia, Tennessee, Kentucky and Illinois, to Chicago ; then possibly through Michigan, and perhaps into Canada." " Oh, bedad," said Phelim, " are you goin wid thim Kanucks ? That reminds me whin I wuz there, in '65, wid Gineral O'Naille, how we loike to hev' tuck the whole cunthry from thim." This remark decided me, and I mentally determined shortly to be *en route* for Canada.

After once deciding to leave the beautiful Crescent City, it becomes quite a task to fix upon which route to take to the North, each having its own particular attractions and delights : to those who enjoy a sea

voyage a pleasant and healthful trip is offered by the
steamships of the Hudson, Cromwell, Morgan and
Alexander lines, following up the course of that remarkable ocean river, the Gulf Stream; whilst the time allowed
when calling at the sea ports of Florida, or at the City of

LEVEE NEW ORLEANS.

Havana, is amply sufficient for a general inspection and
acquaintance; and long remembered will be the remarkable beauty of the rising and setting of the sun in these
balmy lower latitudes, when

                " The glorious orb of day—
In southern climes, o'er ocean's waveless field, sinks sweetly smiling:
Not the faintest breath steals o'er the unruffled deep,
The clouds of eve reflect unmoved the lingering beam of day,
And vespers image on the western main is beautifully still."

Passing closely to the coral reefs, and again skirting the sandy beach, the journey north is pleasant and agreeable. For those who are in a hurry and who must save time there are the various all-rail routes both by the sea-board and coast lines, the inland air lines, and the roads over the mountain ranges north and west; whilst the palatial river steamers, so numerous and closely packed along the levee, bring vividly to memory the delightful journey up the Father of Waters, the great Mississippi. The trip up this river from the latitude of the sunny South to that of the frozen North is unexcelled by any in the world, whilst the enjoyment and comfort those floating palaces such as the " Great Republic," the " R. E. Le3," "Frank Pargoud, " Natchez " and others afford cannot be excelled.

Ascending the stream in the spring, the traveller follows the line of vegetation, and enjoys in succession all the products of the earth, from the golden orange, the luscious peach, mellow banana, juicy mango and dainty apricot of the South, to the hard apple and tasteless chestnut of the North. Ample time is often given to acquaint the passengers with the towns *en route*, and you remember with feelings of pleasure the quaint former capital of Louisiana (Baton Rouge), the pleasant stroll along its shady and tree-lined boulevards, the cosy City of Natchez under the Hill, the historical Vicksburg on the Bluffs—the city that was at one time thought impregnable, but whose citizens during the days of the Confederacy were called upon, like those of Paris, to endure that most terrible of seiges, the seige of famine and starvation, in addition to the scourge and terrors of war. Journeying upwards, the ruins of the fine and costly sugar houses and cotton gins are still met with at intervals on either bank of the river, and thousands of acres of valuable land are filling up with rank growths for want of cultivation, although at points and plantations where landings are made the crowds of laughing frolicsome negroes and groups of country whites, who come down to watch the boat, make the landing assist to form the idea that a vast amount of land is still being cultivated. The country here being very low, in the spring floods, and some times during the June rise, if there happens to be a crevasse in the levee, you can be landed at Chicot, on the second story of the hotel or residence, being carried by a dug-out to the platform of the cars of the L. R. M. R. and T. R. R., the speed of which road, bye-the-way, is only surpassed by Morgan's Line, from Victoria to Port Lavacca, Texas. The cars, being drawn by mules, average some 5 miles per hour.

70 miles from Chicot, lands us at Pine Bluff on the Arkansas River, thence, 90 miles further, and we arrive at the City of Roses, Little Rock, the capital of the State of Arkansas, then by the Iron Mountain road, 22 miles to Malvern, where change is made for the Hot Springs, 25 miles distant, the cars then being narrow gauge, or, as the road is familiarly called, "Diamond Joe's narrer gouge," and is certainly a gouge in fare, for the tickets are $2.50 each way, so, as the Irishman observed, "If a man's in good health sure he'll save a day's wages by walkin," whilst "dat's so, dese ere keers ought to be busted up," came from the other end of the car. Although it is probably not the proper thing to do to smile at human misery, still the scenes on those diminutive cars are constantly inciting humor. When the change is made at Malvern, the suffering and ailing of humanity from all parts of the universe who are making or the renowned Hot Springs congregate in a seemingly harmonious democratic throng, each too much engrossed

with his own ailments to care to argue upon caste or religion with his neighbor, the majority being as peevish and cross as the mythical bear; so, as rheumatic twinges are felt, such remarks become frequent as " Ouch!" " Dam all Hades!" " Oh lordy, take dem hoofs outen my back!" whilst the old man in the corner consoled himself with, " Oh, if I wuz only at home in my father's palace, bad luck to it!" whilst the consolation was offered by a fellow sufferer, ' Bedad, if you wuz, sure you cud put yer han down the chimney and undo the latch uv the doore." Soon the car, to the olfactories at least, becomes an apothecary's shop, redolent with balsams, whisky, liniment, juniper and a confusion of other well-advertised equally sure remedies for suffering.

The story of the discovery of the Hot Springs is told as follows: A Dutchman and his family were journeying with their team from Missouri to Texas, and after a day or two spree at Fort Smith continued his route through the valley. Having punished a considerable quantity of Missouri Red Eye he was naturally very dry on arrival at the Magnesia Spring, but seeing a clear crystal-looking pool in the rock he said, " Schonney, hold on dem mules vile your olt Fader gets a drink uv wasser. The old man got down, and bending over the basin attempted a good swallow, but in a moment rising with flushed face and streaming eyes he dashed the water off with both hands and shouted," Schonney, drive on dem mules. Hell is but tree miles from dis place."

But soon the journey is performed, and the sufferers landed a mile away from the Springs, which necessitates still another transfer by car or bus to the town of Hot Springs. The town or village consists of one street (Valley street) some mile and a half or two miles in length, and is well protected by the surrounding hills from sudden or severe changes of weather. Hotels, boarding houses, general stores and gambling shops are numerous, and situated chiefly on the south-western side, the north-eastern being the one from which bursts forth the hot water of the different springs; thence the mineral water is conveyed in pipes across the road to the public drinking fountains, and also to the bath rooms of the hotels. On the side of the hill situated above the Magnesia Spring is the Pool of Bethesda, familiarly called the Ral Hole, free for all who are afflicted, and numerous camps and tents are erected for the accommodation of those who are too poor to reside at the hotels and boarding houses. Of the hotels the Arlington, French's and the St. Louis are about the best; and their storerooms, piled with crutches, sticks and other adjuncts of recent sufferers, bear unspeakable but earnest testimony to the efficacy of the healing waters. In undergoing the bath (the patient gets one each day) the water at first is from 90° to 100° F., but in a few days the heat is increased to from 140° to 160° F., so that the invalid emerging from his 10 or 15 minutes cooking resembles, in color at least, a boiled lobster or a ripe tomato, whilst the truthful colored deacon who rubs him down entertains him with the remark, " dat we had a man frum way up North somewhar dat we had to bile free weeks befor we got it outen him."

Taking the train again, 120 miles east across the State of Arkansas (that will at no very distant period become one of the finest grain and fruit growing states in the Union), and we are landed at Hopefield, opposite the City of Memphis, Tennessee. This formerly thriving city that a few years ago suffered so severely from the visitation of yellow fever has now undergone a most thorough and complete change for the better : miles of sewer pipes are laid under ground; the swampy lands around the old Memphis and Charleston Depot filled in and drained; the negro shanties and wooden houses, where fever could find a lurking-place, burned down; the Nicholsen block pavement, that breeder of disease, torn up and cremated; and the experience of the past two years demonstrates conclusively that the germs of the dread disease have been entirely eradicated from the city; and once more its wharves are the scene of life and activity—the various lines of steamers continually calling, and lining its levee, recall the old-time bustle and confusion. So, coming back in memory for a day or two longer, we linger in our loved city, idly wandering and enjoying its attractions, roaming Canal street, probably the finest, widest and best kept street on the continent. Driving on the shell road to Lake Ponchartrain—a road equalling the famed Champs Elysee of Paris or the beach at Galveston, revelling at the Spanish fort, and on the old battlefield, fishing, lounging and boating during the day, whilst evenings are spent amidst the excitement of the masquerade. Still but a wandering son, thy sunny Southern land we love; and, although for a while an exile from thy bright clime, still the heart longs and aches for the time of its return to the smiling faces and true hearts of friends of the long ago !

During the season New Orleans presents a scene of, seemingly, the wildest confusion : at every hour, night and day, shipping from every portion of the world, steamboats from the great rivers and their tributaries, are constantly arriving or departing, whilst work goes on incessantly up town; the long freight trains loaded with grain, cotton and sugar, come steadily rolling in. At present the population is some 220,000, and is yearly on the increase.

Bidding adieu to New Orleans, we are soon passing its summer resorts of Biloxi and Mississippi City. In the spring a journey through the Southern States is most delightful and invigorating, and, with the hearty welcome the traveller receives at each new stopping-place, the anxiety of the citizens for news, both political and general, from other States, stamp the people as being both hospitable and highly intelligent. Stopping respectively at Mobile, the coming seaport of the Gulf; then again at Montgomery—the first capital of the Southern Confederacy and the prettiest laid out town in Alabama—at present containing some 25,000 inhabitants, pleasantly situated on the banks of the Alabama river. In its streets are several artesian wells, that supply clear cold water even in the hottest weather, whilst the country· surrounding is excellent for farming. What a contrast is the present aspect of the city to that presented in the fall of 1860, when Jefferson Davis was nominated as the president of the new-born Confederacy, representing 6 millions of Southern people; and how many changes has it seen from those wild, stirring and heated scenes that took place on the raising of the flag until the time when force decreed the banner should be forever laid aside.

> " Furl that banner! True 'tis gory,
>   But 'tis wreathed around with glory,
>   And 'twill live in song and story,
>   Though its folds are in the dust;
>
>   For its fame on brightest pages,
>   Penned by poets and by sages,
>   Shall go sounding down the ages,—
>   Furl its folds, for now we must."

Again a few hours' run, and we arrive at the flourishing Gate City in Georgia, which, in spite of the havoc made by war, is now fast rivalling New England with its manufactures and industries. Remaining over at the Kimball house, we took advantage of the opportunity to hear that sensational preacher, Talmage, who was to lecture in the evening. Although having heard him on several former occasions in Brooklyn, both on his Chinese Question, the Night Side of New York, &c., the idea was formed that he would be both liberal and eloquent, but his lecture proved very tame and uninteresting, until his final peroration of his prayer, winding up as follows: "Oh Lord, when in that day we all assemble before thee, may each of these Georgians wear upon his head a crown of glory, and hold in his right hand a star." "That's taffy," said an old farmer close by, "to give these goober grabblers a little crown for a cent is all right, if it fits well, but, fancy, a man must have a hand like the hand of Providence, and a back like the back of Atlas to support the smallest star in the orrory. I reckon they would soon be sick of toting that star around."

Hurrying on we reach Chattanooga, the Mountain City of Tennessee, and there were treated to an unusual sight for a citizen of the sunny South. A first-class snow storm was in progress, and the mountains surrounding the city were covered with the fleecy white crystals. Lookout Mountain looked especially grand and majestic, clothed in her winter drapery, but the transition from summer to winter was so short, twelve hours only, that it seemed hardly realistic, and, but for the sensation of cold experienced, we could hardly reconcile ourselves to the fact.

From Chattanooga we were fortunate enough to embark on the first passenger train on the New Cincinnati Southern Railroad, at that time under the manage-

ment of Mr. T. C. Gabbitt. The road runs through
some of the wildest scenery in America, and is certainly
one of the triumphs of engineering science. Its construction has cost the City of Cincinnati alone some $13,000,000.
The High Bridge over the Cumberland River is said to be
the highest trestle in the world, being over 160 feet above
the bed of the river, and certainly demonstrates to what
perfection iron bridge building can be brought, for in crossing the feeling of the traveller is that he is gliding through
mid-air, and is really without " visible means of support."
It was stated that should the passenger drop a rock or
piece of coal, whilst the cars were in the centre of the
Bridge, the train would arrive at the other side before the
missile struck the water. Of course there were plenty of
experimenters, but results were unsatisfactory.

Arriving at Lexington, the Capital of Kentucky, sampling
the white wine of the country, its famous sour mash, it was
but a short trip to the " Falls City," Louisville, prettily
situated on the banks of the Ohio, about 120 miles south-
west from Cincinnati, thence through the fertile States of
Indiana and Illinois, to the future great metropolis of the
West, St Louis. This city lies in N. lat. 28° 37′, and long.
west (from Greenwich) 90° 16′; distant from New York City
1,050 miles. Is the chief port and business centre of the
State of Missouri, which State lies between 30° and 40°
30′ N. lat. and 11° 45′ and 18° 50′ W. long. (from Washington), and is most prolific in its production of woods and
minerals, lead, iron, copper and coal mines being actively worked, and contributing much to the wealth of the
State. The taxable property alone, not including the City of
St. Louis, is estimated at $500,000,000, and the yield of
wheat some $45,000,000 bushels. Its elevation above

tide water is 461 feet. Frosts commence about the middle of November and continue until March, giving some 115 days of cold for a winter; its summers are short and hot. In 1775 the city was a mere fur-trading post, with but 800 inhabitants; in 1817 it had increased to 5000. In 1850 it contained 40,000 inhabitants, but now is a busy hive of human industry, and numbers over 500,000 people. Its commerce is great and constantly increasing, the trade of the Mississippi and Missouri centering at its port, whilst no less than eighteen trunk lines centre in the city. Its industries are both staple and enterprising, whilst its public buildings and parks command the admiration of the entire western people. Lafayette Park and Smith's Garden, the latter owned by an English resident, rivals some of the boasted parks and gardens of the South of England. The bridge across the Mississippi River connecting the States of Missouri and Illinois was erected by Capt. James Eads of Mississippi Jetty fame in the South, and is a most substantial structure. The cost of the building in all, with the approaches on either side, amounted to some $1,350,-000, and for the privilege of crossing in the cars passengers are taxed 25c. in addition to the ordinary railroad fare. The taxable property of the city in 1879 was $132,785,-450, although it has considerably increased since then.

Breweries, both lager and beer, are numerous, Anheauser alone having an establishment that would compare favorably with Bass or Allsopp; whilst the American Wine Company, for the manufacture of "Cook's Imperial" Champagne, possess cellars that would be creditable to Mumm of Reims, or Cliquot of Epernay. Under the guidance of the genial secretary, who is untiring in his efforts to please and entertain his visitors, we wandered through their fine vaults or cellars, where the manufacture of champagne is carried on, and, as the process may be interesting to the reader, I will attempt to describe it. These vaults, which are claimed to be the largest in the United States, occupy

BRIDGE AT ST. LOUIS.

the entire space between Cass and Garrison avenues, and are divided underground into various departments, in the first of which we see the large casks of this season's juice as it comes from the grape press, the wines from each district being kept separate. Then we notice the large vats in which the wines from Ohio and those from Southern Missouri and other favored localities are blended. The wine is then racked off into bottles, well corked and arranged with their necks downwards in rows on *pupitres* or stands, where they undergo for several months the moving process in order to settle all the sediment from the wine on the cork. After viewing the labyrinth of underground vaults, filled with thousands of bottles of wine admirably binned, we return once more to the light of day, passing through walls of barrels of last year's vintage, still in the wood. We then pass on to the finishing room ; here we find, seated in a row, each before his special machine, skilled workmen ready to give the last touch to the bottle before it passes into the hands of the consumer. Workman No. 1, called a *dégorger*, had to practically solve the difficulty of expelling from the bottle the accumulated impurities lying on the cork, and forced into that position by the skill and watchfulness of the movers or remeurs; this he accomplishes by a skilful withdrawal of the cork, when the force of the explosion forced out, with a wonderfully small loss of wine and gas, the obnoxious deposit. This done the bottle is passed on to workman No. 2, who proceeds to infuse into the wine a small but fixed percentage of a luscious nectar, technically called a liqueur, the quantity being determined according to the taste of the market, thus solving the mystery of "Dry" or "Sweet" Champagne. Workman No. 3 then proceeds to replace with a new cork the *bouchon de service*, powerful machinery compressing the yielding wood, and inserting into the narrow neck of the bottle a cork that appears quite out of proportion to the duty required. Workman No. 4 is the stringer who skilfully adjusts the twine, making, by physical force, the cork assume the mushroom appearance with which we are all so familiar. No. 5 then wires the bottle. No. 6 then deftly adjusts the gold or silver leaf; and to No. 7 belongs the duty of affixing the label or brand of the firm, thus completing the work, and leaving the bottles ready. for the packing room, prior to exportation for champagne drinkers found the wide world over.   In New York city the manufacturers do not go to all that trouble; they merely procure Jersey cider, condemned wine and sulphuric acid, sweeten it, and charge it with carbonic acid gas like a bottle of soda water, label the bottle, and place it on the market, thus saving both time and expense, and materially assisting the spirit merchants in their sales of brandy to relieve the pains consequent on the absorption of a bottle of New York champagne. Other wines, such as Catawba, Virginia Seed- ling, Concord and Clarets, the native wines of the west, are stored in immense quantities awaiting a market.

From St. Louis, stopping but at Springfield, Illinois, to . pay our respects at the shrine of the martyred president, Abraham Lincoln, and to meet the jovial, good-natured ex-Governor, J. M. Palmer, and to wish him success at the nomination in Cincinnati, for which the Palmer Club and his friends throughout the country were actively working, a twelve hours run across the fertile prairies of the State of Illinois brings us to that energetic, pros- perous and bustling city, the grain emporium of the world, Chicago.   The city claims 137,616 more in population than St. Louis, but the latter city most strenuously denies the claim, and offers to prove in every way imaginable her own supremacy in the matter of population.   It is stated that such interest is taken by the people in this matter that the sight of an emigrant train with women and children bound through to St. Louis is enough to make a Chicago man turn green with envy.   The site of the present city was located first in 1804, and a fort called Fort Dearborn, erected, afterwards destroyed in 1856. The city was incorporated in the year 1837, with a population of a little more than 4,000. From that time onward its growth was marvelous, until checked by the terrible fire which

CHICAGO FROM THE LAKE.

occurred in October, 1871, occasioning a loss of property estimated at $190,000,000, destroying 17,450 buildings, rendering homeless 98,500 persons, and leaving a death record of over 200. During this terrible calamity the sympathies of the entire civilized world were aroused, and contributions

2

and supplies were forwarded to the stricken city from all parts of the earth. Two years afterwards, in 1874, another fire, although not so disastrous in its results, occurred, but to-day all trace of ruin is obliterated, and the city itself stands forth, a monument of men's pride and energy. Being

LINCOLN PARK, CHICAGO.

located at the mouth of the Chicago and Calumet rivers, and on the Western shore of Lake Michigan; its situation as a lake port is unrivalled: during the past year the clearances from Chicago alone have been more than any three ports in the United States, New York City included. South Park,

Lincoln Park, and Haverly's are its chief recreation grounds; some forty-five Railroad lines centre in the city, and its stock-yards and pens, for the shipment of cattle, cover

CALUMET RIVER, CHICAGO.

146 acres. Being the metropolitan centre of trade for the west, business agencies, commercial agencies, Eastern branches, etc., etc., are to be met with in any number; some

of these business agencies profess to protect the business man in his credits, etc., informing him whom to trust and whom to refuse. A young pushing representative of a close-fisted firm, on his return from a business-trip is sometimes confronted with such a report as, "he's seemingly at work all the time, but he spends a good deal on the road." Of course the employer has the edge on that young man, and he is set back a year or so. A salesman for one of these agencies enters a business office, and a colloquy such as follows occurs : " Are you Mr. Jacques B. Scooter ? " he asks, " I am," is the reply. "Then I would like you to subscribe to the Agency reports of Messrs. Slyman, Skinem & Doem ; the cost is but one hundred dollars each year, entitling to two volumes and weekly reports, whilst for $25 more you can have a traveller's letter of introduction to our agencies, so as to obtain our latest reports of the men, their habits and standing, with whom you come in contact. You see we furnish information to our subscribers, but of course we only give it in homœopathic doses, like justice to a work-man in Quebec, especially so if the one enquired about is a city subscriber of ours. You being a newly established firm, I've called also to give you a rating, and improve your credit, also to inform myself if you are the J. B. Scooter, late president and treasurer of the Golden Bubble Mining Company, as we have an enquiry from a party East who invested somewhat heavily in the stock.". "Oh yes," replies the party accosted, " I have heard of your business proclivi-ties, here's $50 for yourself, and you can put our office down for four of your volumes, and, by the way, just let those anxious enquirers know that J. B. Scooter, formerly of Silver Cliff, went into the cattle export business, and was lost at sea." "Oh, certainly," was the reply, and the way that agent classed the office as A A X X 1 wasn't slow. The scene changes to Dutch Pete's, where two enterprising citizens are seen quaffing their beer, and concocting a new lay, for the benefit of the fraternity and themselves in particular. "Well, how goes it?" queries Sam. "Bully, you bet," is the answer; "you see I guyed the gillie up to the agencies, and I slung him a half a century, and he give it all away; the cashier (the masher) of Grab & Dodgeout, the contractors, is going up to pay off the hands to-morrow. Well his nibs and me got acquainted and I slung the lush around pretty .lively; so I put Lady Liz and Parson Joe, for the Pullman, and if they don't stagg, Miner Sam and Manitoba Megs will meet him at St. Paul, then if he don't come down, they'll slug him A century each to the 2 D's that work that end of the road will fix the biz, so I say, fill em up agin, and long life to the Agency men!"

Still hurrying onward, twelve hours from Chicago, and we reach the thriving city of the Straits, Detroit, the river alone separating the State of Michigan from the domain of her Imperial Majesty, Queen Victoria. It is probably at this point the visitor first notices the wide difference between the enterprise of the Americans, and the seeming apathy of the Canadians. Although Windsor was the terminus for many years of the Great Western Railroad and the nearest town to the Western States, still enterprise seems dead, and the ennui of the people so pronounced that they seem disinclined to make any exertion in their own behalf or for the advancement of the town they live in; there, however, is some reason for this: the younger people all cast a longing eye towards Uncle Sam's possessions, and hope to some day explore for themselves the wonders that are so freely talked about on the return of those who have visited the States and settled there—for of the numbers who yearly visit their relatives, but few ever express a desire to return to live, whilst the older people don't care, so long as they have enough for the time being, for, as one old gentleman remarked : " What is the use of " the Dominion Government expending vast sums of money " for emigration if we can't keep either the laborers or " domestics over here ; and it is my belief that Canada is " just becoming a recruiting ground for the United States, " and will eventually become annexed to that country; " for emigrants discern the difference between fair " speeches and champagne in Europe, and hard labor and " poverty here." Still visitors and the public generally, on arriving at the terminus, as it were, of Uncle Sam's domains, naturally cross over, expecting to know something of the habits and peculiarities of their neighbors on the Northern boundary, so numbers of them sojourn at Windsor, or even into the interior of the Province. Although, to a certain extent, there are symptoms of a business rivalry and jealousy between the City of Detroit and the Town of Windsor, still for comfort, cleanliness and a genuine attention to the wants of its guests, the Crawford House, under the management of Mr. C. C. Green, stands pre-eminent, whilst the courtesy of its clerks, Messrs. A. C. Walters and Kilburn Pierce, assist materially in establishing a name and reputation for the hostelry at Windsor equal to any ,in the Provinces. Constant communication is kept up by an admirably conducted ferry service, the steamers are commodious, the employees attentive, such a contrast to the Suspension Bridge, Prescott, or the river towns below ! For a time the idea was prevalent that the Wabash would ,purchase the Great Western road, but that enterprising corporation now having perfected their arrangements constitute a trunk line from Boston, New York and the cities of the East to Chicago, draining as they pass through Canada a good proportion of the trade of the Province of

SOLDIER'S MONUMENT, DETROIT.

Ontario, which Province, at the last census, numbered some 1,913,460 inhabitants.

Crossing once more to Detroit, which in the year 1845 contained a population of but 10,948, but at the present time numbers some 132,720 persons, the taxable property of the city alone amounts to $5,859,488.25.

We wander through its spacious thoroughfares, admiring its public buildings, paying a visit to its excellent Free library, which deserves more than a passing notice, being not only a popular public educator but the finest institution of its kind in the West. The Library was founded through legislative enactment more than forty-five years ago granting a proportion of the fines of the criminal courts throughout the State for the erection and support of libraries in each district. These fines falling off so rapidly owing to the diminishing number of criminals, the Legislature levied a special library tax of 1-5 of a mill on the dollar. The cost of the edifice was $137,000; it contains 43,000 volumes exclusive of pamphlets, has a free membership without fee or subscription, and is well patronized by the working and mercantile class. Under the superintendence of Mr. Henry Gilman, the library has become a model of neatness and order; it is pointed to with pride by the residents, and is quoted as worthy of being patterned after by other institutions of its class. It seems hardly possible that the people across the river could knowingly have allowed such an opportunity of building a western terminus to slip through their fingers, but the fact is apparent to each visitor. Of course we called at the *Free Press* office, occupying Em Quad's time, and viewing the notable and heterogeneous collection of curiosities, his ghastly relics of the battlefield and the numerous presents sent from all parts of the universe by admiring friends to Brother Gardner, the worthy president of the Lime Kiln Club. Some little chat with Signor Max on human nature, and then of course "Bijah" was visited. Although the old man is tolerably well advanced in years, and since his episode

with the widow, care has been actively engaged in plough-
ing furrows, but he has been promoted from the Central
Station to one nearer the outskirts of the city, affording a
better view of the country and a purer and clearer atmosphere, still he carries his years and his troubles with grace
and unostentation. Being of a kindly and good-natured
disposition he bears the infliction of numerous callers
without outward manifestation of pain, and about the only
thing that really "riles" the old man is when a visitor,
who happens to have travelled a few thousand miles,
solemnly asseverates that he undertook the pilgrimage to
silently weep and piously gaze on the old man's feet, then
the thunder cloud darkens on Bijah's classic brow, and visitors know the levée for the day is over, so they quietly
pass out, indulging in feelings of pity for the next unfortunate who takes refuge until morning at the station.

Whilst noticing the enterprise of the public journals, and
the persistency with which each resident seems to advocate and advance the interests of this model city, it should
be stated that Mr. Silas Farmer, an old resident of the
State, and thoroughly familiar with its growth, has for the
past seven years been actively engaged in gathering material for his forthcoming work on the " History of Detroit."
The work is most thorough and complete, embracing
almost every incident of moment, from the earliest settlement of the post until the present time, with maps, illus-
trations and charts, depicting the changes under the
French, the English, and American Regime. Mr. Farmer
has almost made his history a life work, and looks forward with confidence to its being read with interest in
every land where the fair name of Detroit has established
a reputation amongst its people. Mr. Lewis has also been

collecting data, and will publish a history of the war, and from the numerous enquiries and encouragements it bids fair to become the most popular as well as most truthful of any work on that subject.

Taking the night boat "City of Detroit," we enjoy a pleasant two hours sail down the river before entering Lake Erie, then turning in enjoy an excellent night's rest whilst making the run of 110 miles to Cleveland, a city of some 60,000 inhabitants, and situated on the Southern shore of Lake Erie, arriving in time for an early breakfast at the Kennard, under the proprietorship of D. McClasky. This city being a central point for shipment its business is large. The city is well laid out and pleasantly situated, whilst at night its leading thoroughfares and square are lighted by the electric light.

Taking the cars of the A. & G. W. R. R. we arrive at Buffalo, the Lake outlet of the Erie and New York Central railways. A twenty-two mile run further on brings us to the famous Falls of Niagara, but, after crossing the Suspension bridge, we conclude to stop at one of the fine hotels, so numerous on the American side.

Whilst at the Spencer House it was my good fortune to become acquainted with Sir Arthur Kennedy, who, with his amiable daughter and attendants, were doing the Falls *en route* from Australia to London. Sir Arthur, who was the Governor General of Queensland, has been an official in Her Majesty's service some thirty-eight years, and was now on his return to his native country. I found him a studious and close observer of human nature, agreeable, and a perfect fund of information and anecdote. His satire on the selfishness of Canadian politicians and its grasping capitalists was certainly pungent and pointed.

The contrast between the magnificent hotels on the American side, their reasonable charges for the accommodation offered, and the charges on the opposite is most marked. The hotels on the Canada side affording a good view of the Falls are few in number, and comprise the "Table Rock," "Prospect House," "Clifton House," which of late years has been generally run by speculators, the "Brunswick," and possibly another. The following, published in the last edition for the information of intending visitors, is a correct copy of a one day's board bill on the Canada side :

Room 115,———1880.
Mr.———   Dr.
Board 1 Dy., Lodg., Bkft. & Din...........7.00
 · Dinner claret, $1.50; Extras, $1.15...$2.65
  Bus 1 way, 50c. ; 1 way, 25c............ 75
                                    ————
                                    $10.40

But when the mild-eyed visitor expostulated, and informed the clerk that he but arrived at 5 o'clock a.m. and would be away again by 5 o'clock p.m., too early for either tea or supper, he was assured by that white-bosomed, diamond-pinned gentleman, "that it was all right;" the charges were all the same, whether meals were taken or not, and, as a matter of great condescension, the visitor was confidently informed that the next time he came to the hotel they would give him supper free of all charge, which promise could with safety be made, knowing well that the visitor seldom returns a second time during the season. The charges are ordinary ones for every-day guests on other occasions ; extraordinary charges are fully equal to the demands, for the average pile of the stranger is well gauged. No wonder that people generally no longer sigh to "do" the beauties of Niagara for the summer, for the only way to travel would be the Kaintuckians : pay the bill but kill the clerk, and so check high-handed despotism for the future.

Niagara Falls, once so noted and well patronized has, it seems, of late years, fallen into disrepute with the summer travellers, and the cause is still left unexplained, although numerous theories are advanced; whether it originates from the grasping propensities of the hotel proprietors, or whether it is a natural consequence of the scarcity of really good views without large payments is one of the facts for the public themselves to determine; or, possibly the younger generation have an idea that it may become international property and become a Park-like rendezvous for the citizens of both countries and the sights enjoyed without expense. A New Yorker, quoting his visit, says : "The first impression of the traveller arriving at Niagara is profound astonishment, that so many distinct and separate sights with corresponding fees could have been found in any one place. As far as discovered up to the time of writing, they are as follows :

Goat Island	$0.50
Cave of the Winds	1.00
	$1.50

Prospect Park, Admission	$0.25
" Art Gallery "	25
Inclined Railway	25
Ferry to Canada	25
Shadow of the Rock	1.00
	$2.00

↓To go behind Horse Shoe Fall........................	1.00
Museum..	50
Burning Spring...	50
Lundy's Lane Battle Ground............................	50
Whirlpool Rapids...	50
Whirlpool...	50
To walk across Suspension Bridge.....................	25
Railway Suspension Bridge.............................	25
	$7.50

Besides these fees there are, for the lovers of old English customs, two toll gates on the Canada side, which the traveller, of course, pays in addition to his $1.50 per hour, the legal rate for the hire of a hack; but that patronage has fallen off most lamentably of late is a fact well attested, although I was assured by one searcher after truth, a theological student, that a great sensation would be produced next season, that would once more awaken an interest in the Falls, for the leading inhabitants had subscribed to a fund for bringing scientific men to visit in a body, and as for sometime past carters and others have been actively engaged in dumping rock, both in the waters above and below, it will soon be scientifically demonstrated to a confiding public, and the figures accurately given, to prove how fast far-famed Niagara is receding towards Buffalo, and the sight of the immense pile of rock dumped from one end of Goat Island will be ample proof to demonstrate the astonishing foresight of the learned gentleman.

The effect at night when the rays of the vari-colored electric light are cast over the Falls from the Park is one of striking beauty, and makes up in a measure for some of the many disappointments experienced, whilst the quietude of the surroundings and the solemnity of the mighty rush of waters leads to earnest and devout contemplation of the wonderful and terrible in nature. A walk across the New Suspension Bridge, almost in the midst of the vapor arising from the Horseshoe, and a ramble along the Niagara River to Clifton, two miles below, is really delightful and pleasant.

The village of Clifton was formally the Eastern terminus of the G. W. R. of Canada, but it now crosses the Suspension Bridge and connects with the New York Central Railway, thus forming a continuous route East to New York and the New England seaboard. This village, together with the village of Suspension Bridge on the United States side, and the Falls on both sides of the line, are the location of the Custom House Officers, who are naturally very vigilant in the prosecution of their duty in the interests of their respective Governments. But the locality is also the stamping ground of a class of men known as "dogs," or in other words detective or agency informers, men who are banded together, with their signs, counters, etc., and who make money by various questionable ways and devices, and who are aided in part by their patrons, even so far, it is stated, that a portion of Government funds go to support these "thugs" or informers, whereas it is this class of men who should be well looked after by the Governments on both sides of the line, for instead of detection becoming a preventative, it rapidly becomes the nursery of crime and the shield of criminals. Among this class, to "put up a job on a man" is considered quite an achievment, and a matter worthy of emulation. No sooner does a visitor arrive at one of the numerous hotels than he is "spotted," and should he be at all convivial in his habits, then the word is passed to the " gang," and he is followed, dogged and crowded, until out of sheer desperation he pays something to escape the trap he finds laid. Should he cross the bridge and be suspected of having money, then the word is passed along the line and over the borders, and the " dogs let loose," and the manner in which these " dogs give themselves away " is certainly ludicrous to the subject if he has sense enough to penetrate their meaning. And, therefore, if we drift through life in the midst of secrets, and are encompassed with mysteries, an observing mind knows to a certain extent what is taking place in the atmosphere that surrounds us, and the relation it has with our minds is to assist in more fully developing the feeling of distrust and suspicion.

Seeing a gentleman spend a little money on the American side, and then crossing apparently without baggage, is enough and he is "spotted." Taking the cars he will generally find himself followed by three strangers: the apparently laboring man, with a bottle and empty valise, the fresh-water sailor and the shabby genteel. These three worthies range themselves on either side, and as near as possible to the stranger, and then commences the system. After several ineffectual attempts to enter into conversation, they commence an interchange of words, apparently between themselves, but talking *at* the stranger, such as, " Is he good "—" Wife," always disjointed fragments, the key to which is in their own possession—" played "—" Emigrant " —" Did he stop first floor "—" Cully, he's a slouch "—" work him "—" Daresn't cross "—" Straight "—" Cash "—"See him with taffy." Then should the stranger, thinking he was in with " a hard crowd," or had fallen into bad hands, attempt to conciliate " the gang," then, indeed, is he to be pitied, for no sooner does one withdraw than he telegraphs the word that "a soft snap is on board," and almost at the next station he meets another crowd, well posted, so that, if rascals are inclined to cross the line they had better confess before leaving, and not defer until after being harassed like the Western defaulter, who originally appropriated $500, was followed by two Chicago detectives, and disgorged $400 to them as the price of his liberty; was almost immediately assailed by another, to whom he parted with $300; but when the third commenced his attack out of sheer despondency he went back, confessed his fault, and chose rather to go to prison than to be so hounded. It may possibly work very well in the case of criminals from justice; but when each passenger or traveller is given to understand that he is suspected of being nothing but a thief or a rascal, with the only honest men (?) those watching him, then it is about time that some reform along the borders was indulged in, even should it result in annexation itself to either country. At the hotels in some of the border towns these parties will parade before the door, or scrape a casual acquaintance at the bar, or on the street, and with one hand behind them inform the suspect that "possession is nine points of the law," "and they are for sale." It is from this class that Guarantee Societies, detectives and agencies obtain their information as to men and character, that sometimes results in the blighting or tarnishing of a young man's name or prospects for life, and on which testimony, as a chief remarked on oath at trial, that he was prepared to go on the witness stand and swear that such information gathered was the truth, the whole truth, and nothing but the truth, so help him God! Is an oath taken by such a class of men worth the

time spent in subscribing to it? Or is the poor victim
convicted on such obtained testimony entitled to any pity
or sympathy from the public at large? Is not every man
who is thought to possess a dollar liable to become a
victim of the avarice, cupidity, or even spite, of such people.
At the bar should they be treated sociably then there is
every probability of being "railroaded," but should no
notice be taken, and they, smarting under the mistaken
impression formed regarding the stranger, then loud and
pointed talk is indulged in, and remarks such as : "He'll pay
for giving the boys this racket," "you bet this excursion's
charged;" and, finally, when the fact was discovered that
the stranger was a business·man, it was then, "Can we
sell him?" "we can't drive him," and when the answer
came. "Oh, he's too strong," the resolve was "then let's
give him away," and when these self-constructed guardians
of a man's honesty think it necessary or advisable to take
away his character, they try to do it and "no mistake." Now to "give a man away" in their parlance
means to ruin his prospects, or to denounce him; so the
disappointed "thugs" hurry off to some of their friends,
and enlist the aid of such as reside in the town, who commence at once to convince all that he aint no use to any
body, and these gentry with their hangers-on, both male
and female, follow the business man from store to store,
generally one entering with the stranger, the others carrying on an animated conversation at the doorway, passing
such comments as "He's a bad un," "You bet." "He's
caused a good deal of trouble, but he'll be fixed," "they
got him this time," with other inferences of like nature
so that, if the stranger even stands the pressure, he finds
that, by the time he is ready to leave town, he has

acquired quite an unsavory character at the hands of these gentry.

Now is it not fully time that either or both Governments should institute some enquiry into the actions of such a class of men as these, who both are perpetrators and protectors of crime, and assume the charge of all citizens who may come within their ban. The Government Secret Service, for the support of which, with the Dominion and North-West mounted police, the people annually pay some $355,945.35, may be well enough, and, under the control of Chief John O'Neil, is most creditably managed, but the fostering of this so-called system of private detection is bringing odium on the citizens of both borders; and were I a juryman, and the evidence alone to consist of the testimony of these sellers of men, then I for one would never convict.

Seven miles below, on the American side, is Lewiston, opposite which is Queenston, on whose heights is erected " Brock's Monument," commemorative of the early struggle for independence. Thence across the lower river to the village of Niagara, some sixteen miles below, and on the borders of Lake Ontario. This town is one of the oldest in the Province of Ontario, and was in former days the seat of Government. Here we found rest and quietness, good fishing—both black bass, herring and white fish in abundance—quiet, and seemingly contented, people, and moderate charges, a consummation most devoutly desired by all summer travellers. And were tourists aware of the many advantages that are offered by this almost forgotten little town, of the pleasant sights and trips on the lake that can be indulged in, and the *real* enjoyment obtained from a short stay, visitors' would flock here in thou-

sands, instead of passing by almost without a notice.
But to enjoy a week's rest, and to catch the fish
yourself for meals, and find them served on the hotel
table, piping hot, thirty minutes after they have left the
water, is an experience worth miles of travel. The town,
although so near the great highways of travel, is completely
isolated, but still containing several good hotels a conservative class of patrons annually resort here. The "Queen's
Royal," owned by the Queen's of Toronto, is an elegant
hostelry, and during the season is well filled. Business—
the little that is attempted—follows the same routine from
year to year; no energy is evinced, and consequently no
desire for improvements. Here the lone fisherman is
found in his primitive state, and even the bustling business man after a short residence generally busies himself
by endeavoring to forget his worldly education and enjoy
the universal quiet of the surroundings.

Opposite to the ruins of old Fort George and on the
American side, some seven miles below Lewiston, stands
Fort Niagara, silent, grim and sentinel-like, to guard the
entrance to the river in the interests of Uncle Sam. It is
stated that a Frenchman, one M. De Salle, enclosed the
spot with palisades in the year 1679, and a fort was
erected in 1725, which was taken by the British in
1759, and they held possession until the year 1796, when
it was evacuated and given up to the United States.
But on the 19th December, 1814, it was again
taken by the British, who held it until March, 1815,
when it was finally surrendered to the Americans.
The fort is very strong, being of regular construction,
and mounting many guns, with stone towers at the west,
south-west and south angles, and is now under the

command of Capt. J. L. Tiernan, who has seen such active service on the plains and in the far west, and who at present is resting on his laurels in peace and quietness, which must contrast strongly with his lately adventurous life, but who in time of danger would be probably wider awake than to allow such a sacrifice of life as that permitted by Capt. Leonard, whose command were mercilessly butchered in December, 1814, by the *Christian* soldiers of a *Christian* king. The attack by the British on the night of December 19th, 1814, is thus chronicled: "The attacking force comprised the 100th Regiment, the Grenadiers, companies of the first and the flank companies of the 41st, with some artillerymen, the whole under the command of Col. Murray of the 100th. Bateaux having been secretly conveyed overland from Burlington Beach to a point about four miles up the British side of the river, the troops silently left camp about ten o'clock at night, concealed their march under cover of the adjacent woods, embarked without noise, and landed undiscovered on the opposite side, whence they descended cautiously towards the fort. At that time Youngston, a village about two miles from the fort, served as an outpost, and was garrisoned by a small detachment from the fort. The attacking party thought it necessary to surprise this outpost without alarming the main body; so a picked number were sent in advance, followed closely by the remainder of the attacking party. When they arrived in Youngston, some of the former crept up stealthily to the window and peeped in; they saw a party of officers engaged at cards. 'What are trumps?' asked one of the Americans. 'Bayonets are trumps,' answered one of the peepers, breaking the window and entering with his companions, whilst the remainder of the detachment surrounding the house rushed into it, and bayoneted the whole of its defenseless inmates, that none might escape to alarm the fort. Not a shot was fired on either side, the sentries having retired into the building to shelter themselves from the extreme cold, giving them no time for resistance, and therefore allowing their assailants to finish their work of human destruction in grim silence. Resuming their march the attacking party drew near the fort, not a word was spoken, the muskets carried squarely so the bayonets may not clash; the ice and crusted snow crackled beneath their tread, but the sound was borne backward on the gusts of a northeast wind, when suddenly the charger of Col. Hamilton neighed loudly, and was answered by a horse in a stable not far off from the front gate. The force instantly halted, expecting to hear an alarm suddenly given, and the sound of drums and bugles, and of the garrison rushing to their posts, but all remained quiet; the sentries, crouching in their boxes, take the neigh of the charger for that of some horse strayed from its farm house, or from some neighboring hamlet, and they felt no inclination to shiveringly explore the thick darkness of a moonless, wintry night. The approaching force, finding all was still, put itself in motion, went hastily and silently forward, and the crisis was near. The 'forlorn hope' was commanded by Lieut. Dawson and led by Sergeant Spearman. Halting about twenty-five yards from the gate, the Sergeant strode onward, and strange to say found the wicket open. The sentry, hearing some one approach, issued from his box and asked, 'Who comes there?' Spearman answered, at the same time introducing his shoulder through the half-opened wicket, 'I guess, Mr., I come from Youngston.' The sentry, perceiving from his accoutrements and actions that he is an enemy, turned in-

wards, exclaiming, 'The Brit—' the poor fellow said no
more, Spearman's bayonet was in his side. The Sergeant then
called the 'forlorn hope,' which swiftly entered, followed
by the column; the light company of the 100th made a rapid
circuit, and escaladed, and the whole attacking force in a
moment were inside the fort. Once inside they uttered a
terrific yell which roused the sleeping garrison and occa-
sioned a slight show of resistance. Lieut. Nolan of the 100th,
a man of great personal strength, rushed into the lower part
of the tower in order to bayonet the slumbering inmates.
Next morning his body was found, the breast pierced by a
deep bayonet wound, at the bottom of which were a musket
ball and three buckshot; but he had taken the lives of three
sleepers before he was stopped. One American lay at his
feet whom he had killed by a pistol shot, whilst the cloven
skulls of two others attested his strength and the rapidity
of his actions. Some of his men followed him and took the
tower, slaying its defenders to a man, and so brutalized
were the victors that they rushed wildly into every building, bayoneting every American they met. In half an hour
the fort was captured, and the blood-glutted victors sought
to drown their excitement in drink and sleep. The short con-
test cost the British, Lieut. Nolan and five men killed, and
two officers and three men wounded. The Americans lost
65 men, and two officers killed and twelve men wounded.
Thus fell Fort Niagara, and with such unexpected facility
as gave rise to the report that treason had contributed to
its capture, and it was charged that Capt. Leonard had
betrayed it by giving to the British all the necessary information and countersigns. It was also known that a large
sum in specie was in the fort at the time of its capture, and
it was openly charged, and ever afterwards believed, that

some of the officers had embezzled 'the' specie, and their increased expenditures justified the accusation. No enquiry, however, was made by the British, and the prize money which had been expected to be large was disappointingly small.

The old fort is also noted for being the theatre of crime and tyranny as well as for military exploits, During the time it was in the possession of the French its use was that of a prison, and for many years afterwards in its dark and dreary dungeons, where light was not admitted, ample proofs remained of the instruments used for torture, execution or for murder. During the war of Independence it was often quoted and dreaded as being theh eadquarters of all that was barbarous, unrelenting and cruel, it being the rendezvous for assembly of those savage hordes who carried death and destruction into peaceful and far-off American settlements ; and even after peace was proclaimed the old fort still held its reputation for enacting scenes of tyranny and murder; and the abduction of William Morgan, who was supposed to have been lodged in its magazine, kept there three or four days and then inhumanly drowned, once more awoke public interest in the old fort." On the shoals near the fort are most excellent fishing-grounds, and the chief recreation of the summer visitor is to sail out to the shoals, anchor the boat, and lazily read or dreamily pass the long summer day away. In the evenings and on Sundays of course other recreations are indulged in.

The people of Niagara are friendly, hospitable and entertaining in their way. A retired Scotch gentleman who had resided here for the past four years, and with whom I had become on intimate terms, after solemnly assuring me over and over again that I was standing on historic and almost holy ground, volunteered to show the sights,—so, after accepting his kind offer, I accompanied him to the little church on the rise, where he pointed with pride to the graves of seven young men who were drowned whilst engaged in the unholy sport of yachting on Sunday.. After drawing conclusions, and pointing out the moral for my benefit, he then proceeded to show the beauties of the. battle-ground and recount how many fell, indulging, meanwhile, in numerous comments on the perversity of the people of those times·

Seeing so many evidences of dissolution around me, and the near approach to that somnambulant state by those still in the flesh, we bid adieu to the peaceful little town, and a fourteen mile drive brought us to St. Catharines, but twelve miles across country from the Suspension Bridge. Here we see the spirit of enterprise, contrasting strongly with the town just left,—all are agreed and are loud in their anticipations of the great benefits to be derived by enlarging and making the Welland a ship canal, for the development of direct trade from the West to Europe, each one be speaking for this bustling little town a grand future, with increasing prosperity for the country around about. For some years past the town has been quite a fashionable summer resort, partly caused by the celebrity of the curative properties of their artesian wells and mineral springs, said to be most successful in cases of rheumatism, etc. The hotels, the Springbank, Stephenson and Welland — the latter managed by a gentleman formerly of Richmond, Va.— with the Norton, are about the principal.

The canal connecting Lake Ontario with Lake Erie is some 28 miles in length, was built to overcome the Falls of Niagara, the fall between Erie and Ontario being some 330 feet, which is met by 27 locks, 150 feet in length and 27½ feet wide, the building of which cost nearly $5,000,000, or, in English money, £1,061,497.

The town is about 38 miles south of Toronto by water, and 32 from Hamilton by rail. Its population is 9,631. It contains fine churches and private residences, with a general and marine hospital, the convent of St. Joseph, and several large manufactories, for which the town is pre-eminently adapted, having an inexhastible supply of water-power. Shipbuilding is an industry, and several fine yards are located here. The town has constant steam communication with the Upper Lakes, the United States, and Lower Canada, the Merchants Line running regularly during the season from Chicago to Montreal direct, and comprises the handsome and commodious steamers, Prussia, Ocean, Celtic, California and Africa — as fine vessels of their class as any that sail the lakes. Steamers of the line also run between Cleveland, Ohio and Montreal, and have become very popular with travellers, owing, in part, no doubt, to the enterprise of their Agent, Mr. H. G. Hunt, with whom the public have been for years familiar, and who recognize the genial smile with which he will book you either for Montreal, Hades or Chicago, or, in fact, to any railroad or steamship point known to the travelling world.

From St. Catharines it is but an hour's run by rail to Hamilton, which city is located on Burlington Bay, in the bight of Lake Ontario, at its south-western extremity. Hamilton was first laid out in the year 1813, during the American war for Independence, but in 1841 contained but 3,446 inhabitants; during the next ten years its population had increased to 10,246. When the Great Western Railway commenced operations it lent a new impetus to the growth of the city, for in 1856 its population numbered some 25,000, since which time it has been steadily increasing, until at present it numbers 35,961, and its real estate represents a value of some millions. The hotels are good, the St. Nicholas, Royal and American being the most prominent. The harbor is also the terminus of the Mail Steamer line to Toronto, Kingston and other ports, on both shores of the Lake, and down the St. Lawrence to Montreal. Being the headquarters of the G. W. R. the town is essentially a railroad one, and the citizens have much to thank that enterprising corporation for the benefits they have derived. The depot is a fine and commodious one, in strong contrast to the G. T. station at Montreal. Here also are located the principal offices and workshops of the line, and at times, and on special occasions, the amount of work transacted is something enormous ; but, under the able management of F. Broughton, Chas. Stiff, Wm. Edgar and others, the British owners rest quiet and contented, knowing full well that competent men assume the management, whilst the interests of the corporation and themselves are fully looked after. The Great Western Railway of Canada has become a favorite one with the travelling public, its passenger equipments are first-class in every particular, whilst its road-bed and track is one of the best on the American continent. Being the direct route between the East and the West, via the Falls of Niagara, on its system are all the principal cities and towns of Ontario, which, with its connections through to Manitoba, make the route one of the most desirable, as for speed, comfort and safety it cannot be surpassed. The road actively contends with the Canada Southern and Grand Trunk for a considerable portion of the carrying-trade.

It was rather a curious fact to notice whilst in this city the hold that Democracy has upon the people themselves: for several days it had been announced that H. R. H. Prince Leopold, the Princess Louise and suite, together with the Governor General, would pass on their journey to Niagara Falls, and a tour through a portion of the States; still when the train arrived at the depot scarce fifty persons were assembled to pay their respects to Royalty, and the few attended mostly from motives of curiosity alone. About the only ones to greet the party were the railroad managers, the American vice consul and a few American citizens. No enthusiasm was evinced; not a cheer rent the air as a welcome; silently the Royal party arrived, and as silently departed, but the episode served to convince us more thoroughly that the people do not so firmly pin their faith on the Divine right of Princes as official sycophants would have us believe. At the time there was a wordy war progressing between the rich and poor on the subject of the Scott Act, debarring the sale of beer, wines and spirits in small quantities. The poor people look upon it as a curtailment of their rights, and assert that, as they have been brought to this artificial mode of life, they are only following scriptural advice, and trying to "drink, and forget their poverty and remember their misery no more." It must be here added that when the voters were mustered, the non-abstinence men came out ahead, re-echoing the cry of Solomon the Wise, "to stay me with flagons and comfort me with apple's (juice), for I am sick of love."

The city itself lies some half mile back from the station. The people are an odd mixture of Yankee energy partially developed and old-time tardiness, thus giving force to the statement that the constant amalgamation of the races of the old world would bring forth even in one generation the inevitable Yankee, preserving the best and noblest characteristics of all, and probably eliminating from them their worst and evil habits. However, several enterprises are established, and at present are in a paying condition. There is a large proportion of Scotch among the population, and they seem to vie with each other in emulating American ways. The city is a pleasant one, and the people congenial and social, who look forward to renewed prosperity in the near future.

Brighton and Burlington beaches, situated between the bay and Lake Ontario, are the favorite resorts during the summer.

From Hamilton a most delightful sail is by the steamer " Southern Belle " or " Rothsea Castle," two of the old-time blockade fleet, to Toronto, forty-miles distant. These vessels during the American war achieved notoriety for speed as blockade runners from Nassau, and still retain somewhat of their old reputation.

Dundas, distant some five miles from Hamilton, is located on the slope of the hill, has fine water power and numerous mills and factories, and occupies a fertile tract of country. Being so close to Hamilton, and with constant communication by rail and boat, no doubt at some future time the one will be but the outer ward of the other.

Passing Harrisburg, merely a junction, we arrive at the town of Brantford, containing some 10,000 inhabitants, and named in honor of the noted Indian Chief of the Six Nations, " Brant," who, with his tribe and allies, supported the British during the American war; he was feared and dreaded as being the most cruel and implacable Indian foe that Americans had to meet, and in " Gertrude of

Wyoming" he is thus alluded to, "The mammoth comes, the fiend, the monster Brant," although later it has been several times denied that he took part in that horrible massacre in the peaceful valley on Pennsylvania soil.

The town is situated at the junction of the G. T. and G. W. Railways and was formerly connected by the canal to Grand river, and thence into Lake Erie, but since the advent of railroads the canal, some 2½ miles in length, has fallen into disuse, and the locks at the entrance to the river are in a state of decay. The scenery along the banks of the river and canal is fine and varied; high rolling lands, well wooded with hard timber, lend a charm to the scene in summer, that makes the banks appear delightfully cool and refreshing. At the locks there were formerly fine mills and factories, but lately, the largest having been destroyed by fire, it is not considered necessary to rebuild so far from town. This town was formerly a good market for wheat, but the railroads have destroyed it somewhat, still it has other elements of prosperity and life, has excellent water power, and is situated in the midst of a productive region. Manufactories and various works are numerous, whilst other industries yet to be added are in contemplation. Floriculture was introduced by Mr. J. B. Hay, and his greenhouses in the midst of the city, well stocked with *Flora* and *Fauna*, are evidence of what perseverance can do in the way of attractions. Churches of each denomination are found and well attended. It is curious to note that the industries of Brantford for some time past have been very unfortunate, not through inability to compete with others, or the inferiority of their products, but, as the native assured us, "from bad luck and the fire fiend." Phœnix-like they arise from their ashes, and one set of mills seem to have suffered quite a series of disasters which almost equals retribution. It happened some years ago that a number of capitalists erected a woollen mill some distance from town, had first-rate workmen, and with good water power and amid pleasant surroundings for a time all went well and satis- factorily, and prosperity seemed to smile on all connected. The mills paid dividends and the men worked well, knowing and doing their duty, but unfortunately one day some woollen goods were missed, and suspicion crept in amongst the workmen. The sharp-sighted manager placed the "men of clues " on the track, and had the sin of theft fastened upon two of the employees of the mill. The proprietors pursued them to the bitter end, had the men convicted and sent to the Penitentiary for a number of years, which time has since expired, but from the era of that unfortunate occurrence misfortune seemed to hover over the industries of Brantford, so that after a siege of bad luck and other calamities, the mill in which the loss occurred was during 1881 burnt to the ground, whilst the other factories are either in the hands of the Sheriff, or converted by the present owners to other uses not designed by the proprie- tors. The Exhibition grounds are well laid out, and include a fine race track and buildings with stabling for stock. The Exhibition, under the presidency of the Ex-Mayor, J. S. Hamilton, has been of late a successful and attractive one. Numerous improvements are going on, the G. T. R. are building a new depot, more churches and numerous substan- tial buildings are in course of erection. The drill shed and armory of the Dufferin rifles is as large and commodious as any in Ontario, and taken altogether the vicinity is a delightful one in which to settle. The hotels are first-class and the cuisine good. The Kirby House, under the

proprietorship of Mr. J. C. Palmer, is all that can be desired
and is well patronized during the season, by American
visitors. The walks and drives are unsurpassed, the
scenery of river, hills, woods and valley is unequalled in
Southern Ontario, whilst six miles distant is the Indian
Reserve, where the remnant of the tribes of the once famous
Six Nations still reside. Near it is the Mohawk church where'
the Indians worship, and one of the oldest churches in the
Dominion; near it is Brant's grave and monument. On the
reserve are located the Sour Springs, the waters of which
being strongly impregnated with iron, possess considerable
curative powers, and have been considered the Indian's
panacea for all ills ; whilst sulphur and other mineral springs
abound.   Boating and fishing on Grand River are excellent,
and are favorite pastimes, and taking a canoe and running
the rapids is exciting pastime, and freely indulged in by
the venturesome.   The Commercial, under the proprietorship of H. T. Westbrook, is also an excellent hostelry, and,
being both a sportsman and naturalist, a visit is both entertaining and instructive.

Seven miles from Brantford is the town of Paris, so named
from its contiguity to beds of gypsum or plaster-of-Paris,
sometimes called the Harper's Ferry of Canada. It is a pretty
little town of some 8000 people, situated also on the
banks of the Grand River, amid scenery quite romantic in
character. The town lies away from the line of rail, and,
like other towns through this fertile portion of the province,
gives every evidence of thrift and prosperity. Nothing
could more fully attest the productive nature of the soil
of this locality than to see so many towns close together
and each seemingly enjoying a fair share of commercial
prosperity. The commercial agent for the United States

or this district is located at Paris, and Uncle Sam is represented by E. M. Sharpe of Michigan, a courteous and entertaining gentleman, who thoroughly believes in the absolute ultimate greatness of the country he represents.

Passing Woodstock, a bustling little town of 5000 inhabitants, and the junction of the Port Dover and Lake Huron Railway, we arrive at London, 119 miles from Suspension Bridge and 110 from Windsor, a stirring and enterprising business-place, and is actively competing with Toronto and Hamilton for precedence in supplying the country trade. No great wealth is apparent on the surface: it is populated by a class of actual settlers, men who have risen by their own efforts, starting clear from the stump, and presents another instance of energy and enterprise of the Canadian when in close proximity with the citizens of the United States. In the year 1846 the then very small village was entirely burned down, but within ten years arose in the shape of a flourishing, well-built city. Several large importers are located here, whilst the people generally are enthusiastic as to the future of their pretty city. Its people are probably the most democratic in the Dominion; the acquirement of wealth here does not mean the putting on of " frills " and the assumption of " style ' so noticeable in the older cities east, whilst the Society and respectable poverty class are also invisible : they are all seemingly workers, their interests, to judge *en passant*, seem mutual. The city and surroundings are well watered by the river Thames, which is navigable to Chatham, sixty miles distant. During the past summer this little river, with apparently no depth of water, was the scene of a terrible disaster, by the wrecking of the Steamer Victoria, which vessel foundered with some 600 people on board, occasioning one of the greatest calamities and loss of life that has ever happened to the city. London is well laid out, and contains within the area of the surrounding country all the elements requisite for its success—factories, workshops, and other industries that bid fair in time to enable it to become one of the most energetic business places in the country. Numerous societies and associations are here for the benefit of its people, and they materially aid in the city's prosperity and advancement, although some of its public offices are denounced by its people, as, for instance, it is claimed that some associations and individuals are so unscrupulous that, having an entry into the Post Office, they manage to open letters in order to facilitate them in working their "*points.*" This charge has also been made with reference to the same office in larger cities than London, and it was even acknowledged by an official " that handfuls of letters were taken *en route,* but always on the other side of the Line." Probably the fact will become so noticeable and apparent that the Government may in time take steps for its prevention. The brewery owned by John Carling, M.P., comprises the finest block of buildings used for brewing purposes in Canada; they occupy one entire block, built of gray sandstone at a cost of over $200,000, the buildings are complete in themselves, each department being separate and all large and commodious. Of late the light lager beer of the United States has been introduced here for summer use, and with Ludwig, an old employee of Anhauser of St. Louis, the venture will, no doubt, prove a success. The capacity of the lager department is over 7000 bbls each year, whilst the ale and porter sends out some 25,000 bbls, using in the production some 120,000 bushels of malt. The city contains two fine parks and recreation grounds, Victoria and Queen's Park, and also extensive exhibition grounds, well laid out with beautiful flower beds and fine lawns, making them quite favorite resorts for all. The hotels are excellent —the Tecumseh and Griggs are the most prominent. The Griggs House, under the proprietorship of Sam Griggs, is perhaps the best known house in the Dominion ; everything that can add to the comfort and enjoyment of the guest is carefully studied, whilst, should it ever be the ill fortune to be away from home and taken sick, one of the few hotels that provides every comfort, with tenderness and good nursing, is the one presided over by the good-natured, whole-souled, genial Sam Griggs.

Leaving London we pass the pretty little town of Strathroy well situated, with a good surrounding country, and soon are landed at Wyoming, the junction of the Petrolia branch, and 5 miles distant from that bustling, lively little town. Probably more business is transacted and more speculation entered into in Petrolia than any town of its size in the Upper province, the value of crude oil shipped during 1881 being some $ Being situated in the midst of the oil regions, wells with their unsightly frame work are visible from every point of view, and should a tender foot be smitten with the oil fever, he will find he can become the owner of a well already sunk at any price to suit his means, from fifty dollars to ten thousand. The only difference for the amount paid will be the fact that at the particular season of purchase the cheap wells are just stopped running, but there is plenty of oil, as soon as the rise takes place, which may keep the investor in hopes and expectancy as long as he wishes. The people are plain, hardworking, friendly and hospitable, always ready to aid the

NORTHWESTERN NAVIGATION CO.'S STEAMERS

stranger in securing a valuable property, and full of good
advice. This is also the central market for the purchase of
hogs for shipment to Chicago. Merchants carry heavy
stocks, and business at all seasons is good. The hotels are
fair for the country, the Anderson House being probably the
most prominent. Cheese factories and other local industries
are to be met with all over the country.

From Petrolia we run on to Sarnia, a substantial, well-
built little town on the River St. Clair, opposite Port Huron,
State of Michigan. Being again on the borders, the Customs
and their inevitable adjuncts are again met with, and the
same experience is undergone as elsewhere. After encour-
aging one of the gentry to follow, on arriving at the hotel you
find him there, and very anxious to make acquaintance, so,
after whiling away an hour or so with him, you will notice
the look of intense disgust depicted on his countenance as
the clerk returns him his small travelling satchel, when the
remark is made, "there's no use for me here," the clerk
informing you shortly afterwards in confidence that "the
gentleman was only a Dr. Smith of Port Huron." Even the
Sarnia *Chronicle* at times denounces this mode, for it
remarks, that " travellers and business men seeking to
benefit the town should not be regarded as though they
came to beg, borrow or steal something, but should be
cordially received and listened to with patience." Mer--
chants here are of a substantial class, many being their own
importers, enterprising and discriminating ; the population
is about 3000. The town is well provided with good hotels,
the Bellchamber taking the lead, being moderate in price
and a good house generally,

From Sarnia a very pleasant sail by the Northwestern.
Navigation Co.'s steamers up Lake Huron is made to

Goderich, a summer resort, situated at the mouth of the
Maitland river. In summer a residence along the borders of
Lake Huron is delightful. High winds prevail nearly all the
season, keeping the atmosphere clear and cool, rendering
the stay both invigorating and very beneficial to health.
Fine views are to be had on all sides, whilst an excellent
park and good drives are offered for resort and recreation.
Several hotels, with the Albion and British American, afford
ample accommodation for visitors, the towns on the lake
being easy of access both by rail and steamer.

Further up the lake is Kincardine, also a popular resort,
well located on rising ground, and transacts a large amount
of business, connected with the central cities by the
Wellington, Grey and Bruce Railroad. In this portion of
Ontario there is still room for numbers of settlers; the soil
is a sandy loam, and is regarded as excellent for the production of wheat, farms being valued at from $50 to $60
per acre. The Salt works are extensive, which with other
industries afford employment to a large number of persons.

From Kincardine 45 miles up the lake and we arrive
at Southampton. This town was formerly the most popular resort as well as the best business town on the lake,
but of late some jealousy seems to have existed, and a new
town of Port Elgin, 4¾ miles distant, has sprung up as
an active competitor, and is certainly making some progress.
The winters here are severe, the cold at times, (especially
when the wind blows off the lake, being intense,) from 28°
to 40° below Zero, the snow being in drifts to a depth of
over 17 feet, but a steady winter provides good and
uninterrupted sleighing. The soil is good and the land
somewhat rolling in character, whilst the gravel roads
throughout the country are kept in excellent condition.

It is said that game, wild fowl, etc., were at one time plentiful in this vicinity, but at present it looks as if they had anticipated Horace Greeley's advice and gone West toward the setting sun, or probably the country had been visited by the H. B. Company or their agents, and consequently denuded of every thing of value. The Saugeen river empties into the lake at this point, and when the ice breaks in the spring, the panorama presented is grand. It is astonishing to notice at that season the rapidity with which the vast expanse of snow disappears, a day or two of hot sun and then a two or three days of soaking warm rain and the sixteen to twenty feet drifts have disappeared as if by magic, leaving the ground bare for the summer's work. Near the lake there are several springs of water strongly impregnated with iron and salts, magnetic in their properties, and so strengthening to the debilitated is this water said to be, that thousands are attracted to Southampton to drink of its waters and indulge in its baths, the sick and puny returning home apparently in robust health. The island and St. Lambert light, but a mile away, is a pleasant spot for recreation during the summer, there being a fine orchard of some 50 acres on the island; it has become a favorite spot for picnics and other parties. Three miles pleasant drive from the town lands us on the Chippewa Reservation, and amongst the "nation's wards," the remnants of the tribes. The Government policy is here seen in full operation under the supervision of the Indians agent Denny, probably one of the most wealthy men in the place, he being the owner of the store at which the Indians trade, the mills, and hotel on the reservation. It is stated that the agent is possessed of the happy knack of keeping the Indians constantly indebted to him through the medium of the store, etc., and although the childlike Aborigine when the paymaster arrives has the pleasure of putting one finger on the annuity generously provided for his use by a paternal Government, still that is all, for his I.O.U.'s are presented, and the treasury notes swept away into Denny's general fund, thus establishing a little monopoly of which the agent is said to be not unaware. Stages run daily from here to Owen Sound at the south-western extremity of Georgian Bay, and distant some 34 miles. Hotels are numerous, the leading one being Busby's.

Down the Wellington, Grey & Bruce R.R. we pass respectively Paisley, Walkerton, Palmerston and Elora, all situated in a good productive country. Although at present cereal crops are the staple, still some departure is being made towards making this a stock-raising district. We arrive at Guelph, a flourishing little manufacturing town, well connected by rail with other parts of the Province. On market days the town wears quite a city appearance; there are several hotels, but having stopped at the Royal we would advise the guest to be sure to deposit with the proprietors, taking a receipt for whatever of value may be wished to have retained.

Leaving Guelph the Grand Trunk brings us shortly to TORONTO, the chief city in the Province of Ontario, at present containing a population of some 86,445. It is situated on Toronto Bay, an arm of Lake Ontario, in N. Lat. 43°32', and W. Long. 79°20', the name being derived from an old Indian term signifying " Oak trees growing out of the Lake." The bay is a sheet of water excellent for boating, about four miles long and two in width, separated from the main body of the lake by a long strip of sandy beach called

Hanlan's island, on which a lighthouse, some few cottages and numerous summer restaurants are located. In 1793, when it was first surveyed, two Indian families were its only inhabitants, and the harbor was a resort for myriads of wild fowl. The city was incorporated in 1834, at which time its people numbered 9,254, whilst in the year 1856 it had increased its numbers to over 50,000, since which time it has rapidly given signs of permanent vitality and growth. Being the seat of Government for the Province it contains a Parliament house, and has a provincial representation of 68 members, who, in order to distinguish them from Dominion Parliament members, are called M.P.P.s, their deliberations being presided over by the Lieut.-Governor of the Province, who devotes his time and service for the benefit of the Province for the small sum of $9,999.96 and little extras yearly, the cost of legislation in the Province amounting to a tax of 5 4-5 cents on each inhabitant per annum. Among the principal buildings are the University, Cathedral, Colleges, Lunatic Asylum (and surely Canada boasts of plenty), Custom House and Post Office. The Church of the Holy Trinity was erected by a donation from a wealthy person in England of £5000, and the seats were conditioned to remain free. As in other places both churches and ministers are merely tolerated, the seeming fondness for both church and pastor are in a great measure merely affectation. Employers attend in order to set an example to their employees, and because, as some assert, " it gives a certain air of respectability to a man, you know ; " their wives and daughters often to display their finery, the servants in order to stand well in the esteem of their masters, but all, with of course some notable exceptions, seem to have no particular love for the preacher. The

city is substantially built, and is claimed to be the most
enterprising City in the Dominion, and is ambitiously
striving to become the depot for lake and ocean trade and a
transfer point from rail to shipping. Whilst watching the
arrival of trains at the Union depot, I noticed two
enterprising Americans meet and greet each other; both
were commercial men, and equally animated with a desire
to introduce their goods and secure a portion of trade on a
reciprocal basis. "Well, Jim,"s aid No. 1, "which way are
you bound?" "Back to God's country," said No. 2.
"What!" exclaimed the first, "back already? Why, I
thought you came here to make business and stay awhile."
"Well! so I did," replied No. 2 sadly, " I tried hard and
thoroughly, and found these Kanucks an uncongenial
set, almost entirely under control of their petty politicians
and masters; they are like the ice on their shores, you have
to break it to get there, and when you arrive you find nothing
but rock, and their hearts are of the same material; in
fact, they are the coldest, most selfish and unsocial people
I ever met, and yet when on our side they are always
asking indulgences." An "Italian," who had been quietly
engaged in sustaining the walls of the depot with his back,
overhearing their conversation, interrupted them with,
"Unsocial is it you call em? Oh bedad, there is wur
ye mak' the mistake. Sure I hadn't been in the city twenty-
four hours before me arm wuz bruck in two places, me
legs wuz carried away from under me, and by mornin' me
head wuz covered wid patches, and the Judge fined me
$5.00, and all fur lookin' wrong way at a police, bad cess to
him! Bedad, they are the most sociabilist people I ever
saw."

· The business men of the city are striving and enterprising, and were it not for the petty officials and so called
leaders of opinion, who are constantly both impeding and
endeavoring to curtail and place obstacles in the way of
the trade development, Toronto would soon be the leading
city, surpassing by far the city of Montreal (although
various reforms recently inaugurated make political evils
far less to contend with than in the provinces further
East).

On the Sunday we had the pleasure of attending St.
Andrew's church, and of listening to a long dissertation on
the history of Job and his patience under trials, difficulties
and despoliation which might have been modernized by the
history of many a God-fearing Southern family during the
late war, for with all the great cry of wrong perpetrated on
the poor negro, the pious wish of the sanctimonious Scot
is often uttered, as Johny Mitchel remarked, "Ah! wae is me!
Why, mon, there's na more to be got oot of puir white labor;
my ambition noo is a Southern plantation and a lot o' fat
niggers." But somehow or another the preachers seem to
have gone back considerably on the blood-thirsty doctrines
advocated by Moses and his Hebrews, whose entry being
pillage and murder are even yet experiencing the effect of
the doctrines themselves which they forced others to accept
and are, even at this day, but receiving a just retribution in
the world—but Israel's fated race receive sympathy
although the sign is 2 to 1—but dwell more and more on
those Gentile or Heathen such as Job whose faith was firm
in adversity, and they freely quote him as an example of
meekness and trust. The book that bears his name is a
pleasant one to read—treachery and murder occupy no part
of it: it is the meditations of a mind strongly impressed

with the vicissitudes of human life and, by turns sinking
under and struggling against the pressure. It is a highly-
wrought composition between willing submission and
involuntary discontent, and shows man as he sometimes is,
more disposed to be resigned than he is capable of being
after finding he has been despoiled by his fellows, but he
seemed determined in the midst of ills and hardships to
impose upon himself the hard duty of contentment. It has
also been observed that the book itself proves to be the production of a mind cultivated in science of the knowledge
of which the Jews were very ignorant, and certainly were
as illiterate as Southern negroes at the close of the war.
According to Mgr. Laudroit a Christian should be a complete
being, having a knowledge of his strength in the order of
nature, and walking under the eye of God to perfection, to
supernatural transfiguration, but *never to the annihilation
of the faculties* (so practice good), Christianity . (*i. e.*
example) is sent not to destroy but to restore human
nature, to renew it, to give to it whilst waiting for the
perfection of glory a part of the attributes of primitive
days but only a part, alas ! The prayers of Job were
touching, and evinced a strong and earnest faith, greatly in
contrast with those of the Hebrews, for the Jews never
prayed but when they were in trouble, and then never for
anything but victory, vengeance and riches.

The sermon was an appropriate one, for in a few days
the community were about to hang to the death an
unfortunate fellow-being who, in a moment of rashness, and
under the influence of a false education, had attempted to
attain what he considered his rights, by firing a shot with
the intent to kill his employer. A wound was inflicted by
the servant's act, and shortly afterwards the employer died—

even then it was stated possibly from his own indiscretion.
The meek and lowly followers of Christianity, bearing in
mind the prayer of their Saviour whilst in His death
agonies, "Father forgive them, for they know not what
they do, " demanded at once the life of a fellow-being. A
judge and jury were quickly got together, the man found
guilty, sentence of death passed upon him, and some of
the newspapers remarked "that the life about to be
sacrificed, even were it a dozen, were nothing to the one
that had gone before." Fie upon the belief that God made
man in His own image and the prayer Our Father, when
such practices on a brother can be tolerated by a Christian
people! And even after the hurriedly passed sentence had
been carried out on the body of the poor wretch, there seemed
to be a grim exultation when the papers noticed the fact
that the man was poor, and no friends had visited him
whilst in jail, and the executioner had tortured the
condemned by strapping him so tightly as to cause him to
cry out with pain before hanging.

In his sane moments, in the year 1791, Maximilian
Robespierre, the thinker, gave utterance to these words," I
will prove that the punishment of death is essentially
unjust, secondly, that it has no tendency to repress crime,
and, thirdly, that it multiplies offences much more than it
diminishes them. In the eyes of justice and mercy these
death-scenes, which are got up with so much solemnity,
are nothing less than base assassinations, solemn crimes
committed, not by individuals but by nations, and of which
every individual must bear the responsibility. When a
legislator can strike criminals in so many ways, merciful
yet terrible, bloodless yet efficacious, why should he ever
recur to the hazard of public executions? The legislator

who prefers death to milder chastisements within his power
outrages every feeling and brutalizes the minds of the
people, and comes into power a newspaper man, a whiskey.
or a beer man.   Listen to the voice of reason: it tells.
us human judgments, especially when weighted with
prejudice, are never enough certain for society to condemn.
a man to death, those who condemn him, being men and
subject to error ; to take away from man the possibility of
expiating his misdeeds by repentance or by acts of virtue.
is, in my eyes, the most horrible refinement of cruelty.;
In order, therefore, to preserve the sanctity of human life
the Government rulers and leaders of opinion should set
the example, and, by prompt punishment for crimes
committed, impress the criminal with the certainty of
punishment and the knowledge that the Government
would reap the benefit of his services for the remainder
of his life.   Already even the city prison is acquiring
notoriety for its cruelties, and whippings of the poor
unfortunates for the slightest infraction of its rules are of
frequent occurrence.   So long as it is confined to their own
citizens it may be all right, but when, once in a while, an
American falls under the lash, and the city has to pay
some thousands of dollars for the privilege, they naturally
pause to consider whether or not they have been too
precipitous and indiscriminate in their favors. Far more
fear took possession of the evil-doer, and more terror
struck the hearts of the Venetians, by the terrible
uncertainty as to what became of the one condemned after
he crossed the Bridge of Sighs than is impressed by the
fighting of modern technicalities.   When the verdict of
guilty is pronounced, the criminal should be forever lost
to the world outside, and his disposal left a matter of mere

conjecture to the community, the mode of punishment being known only to the Government and its officials. Students of psychology assert that, after the sudden removal from life, the spirit hovers near the scene of its execution, and we know that with all its evil thoughts and those on parting still more bitter, that on meeting with a kindred spirit in the flesh with whom it can come in *rapport,* it at once identifies itself with its living " companion, so that the evil thoughts and actions of the last shall be worst than the first;" or not finding a medium to affiliate with, may, like the apparition that appeared in December, 1628, at the Palace of Berlin, call upon the Almighty and was heard to say: " *Veni judica vivos et mortuos! Judicium mihi adhuc superest.*" Come, judge the quick and the dead. I wait for judgment. That the disembodied spirit does for a time hover about the spot of its taking off is a well-attested fact, and as in a short time we shall have to appear before the Almighty power that created us, it is my belief that there is no crime in the category that will justify the taking of the life of a fellow-being. Surely the punishment by the Power that gave us the breath of life will be far more terrible and complete than the pitiful vengeance man can meet out to his fellow, and oftentimes unjustly. Again, the constant repetition and hearing of such scenes brings to the surface and fosters in the heart all the baser passions of mankind, besides breeding a feeling of contempt for the life of another that all the outward forms of Christianity cannot obliterate.

During the winter, Toronto is often the scene of gaiety and pleasure, the winter sports both contributing to the health and pleasure of its people, skating and ice boat sailing, sleighing and tabogganning being most popular.

Younge street, one of the principal thoroughfares, extends from the esplanade or water's edge for several miles into the interior towards Lake Simcoe, and affords a pleasant drive in good weather. The hotels of Toronto are well kept. The Queen's, under the management of Messrs. McGaw & Winnett being the most aristocratic ; the Rossin and American being also popular amongst all classes. The public generally are well catered for at a moderate charge; impositions on travellers are very rarely practiced, and, taken altogether, the city will, at no distatn day, become a pleasant resort for enterprising and s pecu- lative Americans.

Six railroads center in Toronto, and the Great Western here joins the Grand Trunk, thus forming a continuous line through to Montreal, Quebec, St. John and Halifax, N.S.

Toronto Bay is a popular resort for yachting, boating and other aquatic sports, and is well patronized, whilst on Sunday Hanlan's Island is a resort of the "*Boys,*". as the bar at Hanlan's hotel is always open without any restraint, his taxes being remitted by the city council as a slight token of their esteem for his skill as an oarsman, and as a slight testimonial of their respect for his muscle.

Amongst the cosmopolitan population assembled here in summer time, how easy it is to distinguish the cold-blooded calculating denizen of the northern latitude from the vivacious warm-hearted resident of southern climes Mexico or Cuba, but possibly the climate makes the difference, not only with men, but with plants, trees and even animals: the new-comer lately from his sunny clime is full of life and vigor, and liberal in his views, but were he to remain here, no doubt he would become as inert and

and useless in this frigid zone as many of the inhabitants themselves.

Embarking on board the steamer "Spartan," under command of Captain J. S. Bailey, of the Richelieu and Ontario line—which line once famous for its liberality to passengers has rapidly degenerated until its stock was but worth 35; but during the present year the old fogy management has been changed, and an effort for the better is anticipated—we arrive at Port Hope, located on the north shore of Lake Ontario, 62 miles from Toronto. It has a fine and safe harbor, where steamers call daily from different lake ports, and is connected by the Midland R.R. to Peterboro, Midland and Haliburton, all in the Province of Ontario. The trade of the port of late has considerably decreased, having found in the next stopping place, Cobourg, but eight miles distant, a formidable rival, the latter town being situated nearly opposite the mouth of the Genesee River, N.Y., and where the lake attains its greatest breadth; it possesses a good harbor, and is much frequented by steamers and sailing vessels on their way up and down the lakes. The town is a pleasant and hospitable one, containing numerous factories seemingly prosperous. The Hotel Arlington is noted as being one of the best hostelries on the lake shore, and during the summer season is filled to overflowing. The Arlington is spacious and well conducted, with fine grounds, good parlors for dancing and amusements, with library and reading rooms for the studious, whilst the sleeping apartments are cool, comfortable and airy, an attractive point for summer sojourners, situated in the midst of a fertile district; the luxuries of the season are to be found upon its board, and the hotel continues, as it has long been, a favorite. Few places in

Canada present a more beautiful appearance from the water than Cobourg, the landscape being extensive and varied by a delightful background.

Leaving Cobourg, the steamer makes out for the broad waters of the lake, and during the prevalence of storms and high winds quite a sea arises, and many passengers experience their first lessons in fresh water sailing, invariably expressing their sentiments in a wish to go to "New Yauk," but this is soon over, for shortly we make the port of Kingston, situated on a good harbor at the north-east extremity of Lake Ontario, and immediately above its outlet. All along, after leaving Port Hope, the surface of the lake was covered with myriads of dead fish, about the size of a shadine, and numerous theories were advanced by our passengers to account for their sudden demise. The day being very hot a scientific pisciculturist insisted on the theory that the sun shone so intensely, so bright, and so warm, that the fish startled at such an unusual sight came to the surface to ascertain the cause, when, of course, they were sunstruck and died immediately. Upon expressing this opinion the votary of science was unanimously requested to take a back seat and study theology for the balance of the trip. Another theory was that the fish commissioners having obtained a grant of cash from the Government for the propagation of fish in the rivers and lakes had wisely expended the amount, less their own percentage, in trying to acclimate salt water shad to the fresh waters of the lakes and rivers, and, having used all the cash appropriated, were now asking more to further the experiment and enrich themselves.

A few miles above Kingston is met with the first of the islands known as the Thousand Islands, Simcoe, Grand

and Wolf Islands being opposite the city, and, being converted into park and pic-nic grounds, become a popular summer resort for the city people.

The first object to attract the traveller from the west by lake is Fort Henry, and the naval station of Fort Frederick at its base, with its battlements, fortifications, towers and redoubts. The former fort is a favorite resort, and from its elevated position is procured the best view that can be obtained of the city, lake and surrounding country.

Kingston contains at present some 14,091 inhabitants. Its public and business buildings are substantial, its city hall is a fine edifice, which cost originally some $92,000, several industries are in operation, whilst at Navy Bay a shipbuilding yard and marine railway are located. Near the penitentiary at Portsmouth (two miles from the city) is a mineral spring resembling in its properties the artesian well at St. Catharines. Kingston occupies the site of the old French fort, Frontenac, one of a chain of forts or posts extending from Quebec to Mackinac on Lake Superior; and, being the outlet for the Bay of Quinte (Kan-ty) and the Rideau Canal make it an important mart for commerce. The canal extends from Kingston to Ottawa, a distance of 126 miles ; 37 locks overcome a total fall of 457 feet between the lake and the Ottawa river, the canal alone costing the sum of £965,000. In the summer nearly all the pleasure yachts from Alexandria Bay and the American shore call constantly at the port, thus adding considerably to the life and business of the city. It was my privilege whilst here to become acquainted with the late Dr. J. Gilbert Holland, and to take a cruise in his fast little steam launch "Camelia." The launch is built on the finest lines, and is the fastest and best model of any among the islands : trim, neat, clean and well fitted, she looks a perfect model; she sits gracefully in the water and, as the enthusiastic engineer says, " she runs like a scart hound." The " Minnie," owned by a Brooklyn gentleman, and the " Cruiser," of Ottawa ownership, are often here during the season, although the latter yacht is built more for sea-coast trade.   Public buildings are numerous, the Queen's University, the Asylum (it is astonishing to note the number of lunatic asylums throughout Canada, and still the people insist that one half are not confined within walls, but, probably, it is the effect of the climate) and the Penitentiary — although the Kingstonians repudiate the charge that the latter building belongs to them, giving up all claims to Portsmouth, two miles distant, at which place the building is situated.   The Penitentiary itself is a large combination of buildings, occupying an entire block on the lake front, being isolated and surrounded with high walls; on the east side runs the railroad track, on the west are wharves at which vessels are unloaded with convict labor, south is the lake, and north the public road ; the walls are some 16 feet in height, with a pathway on the top ; watch towers are at each corner, and the place well guarded by sentinels. The building contains on an average some 550 convicts, and for the small sum of 25cts., payable at the warden's office, a citizen can have the pleasure of going inside and viewing his fellow-men as if they were wild beasts or cattle on exhibition.   The cost of keeping criminals at the Kingston Penitentiary is some $157,236.54, whilst the revenue derived amounts to $34,409.34; the total cost for keeping convicts throughout the Dominion amounts to $376,177.52, against which the revenue derived from Penitentiaries foots up $50,023.27.   A short distance from the Penitentiary is the Kingston Asylum, a fine block of buildings having extensive grounds of some 114 acres surrounding it. The buildings are pleasantly located on the rise, and are at present under the management of Dr. W. G. Metcalfe; its total capacity is 430, but the average number is 234. The institution is ably and economically managed, but probably one of the worst features is the manner in which it is supplied —the majority of its inmates arriving via the jail naturally detracts some from its reputation of being a hospital for the treatment of a disease, but under present management the treatment accorded the unfortunates is most humane, the food supplied being plentiful, nutritious and varied,—kindness is met with on every hand, whilst medical supervision constantly hovers over all; as a consequence, the inmates not only improve, but in many cases entirely recover. The out-door exercise being ample and conducive to health, the normal condition of the patient soon asserts itself, the inmates being employed in some useful out-door occupation or trade, and from the products of the farm alone, cultivated entirely by lunatic labor, under the guidance of a single overseer, there was realized the sum last year of $3,830.15. Patients are received in two ways, by warrant of the Lieutenant Governor from the county jails and from private homes by application.

In Kingston are several hotels, for the accommodation of the travelling public, but the City Hotel, recently acquired by Archie McFaul, a genial and enterprising host, can be patronized with the utmost confidence, the public being assured of every comfort and attention, the proprietor at present sparing no pains to render the house both attractive and inviting. The rooms are cool and well furnished; the beds excellent, whilst the cuisine is as fine as the

country affords. Delightful drives throughout the surrounding country can be indulged in; the towns along the
lakeside are pleasantly located. The cottages look homelike and comfortable, whilst the surroundings have an air
of comfort and quiet contentment.

Opposite to Kingston, some twelve miles through the
canal, across Wolf Island, or thirty miles around in
the State of New York, is Cape Vincent, distant
twenty-five miles from Watertown, the terminus of
the St. Lawrence Navigation Company's opposition
line of steamers, and a transfer station of the Rome,
Watertown and Ogdensburg Railway. The town is well
laid out, fine water frontage, and is supplied with good
family hotels, for the accommodation of visitors, with whom
the town is quite a favorite. Catamaran sailing and fishing
are most indulged in. As capital is induced to invest at the
Cape to aid in its development, no-doubt, in the near
future, it will be able to compete with its at present more
pretentious rivals. Steam ferries communicate twice each
day with Kingston, and the fare charged is sometimes 25c.
but very often $1, according to whether you are taken
for a stranger or a resident. Small steamers also connect
with Clayton and Alexandria Bay on the American side.

Leaving Kingston we are soon wending our way amidst
the famous Thousand Islands, which stretch down the river
for between forty and fifty miles, for which distance the
St. Lawrence is from six to twelve miles wide. Part of the
islands belong to Canada and part are within the boundary
of the State of New York, the line dividing them about
equally. The islands that now are bought and sold
like other properties undergo with their transfer a change

View on the way from Gananoque

THOUSAND ISLANDS.

A.W.Moore

of name, most generally taking that of their present proprietor : thus we pass Gage Island, on which is a lighthouse ;
Garden Island, a lumber depot; Howe and Carleton
Islands, both having history connected with the fight for
independence attached to them.   The waters of the river
vary at different seasons from three to four feet, exposing
hundreds of islets.   Our passengers, whilst admiring the
islands (at this season of the year covered with verdure),
rather took as a grim official joke the Government notices
that the virgin forests were to be preserved, and affixing a
penalty to any one found felling timber on the islands.
Now about the only ones we could imagine attempting to
fell timber would be some forlorn jay hawker from Kansas ;
they have no timber except willow and corn stalks, and
he would only fell it with his pocket knife for toothpicks;
for on many of the islands if an unfortunate goat were to
land at night he would browse away all the timber before
morning.   Some of the islands are so large that a cat
might sit on them by keeping perfectly still, but to keep
dry she would either have to wrap her tail around her
neck, or else let it drop in the water. (N.B. Some of the
islands are for sale cheap, full particulars from agent.)
The fish most abundant are Maskinongé, pickerel, black
bass, pike, perch, rock bass, catfish and eels ; with the
exception of the pike, they are mostly taken by hook and
line.   On the islands are found rabbits, sometimes coons
and muskrats and in season quail, wild duck and
mosquitoes, although sporting of late years does not afford
as much pleasure as formerly.   Then follow Grindstone
and Johnston's Islands, the latter named after the noted
Bill Johnston.

Wells Island lies above the village of Alexandria, and on the west side has a beautiful sheet of water called the Lake of the Thousand Islands. Numerous residences are erected on the islands by the proprietors, whilst some are free for camping parties during the summer. The outfit for tenting should always include camphor for insects, aquamonia for bites, a few rolls of mosquito netting, whiskey for snake bites; dose, **a quart** to a bite, with a dram every once in awhile to ward off possible attacks matches and tinder to drive away gnats, and sticking plaster for wounds and injuries, for even the mosquitoes partake to a certain extent of the peculiarity of the climate and its people, for, instead of entertaining you with its song, and affectionately calling you " cuzzin " before proceeding to business, these northern invaders approach like a thief in the night, and, without sign or sound, commence at once in silence to extract from your comely form the blood that sustains life itself, moral: use oil of penny-royal to defeat their machinations, but should they decline to be bribed by such sauces and syrups, why take a little rye and soda to nullify the poisons, the rye extract being taken internally, whilst the soda is used outside.

The Admiralty, Fleet, Indian Group, and Amateur Islands lie either on the Canadian or U.S. lines, but below the latter islands the river contracts to one or two miles in width, and the Thousand Islands, of which there are estimated to be some 1400, may be said to terminate, although quite a number, called Brock's Group, are passed a short distance below Brockville.

Landing at Brockville we find it a thriveing litlq town of some 6000 inhabitants, connected with the capital by the Brockville and Ottawa R. R. and by ferry with the town of Morristown. A large amount of business is transacted and several important industries, including the chemical works, are located here. The town is supplied with good hotels, both near the river and also near the G. T. R. station. The Revere, a short distance from the ferry landing and B. & O. R. R., is probably the best patronized by the public. The ferries have a curious way of charging for passage : for nstance, to go to the United States costs 10c., whilst the are to return is 25c., and no doubt this will account for quite a number of citizens and emigrants when once across the line not returning to Canada for want of lucre.

Between Brockville and Prescott or Ogdensburg the river widens considerably. Arriving at Prescott we remain to witness the military manœuvres and the sham fight on Dominion Day, the 1st of July. In no two countries or states can a greater contrast be seen than is here presented by the village of Prescott on the Canadian side and the city of Ogdensburg in the State of New York. The latter is a thriving city of some 12,000 inhabitants and the terminus of the Utica & Black River, Rome, Watertown & Ogdensburg and Ogdensburg & Champlain railways. The city boasts of fiue elevators, good wharfage, saw mills, round houses and machine shops, and contains energy enough to make a prosperous and enterprising community, ostensibly showing American thrift and go-aheaditiveness ; the other looks apparently but a shell or a ruin, although it is stated that soon there will be an elevator on this side which will a1d somewhat to the prosperity of the town. At present it is iu a wretched condition, the streets ill-kept, business is

but small, and, were it not for the small amount of cash
spent by summer visitors and railroad travellers, the people
must either starve or emigrate.   Although the bank is ṣaiḷ
to command a good amount of capital, yet such terms are
demanded for its use that no improvements are ever thought
of, and its merchants have no idea of ever increasing their
trade.   There are two breweries and a distillery in Prescott,
the owner of the distillery is a member of Parliament, and
distils enough whiskey to control every vote in his district
(and here I would remark that the favorites as M.Ps
are the distillers, the brewers and newspaper editors.
Although prohibited from engaging in trade whilst rendering
their country a service, the latter class either sell out to
their relatives or form their paper into a company of which
the brother is managing-director, whilst the Parliamentary
adviser is looking for "fat takes" of the session) ; but the
Prescott member is one of the most enterprising men in the
place, and one who endeavors to keep up with the times
making several trips to the States yearly, and no doubt
adding to his general stock of knowledge, as also to his fine
breed of stock, owning some of the choicest cattle in the
province; he is about establishing a cattle ranche on an
extensive scale east of the Rockies where, if the Indians
and Mounted Police do not raid the stock, no doubt but it
will be found a paying investment—M.Ps having the prit
vilege of acreage at $10 per thousand.   The hotels are
small, and prices proportionately high, living poor, and the
visitor very apt to make foreign acquaintances at almos
any hour of the day or night he may occupy his room.
An excellent newspaper is published here—the *Prescott
Messenger*—under the editorship of Chas J. Hynes; the
paper is bright, newsy and vivacious, thoroughly advocating

and proclaiming the advantages of the country surrounding.
Dominion Day in Prescott was the great day of the year,
the militia were encamped for their annual drill, a sham
fight was to be indulged in, and an attack. made on old·
Fort Wellington, which is fondly imagined by the citizens
to stand as a menace to the people on the other side of the
river. The militia boys—the sons of small farmers—raw
recruits but a few days before, went very creditably
through their work, and aided in convincing me that the
improvised soldier is, *under certain circumstances*, quite
equal to the professional hireling, for, during the civil war
in the United States it was on several occasions demonstrated that a small and patriotic command whipped and
nearly annihilated a well equipped and veteran army of
twice their number; but it is still to the interests of the
rulers of the people to imbue false ideas upon this point.
It is due here to state that the militia were drilled under
the personal supervision of Col. George Shepherd who
after years of active service in the East, is now passing the
evening of life in his pleasant home at Burritts Rapids,
It was by an attack upon Fort Wellington from Windmill
Point, with a small company of liberators, that the gallant,
brave and noble Pole, Col. Von Schoultz, in the year
1838, won for himself a lasting name and a respectful word
even from the lips of his enemies. He was the soul of
honor, and as cool of head as he was brave of heart; and
even though he perished with his faithful band of followers
still he was revered as a foeman worthy of a better cause.
But had he been guided (even feebly as he was supported)
by an intelligence brighter than his own, success instead of
defeat would have crowned his efforts and his cause ; but his
superior officer, Gen. Birge, was the impersonification of

absolute cowardice and a thorough craven at heart, who brought upon himself by his false promises the obliquy of the loss of lives more precious than his own, whilst his name became a bye-word and reproach, for the men who sacrificed their lives even in a fruitless cause were esteemed and respected by all.

The Town of Prescott is connected with the City of Ottawa by the St. Lawrence and Ottawa Railway, one of the most dilapidated roads in the Dominion, but which has lately been purchased by the C. P. Syndicate, who, like the proverbial cat, are bound to have all that's in the house in time; but it runs through an unproductive region, the land being barren and sandy, covered partially with rank growths and scrub timber, entirely unfit for agricultural purposes, but still has good locations for manufactories of various kinds. The inhabitants when pointed out their opportunities and rallied on their lack of enterprise invariably reply, "Oh this is a new country, you know. It will take time to develop it." Still it is an older country than most of the States, and note what they have accomplished in the last one hundred years; or take for example even a section, the Southern States, who, sixteen years ago, at the close of the war, found her lands laid waste, her houses burned, her fences destroyed, her labor scattered or driven off, and her produce carried away out of the country, in fact, she was the realization of desolation itself. Now see the change: her houses are rebuilt, farms are well tilled, manufactories are established at many points, and to-day the southern section is the most prosperous of any portion of the whole country, and the prosperity of the South has materially assisted in causing a return of good times throughout the whole nation, whilst its influence is even felt throughout the length and breadth of the Dominion.

Leaving Prescott we for a time have done with the islands that so thickly studded the lake above us, and which for the most part are bare rocks, partially covered with the scantiest of verdure, varying in size from a few yards to nine miles, although on larger islands, like that of St. John, some farms are cultivated and good pasturage shown. The rocks seem to be either the deposit of icebergs gradually cut through by the action of the water, or are the residue of a volcanic disturbance.   The channel in places is a narrow and tortuous one, but is well lighted at frequent   intervals on both the Canadian and American shores.

On leaving Prescott, which is generally from 9 to 10 a.m. the hotel runners, lightning workers, and the invariable Old Traveller, are found on board, who discant loudly on the merits of their various avocations, the O. T. sagely advising the passengers not to be so fully absorbed in the beauty of the scenery as to take away the appetite, for he calmly assures them that, whatever happens, and whether they arrive at Montreal by 8 p.m. or midnight, it is the policy of the Company, fully endorsed by the steward, to furnish passengers with no meals after the one o'clock dinner. Of course the passenger, on receiving this information, naturally growls, and inwardly resolves never to patronize the Royal Mail line again, but the Company don't care, for they are making money (they believe).

Six   miles below Prescott, we approach the Gallops, (Gallewe) Rapids, a stretch of rapid some two miles in length and the water taking a good hold brings the steamer through in style, but for sailing vessels the rapids form a barrier. At present dredges are employed by the Government to deepen the channel, and no doubt afford life-time sinecures to those in command. On the return these rapids are overcome by a canal two miles in length, containing two locks with a fall of water of but eight feet. The five canals between this point and Cornwall cost the Government £1,052,601, or $5,263,005; then is passed Point Iroquois, with its canal three miles long, one lock and six feet of a fall, then Matilda Landing on the Canada side and Waddington on the American shore. Rapid Platt commences here, and extends some two and a half miles. At the side is a canal four miles in length, with two locks, overcoming a fall of eleven and a half feet, Williamsburg and Chrysler's farm, where considerable fighting between the Lobster Coats and the Rebels was indulged in during the year 1812, come next; then Farran's Point, with its little canal of three-quarter mile, and fall of four feet; Louisville Landing, where passengers land for Massena Springs, six miles distant. During the summer two small steamers, the Algoma and Massena, run daily from Ogdens - burg to the Landing, for which service the passenger is taxed his dollar, with an additional 50c. from the Landing to the Springs.

Opposite Louisville, on the Canada shore, is Dickenson's Landing, just below which the Long Sault Rapids are met, the longest, wildest and most important rapid on the St. Lawrence, having a fall of forty-eight feet, and which necessitated the building of a canal eleven and a half miles in length, containing seven locks, to enable vessels to clear the current; the rapids are divided by islands into two channels —the North and South; for some time the South was the only channel used, but finding that the North Channel, although seemingly more dangerous far to the eye—the waves roll and rush with apparently terrible force, the combing coming over the steamer's sponsons in some quantities is caused by the breaking of the waves upon the projecting rocks—but as the passage is not dangerous it is now run in preference, owing to its depth of water and steady current, for after once passing the point good time is made to Cornwall, at the foot of the rapids.   Barnet and Long Sault Islands, which belong to New York, and Cornwall and Sheeks Island, belonging to Canada, divide the waters of St. Lawrence into two channels, which cause the rapids of the Long Sault.

Cornwall, a manufacturing town of some 4000 inhabitants, and prettily situated, is next reached.   The Indian village of St. Regis, within the boundary line of both countries, is then passed, and Lake St. Francis, with its expanse of water from two to six miles in width, opens to the view,—then we plunge into Coteau du Lac Rapid, which extends about two miles.   Below this the Cedar Rapids some three miles in length are passed, then through the Cascades or Split Rock which plunge into Lake St. Louis, and oncemore, we are in still water.   The latter rapids are overcome by the Beauharnois Canal, eleven and a quarter miles in length containing nine locks, whilst the velocity of the current can be estimated from the fact that the water of the St. Lawrence falls eighty-two and a half feet in that distance.   The cost of this canal was £365,331, or $1,826,655.   At Isle Perrot in Lake St. Louis and mouth of the Ottawa, the dark waters of the latter river join the St. Lawrence; then down the lake some fourteen miles, and we wait for the Indian pilot at the village of Caughnawaga, opposite the town of Lachine. From there we start over the turbulent waters of the Lachine, the last—but called the most dangerous—of the

rapids. Running these as the boat moves onward, almost grazing the rocks, which, as my second mate once remarked of the breakers whilst we were cruising for a pilot off the Gaspé coast, "are pretty enough to look at but rather in the way just now," all the passengers, even to those affectatious ones who "have done so much of the kentry you know, that it is becoming quite a bore, and besides we are going to Yurerope, you know," are all anxiously crowding forward to obtain a good view of the heaving, breaking and seething waters ; and as we are about to plunge into the cauldron we seem to be running directly upon the rocky and grass-covered little Isle aux Diable; and for a moment the bow of the boat is so near that it seems impossible to clear it, but the steamer answers swiftly to the helm, and quick as thought she glides away from the danger it seemed impossible to avoid. The descent depends greatly on the coolness and calculation of the captain and pilot, for one false move and the passengers would experience lively times, for the current is so swift, the seas run high, whilst the boat is driven so rapidly by, that one touch upon the rocks and every plank would be started and the vessel shivered to atoms. But soon the thrill is passed, and leaving Isle aux Heron and Nuns' Island we are gliding under the Victoria Bridge, and rounding up for the wharf at Montreal. These last rapids have a greater fall in their descent than any on the river: the fall between Lachine and Montreal being forty-five feet, making a total fall from Lake Erie to Montreal of 550 feet. The fall from the latter city to tide water at Three Rivers being thirteen feet makes the total fall from Lake Erie to sea level some 565 feet. The Lachine rapids are overcome by a canal eight and a half miles in length, containing five locks and which cost originally £481,736, although far more is being spent on its enlargement annually.

MONTREAL

Montreal, formerly called Ville Marie, claims to be the largest city in British North America, having a population of 140,747, and is an admixture of the greed, selfishness and parsimony of Scotch with the shrewdness of the French. The city lies on the north bank of the river, which at this point is over two miles wide. The bearings of the city are lat. 45° 30' N. and long. 73° 25' W., whilst its site as a port at the head of ship navigation is an excellent one. Its wharves, extending down the river some 3 miles, are substantially built of wood faced with grey limestone. The managers of shipping interests have certainly persevered in order to obtain the wharfage privileges they now retain. A few years ago the "Allan Line" had almost entire control of the shipping interests of this port, and being largely subsidized by both the Home and the Dominion Governments they fast assumed control of the trade, and became a monopoly that smaller companies were afraid to compete with; even now a moiety of the yearly subsidy granted to the Allans comprises the items of $126,533.32 and $28,135.14. It is by the fostering care bestowed upon the line that has enabled it to comprise one of the largest fleets in the world, owning an ocean steam tonnage alone of 77,400 tons, with sailing ships, river and lake steamers as adjuncts. This line during the season of 1880 carried some 11,402 head of cattle, 11,430 sheep, and 1,354,706 bushels or 169,-338 quarters of grain. For a time it was thought the height of folly to attempt to compete or even to obtain a portion of the trade for a season, much less attempt to establish a permanent line as a candidate for public favor; but through the indomitable energy, perseverance, and close management of Mr. Thos. Cramp (David Torrance & Co.) the Dominion Line of Steamships have become a regular and permanent line of traders to this port, and are rapidly growing in favor with both shippers and the public generally, and are certainly well patronized. During the season the Dominion Line carried some 11,305 head of cattle, 21,262 sheep and 2,400,000 bushels grain. The steamers of this line divide their service, a portion of the fleet being regularly engaged in trading to New Orleans. The new vessels of the line will be amongst the finest steamships trading to North America. The "Vancouver," the latest addition to the fleet, is a vessel of 5,800 tons, four-masted, driven by compound engines; her saloons amidships are fitted with every modern appliance for the comfort of its passengers. The "Beaver Line," under the management of Messrs. Thompson, Murray & Co., also obtain a fair proportion of patronage. Their exports may be summed up in general as 6,457 head of cattle, 5,588 sheep, 1,050,-000 bushels grain. The Donaldson Clyde Line, Temperley, together with the outside ships, are roughly estimated to have carried 20,396 head of cattle and 33,263 sheep. The total value of the Montreal exports for the season 1880 was $32,284,240, and for the year 1881 amounted to $31,300,000. A new line has been established through the enterprise of Wm. Darley Bentley, the Consul for Brazil. The line of which the Comte d'Eu and Tancarville are the pioneer steamers are now running from France to Canada, thence to the West Indies and Brazil, and it is thought that if proper interest is taken in the line that it will assist materially in establishing a permanent trade between the two countries, navigation opening here about the end of April and closing early in November.

WHARVES OF MONTREAL.

The number of vessels arriving at the port of Montreal in 1880 was 710, which produced a revenue of
$331,294, but last season there was considerable
falling off, owing in part, with sailing vessels at least,
to the report of excessive charges for towage, for a
stranger here finds his pilotage alone $4.20 up, $2.80 down,
$7 per foot, with discrimination and the usual expense
of breaking in new arrivals, the other tariffs being at the
rate of $1.20 per mile, or averaging $63.29 cents per ton;
the Beaver tariff $1.79 per mile, or $94.29 per ton,
whilst the tariff of 1873 entitled them to a charge of
$3.48 per mile or $188.58 per ton, and under which
latter tariff a vessel of 572 tons being towed 398 miles
would cost $1,096, but old traders and those companies in
the ring are allowed a rebate, which at all events is satisfactory to the owners receiving it.

The business streets and those on which reside the
gentry are well paved and macadamized, and present a
cleanly appearance, for, owing, to the rising ground occupied,
the drainage is good and effective. Notre Dame is the
fashionable thoroughfare for retail trade, whilst on St
James are located the post office—a fine stone edifice
with a revenue of $169,554.09 against an expenditure
of $74,099.46,—most of the banks, insurance and other
business offices, including the fine St. Lawrence Hall. This
hotel, being the property of the enterprising proprietor,
Henry Hogan, Esq., now occupies the entire block, and is
fitted with every modern convenience that may add to
the comfort of its guests; is lighted throughout with the
electric light, and having a fine electric lamp suspended
from the exterior over the main entrance, becomes the
centre of attraction at night, the light being seen from one

extremity of the thoroughfare to the other. McGill street, commencing at Victoria Square and extending to the river, is filled with stores and offices of various kinds; here too are found imposing offices of the Mercantile Agencies, Guarantee Societies and similiar adjuncts of a state of suspicion, affectation and servitude, but whatever may have been the aim intended by the founders of Mercantile Agencies and so-called private detection, or the ends that were to be subserved other than private gain, it is not the intention here to discuss; but one thing is certain, it has either outlived its usefulness, as many young merchants here can testify, or its objects and mode of working have been sadly perverted. Instead of keeping men honest they really aid a man to become a violator of law, and so subvert the very ends for which they were supposed to be created. How many ambitious young men eager and anxious to do the thing that is lawful and right, and good-naturedly try to push themselves and their fortunes along in the world, have found their creditors inexorable and ruin staring them in the face because the report was rendered "That he was too ambitious, and for the good of society must be kept under, or he would rise too rapidly and thus breed ambition in others."

A very good story of tit for tat is told of a bank president who used to have his clerks watched by some of the so-called private detectives, now so numerous, flourishing and importunate, who never work for rewards but sell their services cheap to all for strictly cash in advance. He had hauled up several of the clerks about their improper and extravagant expenditures, and was sitting in his private office, waiting the appearance of the new assistant receiving teller, Charles Augustus Fitzloftus De Gum, who had

MONTREAL.

J.Walker sc Montreal

been duly shadowed and reported on by operative P. Q.
of Judas and Gehazi's secret service. The clerk having
entered the president's office, was accosted with the question, "Young man, what is your salary?" "Nine hundred,
Sir, and I can scarcely live on that." "No, I should think
not. I suppose you know I am a cautious man, and now I
will say that from enquiries made touching your habits I
have been led to form the opinion that you are spending
money altogether too fast for the trusted employee of a
bank. Now do not defend yourself. Let me tell you
where you went last night. You left this office at 4 p.m.,
and with the messenger walked into Isaac's and drank
brandy smash. You played billiards at the hall from
4.37 to 6.42 p.m., and dined at Compain's on saddle
rocks, quail, pommery sec. You went to see the
Colonel at the Academy, went out several times between
the acts, and before the piece was through walked down
to Pete's and lost $5.25 at poker, after which you drowned
your sorrow in several hot scotch's and took the last
car for your room on east St. Catherine street. Now I
want to know if you think that proper conduct for a
servant of a bank like this?"

Now the other clerks, on arriving at this point, had
one and all admitted the truth of the operative's reports,
and after begging forgiveness had promised immediate
and substantial reform. But this clerk was made of different stuff, and he said, "I don't think anything at all about
it. That report is a tissue of falsehoods from beginning to
end; and, as I happen to know, was made by Jim Muggins,
an ex-convict and son of a thief. If ever you want to
know how I spend my evenings, I shall be pleased to
inform you, Sir, at any and all times; but now that this

matter of fidelity to the corporation has come up, let me read you my special agent's report of how you spent yesterday afternoon. At 2 o'clock you met the notary of the bank and told him to send around the rebate on his commissions for the year, and he met you at the Bodega a little later and gave you $366.15, for which you thanked him, and told him the directors would not change their notary for the present. On leaving the bank you met Flimsy, the contractor for the stone and brick work for the new western branch, and he handed you a parcel and said, ' Here's your whack up of the divy,' at which you smiled and invited him to drink, which he declined. At 7 p.m. you told your wife that there was a meeting of bank Presidents at the Windsor that night, and you wouldn't be home until late. Instead of going to the hotel you went to a house on Sherbrooke near St. Denis street, where you passed the evening with the pretty widow you called Evangeline, first giving her a package of new tens and a watch and chain, with the observation that you had promised your wife a watch long ago and hadn't given it to her yet. You reached home at 12.30 a.m., and had to ring the bell because you dropped your latch-key on Evangeline's carpet. You were surprised during the night by burglars to whom Evangeline had given the key of your house, and while they took nothing of value because your dog scared them off, you were so angry that you complained to the Chief of Police that the policeman on your beat was of no account, whereas you were yourself to blame, and then—" "That will do," said the President. "I see that you are a smart young man, it is not necessary to discuss these trivial matters. By the way, what did you say your salary was ?" " Nine hundred, Sir." "Well, it will be fifteen hundred after this, and I will make you cashier as soon as old Kreter goes on his next drunk!" "Thank you, Sir." "Oh, that's nothing to be thankful for. Just go along and attend to your work, and I'll take care of you, and by the by you needn't say anything to the other clerks about my little foolishness with that widow," and the clerk sailed out to his duties.

Water, Commissioners and Common streets extend the entire length of the city, facing on the St. Lawrence and Lachine canal, and are the business centres for commission merchants, ship stores and storage warehouses. When the port and harbor are crowded with shipping and ocean, lake and river steamers, these streets and wharves present an animated appearance, for by the use of the electric light the noise and bustle of loading and discharging is continued both night and day.

The city of Montreal is laid out in the form of a parallelogram, and lies at the foot of an eminence called Mont Royal, from which the city derives its name. This rock, which stands alone in the wide river plain, is some 550 feet in height, and is supposed to have been formed from the deposit of an immense iceberg stranded here some centuries ago whilst the surrounding country was overflowed by the sea. The mountain is ascended both by a winding carriage road and also by a series of some 427 steps up its sides; the steps in some portions of the incline are so steep that resting places are provided at intervals during the ascent. Foreign boulders are perched on the top of the mountain, which itself is scored with glacial *stria*. The view obtained from the various eminences is a pleasing and delightful one, laying the entire city at its feet, further off the majestic St. Lawrence and the various islands, whilst in the far distance the Green Mountains of Vermont and a portion of the Adirondacks are plainly discernible on a clear day. On the top and sides of the mount are laid out the park and cemeteries, which will amply repay the time spent in visiting them, and noting the prevailing customs and man's vanity for interments. The Stations of the Cross in the Catholic portion (fourteen in number) depict incidents in the life of Christ until his crucifixion, whilst on the apex are life-size figures erected on three crosses, of Christ, Barrabas and the young man, who were crucified together at Golgotha by the Jews some years ago, who if living in this portion to-day would be in jail as tramps before twenty-four hours. The dwellings and public edifices of the city are substantially built, being for the most part of cut-stone, giving them a solid and lasting appearance. This peculiarity is accounted for from the fact that immense quarries of rock are opened in close proximity to the city itself; that it is certainly cheaper to erect a building of stone in preference to one of brick, without the consideration that the stone house is cooler in the summer time and warmer during the winter months than one built of any other material. The landlords here have also two seasons of diversion and enjoyment during the year: one in the early spring, when the tenants are signing new leases and paying their month's deposit in advance; the other in the fall, when the landlord, accompanied by the bailiff, are using up the eight days allowed by law, earnestly engaged in looking for that tenant, to collect or distrain for the last four months' rent, which the gentleman forgot to forward when he gently and silently skipped away between two days, taking his furniture with him, and forgetting to forward his new address with the key. Thus are old country customs transplanted to a new, fertile and prolific soil. The winters are severe, and last usually from the latter end of October until May, at times out-door labor being suspended for days together. The poorer classes are either gone to the States or confined in the hospitals or jails, but the merchants who have made enough out of summer visitors, together with the upper ten, are securely housed until next season's sun shall wake them into life and energy once more.

In approaching the city from the river the scene is one of interest. First the mountain in the back ground, then the Victoria Bridge and islands rivet the attention; this bridge crosses the river from Point St. Charles to St. Lambert, on the south shore, a total length of 10,284 feet, or fifty yards less than two miles. It is built on the tubular principle, and so arranged as to allow for the contraction and expansion of the entire mass, a difference between summer and winter of some 6 inches. The bridge rests on twenty-four piers, with two abutments of limestone masonry, the centre span being 330 feet in length, at a height of sixty feet above the summer level of the river, descending from the centre at the rate of 1 in 130 to either end. The bridge was built by Thomas Brassey, the noted contractor of Birkenhead, Eng., for Sir Morton Peto, once well known in railroad circles, who afterwards took a prominent part in the A. & G. W. R. R. addition to the Erie. The cost of construction amounted to the enormous sum of $6,500,000, which many a fair estate and numerous quiet families in Great Britain earnestly regret to this day. The weight of iron in the tubes alone is over 8000 tons; the dimensions of the tube through which the trains pass in the centre span is twenty-

two feet in height by sixteen feet in width.   Half way across
is a golden rivet driven to its place by the Prince of Wales,
upon the completion and formal opening of the Bridge for
traffic in 1858.   The rivet is surrounded by a glass case, and
having telegraphic communication to each end of the bridge,
should the glass be broken or an attempt made to remove
the treasure an alarm would be instantly sounded; had it
not been for these precautions it would be impossible to
ensure the safety of so valuable an ingot, especially in a
community such as are found in the vicinity.

Next to attract attention are the towers of Notre Dame and
the spires of other churches, the bronze cupola of the Marche
Bonsecours, with its fine frontage and buildings generally.
The market, formerly the old City Hall, is the largest of the
six markets that Montreal contains, whose total sales of
farm produce amount yearly to $525,000, Marche Bonse-
cours disposing of some $195,000, and securing a revenue
of $25,000 in rents, against an expenditure of only $3,-
700.   The sales of fish alone are estimated to amount to
$193,000.   Market boats from Berthier, Sorel, and suburban
boats, both above and below the rapids, are regularly run
in summer, bringing vast loads of produce to the city, literally packing the market and adjacent streets for blocks
with country produce, and rendering the housekeeper's duty
a pleasant one, whilst the dealers and habitants alike seem
happy and contented.   During the winter supplies are
brought over the river in sleighs, and everything is changed:
the habitants stand clothed in furs shiveringly beside their
stalls ; and as the purchaser hurries along, he is accosted
with " *avez vous besoin de quelque chose.*"   Upon the selection being pointed out from amongst a number of frozen
blocks which, when thawed, prove to be beef, pork or mutton.

tI e butcher picks up his axe, and chops off a chunk like chopping stovewood; but even his peaceful occupation is not unattended with danger, for a boarding house keeper had her eye put out by a butter splinter, whilst the sausages she was selecting fell down "kerchunk," stunning her so badly that it took fully two hours and a bottle of gin for her to recover. Milk is sold by the yard, and the boys buy milk icicles like cent sticks of molasses candy, whilst birds and chickens might be used successfully as cannon balls during a winter's seige.

Leaving the market, up Jacques Cartier square, is seen the monument erected to the memory of Admiral Nelson, the hero of the Nile. On the sides of the pedestal of the Doric column are bas-reliefs, commemorative of naval engagements in which the Admiral took part, at the foot of the monument, and pointed toward the river are two old-fashioned cannon taken by the British from the Russians during the Crimean war.

At the head of the Square are the splendid pile of buildings, the Court House and the New City Hall, which latter cost close on $12 50 000 The former building was paid for by a special tax on civil cases heard, and so popular did the tax become that it has never been remitted. In the building are the offices of the Court officers, etc., together with rooms in which are held the Civil, Criminal and Marine courts. In the new City Hall the various interests of the city are duly attended to by the Mayor and his Board of Aldermen, although apparently the latter are not much valued by either His Worship or the various corporations with whom they come in contact. On the ground floor are the police offices, cells, and the Recorder's Court, the latter a veritable Star Chamber, the proceedings being decidedly summary. Having managed to get admitted into one of the local stations, a night's experience is thus summed up: After being placed in a cell, that certainly would be benefited by a visit from the Board of Health, every thing went quietly, with the exception of a few energetic remarks made by a gentleman in the next apartment, until the patrolmen returned from their beat; they then surrounded the table and, after imbibing something out of a tin can, called for the cards, and Euchre was the game. Soon becoming interested, remarks were frequent: "Them two bowers wuz played by me," says Officer Doolan. "Dat's zo but I took dem tricks" says, Jacques. "Will yer let me take a hand wid yer?" was the request from behind the bars. "Shall we?" said one." "Oh, no," put in another, "sure he's a disperate man, and might kill and murder us all and make his escape, and thin the Recarder cudn't foine him in the morning." So the poor prisoner had to quietly look on and listen. In a short time the silence was broken with, "Sure its a foine Recarder we have now in the place of Ould West,—There's the ace, and that gives me a march. You bet this is the banner station; didn't we get four men lasht month alone wid from $75 to $200 in their pockets, and didn't the Recarder foine them $25 apiece, beautifully and nathuralloike. Them return sheets is a splendid thing: sure the Recarder has little to do when he looks at them, except to foine." "Its an aisy job he's got, an no mistake; sure last year the Court foines mounted to $11,600," chimed in another. In a little while the patrolmen retired to their bunks and all was silent. At five a. m. all are awakened with the intimation that the carriage is around to convey prisoners to the Central Station at the City Hall, and the various occupants of the stations who, for the most part, were but trembling drunks, are conveyed manacled through the streets to the City Hall, where, after remaining until 10 o'clock, the cases are called on; and the prisoners one by one make their appearance at the bar, to be tried in any language they like, for its all the same remarked one, for "the divil a man he ever lets off." The clerk, a little, fussy old man, with grey hair, then proceeds to read the charge: "Bill Sykes, your charged with being drunk and-begging-on-the public-streets-Are-you-guilty-or-not-guilty? (*sotto voce*) of-course-you-are. No! How's-that-trot-up-the-Highly-Intelligent." The officer, being called upon, steps up and delivers himself: "I wuz on my bate last night, yer Honor, betune the hours of six and eight yer Honor, and two very respectable females informed me that the prisoner at the bar, yer Honor, was axing thim for something." The prisoner here broke in: "Yer Honor awm ony hout from Hingland by last ship, on I wuz ony axing the way to the ships, for if aw con ony git back to Wigan, aw'l never be copt here any more." "Was he drunk?" queried His Honor. "He wuz, yer Honor," replied the H. I. "How do you know?" asked the Judge. "Becase his breath shmelt ov onions, yer Honor," was the answer, $5 and costs." said His Honor, and the case was over. There is one thing very certain,—that is, it matters but little whether it is a servant girl suing the wife of an alderman for wages, a salesman or traveller suing for pay, the poor party and laborer, gets all the law he can stand, whilst the decision may be almost anticipated by "dismissed with costs."

RELIGION.

Tell me not, in mournful numbers,
 "Life is but an empty dream"!
For the soul is dead that slumbers,
 And things are not as they seem.
Life is real ! Life is earnest !
 And the grave is not its goal;
 " Dust thou art, to dust returnest,"
Was not spoken of the soul.

                          —*Longfellow.*

Montreal claims, and certainly deserves, the title of the
" City of Churches," and, as Mark Twain observes, is the
only city on the continent where you cannot throw
a brick without breaking a church window.   There are more
places and forms of worship, with less real Christianity,
than can be found in any other city of its size in America,
but some of them are really notable structures.   The
French Cathedral, Notre Dame, opposite the Place d'Armes,
is built in the Gothic style of architecture, and almost
after the model of the Cathedral of Rheims, France.   Its
length is 255 feet, whilst its breadth is 134; the towers
belonging to the front are 220 feet in height; the S. W.
tower containing the largest bell in America, weighing
29,400 lbs.   The eastern window at the high altar is sixty-
four feet in height and thirty-two in breadth ; the interior
has numerous chapels, confessionals and altars, whilst the
body of the church is separated by shafts into five compart-
ments. The building itself will accommodate some 10,000
persons; who can quickly disperse by the several outlets. The
portal is formed by an arcade of three arches, on the top of

which are placed statues, each arch being nineteen feet by forty-nine in height. Under the church was occupied as catacombs in which the more wealthy of the congregation were interred. The chapels and high altar are profusely decorated with gilt, color and statuary. The Seminary of St. Sulpice adjoins the cathedral. In it the secular affairs, connected with the very valuable business property belonging to the church, as well as parochial business, is transacted. It is estimated that two-thirds of the real property in Montreal is owned or held by religious sects or institutions. There are some fifty-five other churches of all denominations, of which the Catholics own thirteen, with the cathedral, Bonsecours church, Church of the Gesu, St. Patrick's, the Bishop's church, St. James, St. Ann's, St. Peter's, Notre Dame des Anges, Notre Dame de Lourdes, St. Joseph St. Vincent de Paul, St. Brigide, General Hospital church, Notre Dame de Pitié, Hotel Dieu church, and St. Mary's. The Catholics number in Montreal some 103,577; all others, including those with no religion, muster about 36,357, whilst the *Yutes* or Jews count up 811.

The Church of England has eight places of worship, whilst the Dissenters and Jews own the remaining thirty-five, but the reaching for the dollar is prominent at each, for when the stranger goes to inspect the building of Notre Dame and ascends one of the towers he is taxed the sum of twenty-five cents. So remunerative has this practice become that several thousand dollars are annually derived from the visits of strangers alone. The services on Sunday are usually largely attended, but here again spot cash or no religion is the cry ; for each seat occupied the sum of five cents is charged, and, should some piously inclined poor find their way into this edific., hoping to attain some con-

solation in their poverty, they are forced either to stand at
the side of the doorways behind the congregation, or to
kneel on the stone floor of the aisle whilst the services are
being enacted; but the faithful poor are happy in their
ignorance, and submit to indignities and almost insults
without a murmur on their part. The Jesuits have also
located in considerable numbers in the city, and have a fine
cathedral in which to worship, but, whilst criticising the
blind and trustfully ignorant faith of the Catholic portion
of the community, we cannot overlook the Protestants.
Taken as a class, and including all denominations, they
have by far the majority in point of numbers of churches,
within whose sacred precincts the Great Creator is popularly
supposed to be served, and in which it is assumed he
delights to dwell, there being no less than forty-three
edifices from which the Reformed Faith is promulgated.
On Sunday no sight is so edifying and delightful as to
sit and watch the procession of the Saintly, meandering
in groups to their favorite place where the Gospel is
interpreted according to the ideas most suitable and
acceptable to themselves, and the Almighty is cajoled
and conciliated from a depraved and artificial standpoint.
First comes paterfamilias, arrayed in his Sunday-go-to-
meeting suit of black, with solemn mien, leading by
the hand his youngest scion; then follow his wife and
daughters, enveloped in their finery, and displaying
jewellery and gewgaws like South Sea Islanders, followed
by the other members of the family,—each of the crowd,
from the old man himself, carrying in their hands a brass-
bound, copper-fastened, gilt-edged, morocco-backed prayer-
book or Bible, with the family name and number of the
pew emblazoned in prominent gilt letters on the back,

SAINTLY.

for fear, if the books were left in the sanctuary, that
some poor thief might actually be tempted to steal " *the
Word of God.*" Then follow the group as they ostentatiously
march up the steps of a fashionable edifice, and slowly
parade down the aisle to a comfortable, carpeted, cushioned
and hassocked pew, for which the head of the family pays
fifty dollars per annum; notice the self-satisfied look upon
the faces of these pious ones as they criticise in an under-
tone the appearance of strangers and their neighbors generally.   Should a well-dressed stranger desire to take part
in the service he is oftentimes shown to a seat, it being a
matter of policy, for strangers generally contribute handsomely on the passing of the plate in the middle of each
performance; but, should an unfortunate or poorly dressed
wight seek admittance, they are quickly informed that there
are no free seats in *this* church, so they must look for consolation to "the little church around the corner," where
the seats are free.   Then watch the gaily attired clerk of
the works as he ascends with sanctified look and dignified
tread to his perch in the pulpit, bows his pious head in
silent prayer, arises and runs his jewelled fingers through
his well-oiled locks, and announces, in a voice full of affectation, " Bwetherin, we will now sing to the pwaise and
glowy of Gad the fortwy thiwd hymn, commencing with
' We'd plwace our sin; ' "—and the way the congregation respond show they are most anxious and very
willing to place their sins anywhere where they will do
the most good, and on any one who will volunteer to
carry the load.   Then listen to the effeminate exhortation,
and the appeals for cash for the enlightenment of the
heathen, the continual repetition that through Eve's temp-
tation and Adam's fall we were all justly entitled to a

share of everlasting damnation. The responses by the people of "Have mercy upon us, miserable sinners," whilst they are fully persuaded they are not half so bad as the poor trash over the way, brings to mind Holy Willie's prayer or the negro camp-meeting refrain :

> " The sarpint he tempted the woman,
> " An' de woman she tempted de man.
> " If it had'nt a' been for the mussy of God,
> " We'd all been dead an' damn."

Such hypocrisy may be appreciated by the special god who is thought to be served, but the Great Creator of the Universe must view with feelings of disgust the mock solemnity and affectation of a portion of the work of His own hands.

And it was from such affected teachings as these in other times that gave birth and credence to such characters as Johanna Southcote, with her prophetic " Coming of Shiloh," and through that class the fact became apparent, that the public at large were steeped in ignorance, and were a most credulous people, who were imposed upon by this dropsical old woman until they believed that she really was inspired. We are informed that she was a native of England, born in the year 1750; wrote and dictated prophesies, but made money by the sale of seals, said to procure the salvation of those who purchased them. Her commission she professed to have received from the Most High, and what she wrote for two years, from 1792 to 1794, were sealed up with great care, and the box opened only in January, 1803, when opened in the presence of twenty-three persons appointed *by divine command*, as well as thirty-five others without special appointment, who, like politicians watching a square count, came to the unanimous conclusion, "that her calling was of God." She thus practised on the credulity of the people until she became a victim of her own hallucination, for early in her last year she fancied she was a second Virgin Mary, and was to bring forth the "Shiloh" promised by Jacob Bryan. This phenomena was to have been born in October, 1814, so great preparations were made by her enthusiastic converts, and they made her many expensive presents, fine wines, luxurious foods, a bible costing $200, cradle costing $1000, etc., so the old woman, who was a great eater, passed much of her time in bed, gal-oriously entranced, or drunk; was never heard to pray, but could swear like a trooper. She really was not half as smart as old Isaiah, who, when he prophesied that "behold a virgin shall conceive and bear a son," took with him two *reliable* witnesses to certify, Uriah the priest and Zechariah, both of whom he prudently left outside the curtain, and then went in "unto the prophetess" to lay foundation for success, "and in due time she conceived and bore a son" who was called Maher-Shalel-hash-baz, which means "I am here;" so instead of giving miraculous birth to a child, Johanna, after assuring her friends she was "off" for four days in a trance, and instructing them to keep her body warm, filled up with brandy, and laid down and meekly died. Her friends, literally following her injunctions, found the old lady stronger than they had any idea of, and the signs of decomposition being unmistakeable, they had to smoke tobacco to prevent being overpowered, and had finally to bury her, so if the heavenly marriage was ever consummated we poor toilers here below know nothing about the whole affair, and are consequently left out in the cold.

Still later have false teachings been productive

of pernicious outgrowths and fanaticism which, under the guise of Almighty inspiration, appeared at various periods in such characters as Sharp, one of the greatest masters in the English School of Engraving; Bryan, an irregular Quaker, who had engrafted sectarian doctrines on an original stock of fervid religious feeling, and Richard Brothers, who publicly proclaimed himself the "Nephew of God," and who predicted the destruction of all sovereigns, and who also proclaimed the millenium at hand. Then the animal magnetism of Mesmer, the mysteries and holy in-spired theories of Swedenborg, which bid fair to live until the end of time. Then the Newfoundlanders, the Spenceans, who advocated their doctrine under the French maxim of liberty, equality and justice, in both national and religious matters. Then Joseph Smith, the Mormon prophet, with his Urim and Thummin; Wm. Huntington, the coal heaver preacher, with his drafts on the Bank of Providence and Bank of Faith, and the various impostors who, under the guise of spiritual teachers, have administered to a credulous and artificial public. It is on these affected and superficial teachers that the onus of such a state of society as that now existing must fall, for now religion is regarded as a pleasant fiction, fostered and upheld in order to sustain society, and to reconcile the producer with the familiar sight of several living in ease and luxury off the labor of one. Even on this continent numerous communities exist who hold as a tenet of their belief, " that association with the clergy is contamination," and to become " tainted with religion " destroys the finest impulses that arise in human nature; therefore they hold that it is only by overthrowing Christianity that the masses can be emancipated from their present thraldom. For a local example of the power and love

wielded just fill a bag with dollars, call it the Temporalities
fund, and start the branches of the Scotch Kirk after it, the
money being allowed to the only true church.   Then listen
to the truthful claims presented by each section, and man's
confidence in infallibility rapidly vanishes.   In looking
carefully over the various forms and professions, one can
truly say with John Wesley, " I am sick of opinions
(forms and ceremonies); I am weary to bear them ; my
soul loathes this frothy food; give me solid and substantial
religion ; give me an humble lover of God and man, a man
full of mercy and good faith, laying himself out in the
work of faith, the patience of hope, the labor of love." And
many a perplexed mortal cries from the heart :

> " The throng is great, my Father.
> Many a doubt and fear encompass me about;
>   My foes oppress me sore; I cannot stand
>   Or go alone.   Oh Father! take my hand,
> And through the throng lead safely home thy child."

The Church of the Gesu is also quite an attraction for
tourists and visitors.   The church belongs to the Jesuits, and
is a massive stone building situated on Bleury street,
between Dorchester and St. Catherine, and capable of
seating some 4000 persons, but with a party we ascend the
steps and enter the church.   Along the sides are the various
confessionals and chapels, whilst at the end on either side of
the altar are valuable paintings from Rome.   Quite a character in connection with the church is Old Peter the
janitor, most devout in his bearing, and most persistent in
his efforts to induce the visitors to " by a buk," or give
something to the church; he explains, " Gintlemen and
ladies, thim paintings wuz done in Rome by the Italians,
and have the blessing of the Holy Father on thim afore

they kim over." "Who is that little fellow in wax in the glass case?" queries a tourist. "That is St. Charles Borromée when he wuz small," is the answer. Another asks, "What do the paintings represent?" "By a buk, only 25 cents, or if you don't by, I'll tell you, that is St. Charles Borromée receiving the Holy Eucharist from the Archbishop whin he give up his possessions and renounced the world." "Then he was euchred out of all he possessed," suggested another. "Oh sure," said Peter, "aint you afraid of committing a mortual sin? Sure I'll have to say three aves and four paters for your sinful sowl. Sure its a shame for heretics, the likes of ye, to gaze on thim holy picturs." So down on his knees he drops, and the way the beads fly through his fingers is a caution. In a moment, "Wud ye by a buk?" is again heard, and each time he passes the railing or the picture, his right knee bends some six inches; in the fifteen minutes our party occupied him the knee was bent sixty-one times, which, on an average of ten hours daily and six inches each time, would make that one knee travel for the honor and glory of the Saint in the course of a month 12,000 yards, or in twelve months a distance equal to 15 miles more than the other knee, so if the book business does not pay the saint ought certainly to keep a good berth for Peter. Another visitor says, "Peter, you are too devout and too good for this world if you keep on that way. Do you do this thing out of love for the saints?" "Faith I do," says Peter, "and sure it raises my poor heart to think that a Lazarus like myself may lay in some great saint's bosom, and whin I die at pace wid God an man, sure its pleasant to know that I'll not be among strangers at the resurrection." But Peter evidently makes well out of visitors, and so we leave him to the next crowd.

CHARITY.

The Province of Quebec does not rank last in an outward show of charity, for the grants by the Provincial Legislature amount to $158,570.50 annually, whilst an amount estimated at some $361,010.00 is expended for the cause of education, but with all the real object seems to be to provide sinecures for a certain class, and pattern after a worthy Alderman, who, whilst a candidate for election, appointed his secretary, getting full work both night and day during the canvass and subsequent day of voting, his workmen laboring faithfully and well amidst the snow and drenching rains on election day, after being handed by the Alderman the munificent sum of $2.00 to spend amongst the voters of the ward and having $4.00 I. O. U.'s liberally cancelled by a brother, quietly ignored all further claims after obtaining a large majority ; he also was unanimously elected as a member of the Visiting Committee of the Protestant House of Industry and Refuge, a most judicious selection, for if each member of Montreal society pays its workmen as munificently as this Christian Alderman the Refuge will not want or wait long for inmates. This may be deemed an exceptional instance, but it must be remembered he was a wealthy man, owning fully $2000 in real estate, and a thorough and conscientious Christian gentleman.

If Montreal prides herself upon the appellation of the " City of Churches," she certainly also is deserving of the distinction of being the home and abode of the beggars, for where there is so much *profession* of religion and virtue, there is a consequent abundance of pauperism, immorality, vice and crime ; for a land where the purest morals and strictest religion are *professed* is generally that which produces vice, and particularly the smaller vices, in greatest abundance.. The portion of the States and the Dominion with most religious teachers, ruled by ministerial Justices and clerical law makers, are those that furnish the greatest number of the *nymphs du pavé* to the cities on the continent, and even furnish a large supply to the capital of Cuba. From the same prolific soil spring most of the sharpers, quacks and cheat·ing traders who disgrace their country's name. It is but the inexorable result of a pseudo-religion, outward observance, worship, Sabbath-keeping, and the various forms are engrafted in the mind; and thus, by complicating the *true* duties that man owes to his fellow-man, obscure or take precedence of them, the latter grow to be esteemed as only of a secondary importance, and are, consequently, neglected; and in these northern latitudes when a man becomes poor he rapidly descends lower and lower until his manhood and self-respect are entirely obliterated and ·the former *man* becomes on a plane with the brute creation. On the ·streets, at the doorways of the hotels, on the corner of the squares, on the steps of the various churches, and even in the shadow of the great Cathedral, the passer-by is importuned in whining tones and with outstretched hand *to give,* for charity's sake. The number of men, women and children who have lost every particle of virtue and self-respect, in proportion to the size of the city, by far exceed the canaille of Paris or the Lazaroni of Naples itself. Many of these beings so lost to a sense of manhood and independence are strong and healthy, able, if properly employed, to bé producers, and assist in benefiting the community by becoming good citizens and bearing a proportion of the expense of government. These beings, when spoken to

regarding their state, often reply : "We, whilst at work,
receive such a pittance from the hands of employers of
labor that it is impossible to exist on the amount earned,
therefore we would rather follow the practice of begging
with all its abasement, and appeal to the charity of strangers
for means of existence, than work for wages upon which
we could do nothing but quietly starve." And there certainly
is some reason attached to this assertion, for many a poor
clerk who wears outwardly a semi-respectable appearance,
and who labors in a large establishment, lives upon but two,
and at times one meal a day, and even by such economy
as this cannot make both ends meet at the termination of the
month.   Whilst in conversation with a merchant, this topic
was alluded to, and the proposition suggested that some
of the able-bodied laborers and starving clerks should be
encouraged to cultivate a spirit of manhood and assisted to
become independent by having some of the territory west
donated to them, and the means necessary provided and
loaned them to erect homes and dwellings for themselves,
thus enabling them to become active producers instead of idle
and comparatively vicious consumers,—when this merchant
replied :   " Oh, that is entirely against Canadian principle
and policy—we never loan ; sometimes we may borrow,
but we never loan to poorer classes—*we give.*"   In order
to note the prevalence of that charitable spirit of giving, I
watched the actions of a number of well-to-do men who
fondly delude themselves with that assertion, and found
that on one Saturday, out of seventeen applications an old
woman received *one cent,* and still these persons thought
they had done their whole duty, and on the Sunday reverently " thanked the Lord for His goodness," and the profits
they had accumulated in their business, as they would that

others should do unto them ; they were not even as zealous as old Uncle Daniel Drew who gave his note for a large amount to found and endow a religious university and college, and then considerately failed before the note came due, thereby proving that he had no hard feelings against religion.

> " *Life is a jest—and all things show it.*
>   *I thought so once, but now I know it.*"
>   *—Ben Jonson.*

>> " I know my hide's chock full of sin,
>>   But I've fixed Old Pete, and he'll let me in,
>>   So rise up children, rise up in a crowd,
>>   And shout and sing to de angels loud,
>>   An' shout an' sing for de lan' of de Blest,
>>   'Case hell am hot as a hornet's hest."

If ever such infinitesimal souls reach the haven of rest and dwelling place of peace, it will only be by enacting the same strategy that Judge Waxem accomplished in approaching the Pearly Gates, and even after arrival they may meet with the same reception. As it may possibly be information for those who yet inhabit this mundane sphere, I will relate the experience : Judge Moses Aaron Waxem was a learned man of great renown, and hailed from Mexas. In course of time his earthly career was done, and his bones were gathered to his fathers, or planted on the *perarie,* but his spirit went wandering through the ethereal realms of space. Now the Judge was an honest man ; he never took anything whilst living that he could not carry away, neither did he appropriate anything his arms could not reach. He endowed a church, and freed his niggers when he could hold them no longer, and, like Harriet Beecher Stowe, got $300 each from the National Government, and was well acquainted with the fact, before he

departed, that there was a splendid climate for settling in,
also one that was reputed to be red hot and still a-heating
—so, eschewing the latter, he attempted to make his way
to the golden gates, but getting lost amidst the labyrinths
of turnings, and the day being very warm, the Judge sat
down under the shade of some beautiful trees to rest.
Whilst refreshing himself in this manner the air became
suddenly darkened, and a shade appeared who, from the description heard of whilst in the flesh, the Judge immediately
recognized as his Satanic Majesty himself. "Halloo!" inter-
rogated His Majesty; "what is your name? Where did you
come from, and where are you going?" "Well," answered
the Judge, "my name was Moses Aaron Waxem; I've just
come from Mexas, and I want to get up to them pearly gates."
"Oh! oh!!" replied His Majesty, "your name's enough.
I have old Mose and his brother long ago, and you're my
meat, so get ready, and come along." "Well," returned the
Judge, "it's pretty warm travelling just now, so sit down and
make your miserable life happy until the cool of the evening, and then I will go along; meanwhile," he added, drawing
forth a greasy pack of cards, "we will while away the time
with a game of draw poker." Well, they played a long while,
and His Majesty became interested. First, he bet the golden
bosses off his horns, then the golden ring around his tail, then
the silver shoes from off his hoofs, and finally some of the
silver chains belonging to some of his favorite imps. At last
His Majesty was dead broke, the old Judge winning every
time. "Now," remarked he, "I will play you one more time,
and if you beat me, then I will show you the road and put
you on the right track to make the gates." They played
another game and the Judge was again the winner, and the
devil for once in his life acted square, and escorted the

Mexian to within a short distance of the gates themselves ; then telling him he was on the right track and could not miss the way His Majesty departed. Well, after a time, the Judge, tired and weary, arrived at the gates, and took a seat outside on a bench. Being all by himself, he commenced to watch the crowds going in. Old Father Pete, with his long white beard reaching down to his knees, with his big bunch of keys suspended from his girdle, was bustling around quite lively for a man so weighed with years and sorrows. First one company would approach. " Who are you ? " was the question. " We are Catholics," replied the spokesman. " Well, go in that side gate," was the command. " Who are you ? " was the query as another band approached. " We are Protestants," was the reply. " Go in the little door to the left, and sit down," was the instruction. Then a little band came up, and, in answer to the interrogatory, the reply was : " We don't belong to church, we are just Christians and try to help each other ; that's all." With that the old man threw the gates wide open and said, " Walk in boys, and just ramble all over the whole blamed city if you want to." After the crowd had all entered, it being about closing time, Father Peter was about to lock the gates for the night, when he espied the Judge sitting on the old bench and wistfully gazing through the panels of the gate. " Well," said he, " where do you come from ? " " My name was Moses Aaron Waxem," replied the Judge. " I come from Mexas, and I want to get in." " Well, hold on till I look over the record," said the apostle ; then he commenced to hunt for the locality. He took down every book in the office and sent out for the old ones of former seasons. At last it got so late and so dark that Peter said, " I am sorry to tell you, Judge, but you will have to remain outside until the morning, for

I believe that in order to let you in I shall have to *open a new set of books."*

Bon Pasteur Nunnery, Hotel Dieu Hospital, General Hospital, which latter institution is a credit to any city, and admirably managed, are well worth visiting.

THE GREY NUNS AND THEIR MISSION.   THE Y. M. C. A.

The preceding was written before I joined the Y. M. C. A.; and as that institution and also the Grey Nuns accomplish a considerable amount of good in their sphere, they certainly deserve more than a passing notice.

> Then, is there no hope ! except for the saintly ?
> Is there no help for the wild trailing vine ?
> Must the prodigal's voice in the distance die faintly,
> And Man in his misery curse the Divine ?

The Grey Nunnery is situated on Guy street, occupying the entire block between Sherbrooke and Dorchester. The building was founded in 1642, and such a reputation has it obtained that thousands of strangers visit its wards and chapel each year. The plodding man of the world, the business man and others, whose thoughts are tied here below, experience such a relief on entering its portals that it is impossible to anticipate or describe. Although but through two pair of folding doors, the feeling comes over you that you are entirely shut out from the world, and begin to feel at rest and peace. The transition is sudden, but it is complete. No longer are you gazed at with sharp, designing or calculating countenances ; no longer do you remember the rough crowding and jostling, the cutting remarks and treacherous actions, whilst drifting outside. Here all seems perfect quiet, and probably you feel for the first time a spirit of charity to all men rise within you. The faces you see and converse with are those of sympathizing women, and recall the countenance of a loving mother o₁ a tender sister. The Nunnery, now under the care of Sister Reed, probably accomplishes more good in a quiet unheralded way than any similar institution in the Dominion.

> Alas! for those who leave the track,
> How few of the wandering souls turn back;
> For eyes may weep and hearts be sore,
> But the silver lost is found no more.

The Y. M. C. A. have recently erected at one corner of Victoria Square a fine building in Gothic style, with large hall, reading room and library for the use of strangers, and have doubtless been of great benefit to young men, strangers and others, in order to reconcile them to their lot and the habits of the people they found themselves amongst. The institution was certainly needed, and the committee deserve great credit for the manner in which they have accomplished the undertaking, as also does the " Witness," an evening paper that has proved a useful, willing and powerful auxiliary. The rooms are under the charge of Mr. D. Budge, the efficient Secretary of the institution, a courteous, affable gentleman, who does all in his power to enable a moral young man to pass away a few spare hours pleasantly and agreeably.

Probably one of the most able advocates of Temperance, at the same time combining business with profession, is Mr. CHARLES GURD, now the proprietor of the MEDICAL HALL WORKS for the manufacture of GINGER ALE, SODA and other AERATED WATERS. This establishment is the oldest one of its kind in the Dominion, and from small beginnings it has gradually risen to be the foremost in Canada, having weathered the financial storms which a few years ago threatened to engulf nearly every enterprise; and, by pursuing one plain course, relying on the excellence and purity of the articles presented to the public, its success has been almost unprecedented. During the summer months the factory from early morn until late at night presents a scene of busy bustling industry and activity—the works then being taxed to their utmost capacity by orders from all portions of the country; at present the factory can turn out and aerate some 950 dozen daily, or 68,400 bottles each week. During the tourist season visitors are numerous, and from the constant popping of corks and sampling by the busy managers and workmen, confusion seems to reign supreme and profits to evaporate, but out of chaos comes order, and Saturday night all seems so still and quiet that the bustle of the week is soon forgotten. Of course comic incidents occur, as when a visitor from the country helping himself to a sample bottle of ginger ale attempted to draw the cork with his teeth, the full force of the accumulated gas assisted him materially, and as soon as he could clear the cork, which was blown half way down his throat, and wipe the water from his eyes, remarked, "Sure this is a great interprize where they bottle up sweetened stame and sell it fur money."

They were awarded two first Prizes for 1880, and Gold Medal for 1881.

ECCENTRIC CHARACTERS.

It is a matter of surmise to the visitor generally how the name of " McGrab " or McNab seemed to be so prominent and so continually quoted. Many ingenious theories are advanced to prove that the name is indicative of Royal origin. One gentleman, a Sandy not long "fra the auld countree," propounds the following: That in other times " Auld Clootie," "Auld Grabbie " and " Auld Nick" meant really one and the same person, and were popularly supposed to stand in place of the lengthened titles appertaining to His Imperial Majesty of the "lately revised Kingdom," arguing then, from this theory, and from the fact that Mac in Scotch parlance meant the son of, it proved most conclusively that McGrab was the son of Royalty itself, was heir apparent to the throne, and would no doubt succeed with true Scotch dignity to all the titles, privileges and emoluments thereunto appertaining. But let that be as it may. From Halifax, Quebec, Montreal, Toronto and Hamilton, and possibly still further West, streets, buildings, wharves and avenues have been named to do him honor, and, like the Squeezems, the name is to be met with in all kinds of out-of-the-way places, and from a superficial glance it looks as if he had certainly "grabbed" all within reach; but it seems he was a *real* canny Scotch chieftain, and brought the characteristics of his early education over with him; there was no shoddy about McNab, for his father owned slaves (or rather a clan of his own), and he brought quite a number of them with him. On arrival, he received a grant of a Township on the bank of *Lake de Chats,* and at once proceeded to erect the castle of McNab, in order that in a new country he could follow feudal customs and the ancient traditions of his progenitors, and raid, pillage and subdue the communities around about, whilst, in case he was attacked, he would have a place to defend and sortie from. He for some years sold off the estate an immense quantity of pine timber, and having cash to his credit, at once became " tony." He visited the Provinces, and went through putting on style like a bondholder or a Western congressman. Dressed in full Highland costume, had his tail or guard to accompany him, with the piper and assistants preceding him, giving vent to those outlandish and soul-torturing strains so much reverenced and respected as bagpipe music amongst the rocks of Auld Scotia. He held himself a little king, and imported his own chattels in the way of laborers and fine Highland girls, meeting them upon their arrival at Quebec, but his power over the community at large in those old and superstitious days is lastingly marked by their efforts to do him honor, for at that time style, position and bluff " took the cake."

THE DOMINION EXHIBITION.

As the master, so the man,
Name me the judges, I'll tell you who gets the prize.
—*Local Paper.*

There is one noticeable peculiarity about the people of Canada, and that is, if the citizens of one section of the country promulgate an idea, it is instantly seized by the people of the neighboring sections. As the individuals are suspicious and jealous of each other, so each province is animated by the same despicable spirit. The City of Hamilton, Ontario, announced her intention early in the season of holding an Exhibition in the fall, and invited the co-operation of the neighboring Provinces, to assist in making the show a success. No sooner had this announcement gained publicity than the city of Toronto went one better, and advertised an Exposition during the month of September, inviting the people both of Canada and the States to come, see, and participate. Shortly afterwards Montreal certified to the fact that she was going to hold a Grand Exposition, "Open to the World;" and, finally, Halifax awoke and opened her show to the Universe and the entire ororory, and it is the working of Montreal that we shall deal with mostly. In the outset a Committee of Ways and Means had to be provided, for the promoters were not men who were inclined to risk a cent toward making a success out of the experiment—the *prestige* of their names was considered amply sufficient a portion to attract the public. So the newspaper men were duly convened, and the various "fat takes" were distributed amongst them: in the way of advertisements, etc., to insure their co-operation, and to assist in creating an enthusiasm amongst the people generally. In the Exhibition of 1881 the newspapers most liberally set the example by subscribing from $500 to $1,000 each (to be taken out in advertising), and most nobly did they perform their duty, although the Exhibition itself was far surpassed by any country fair. Reporters were stationed on the grounds with instructions to "gush," tents for their accommodation were provided, whilst from them issued column after column in continual streams. A truss from a drug store put them in ecstacies, whilst a home-made bed quilt drove them wild with frenzy, but the sight of a winter apple, tomato or potato put them on the borders of distraction.

Having thus laid the foundation, the papers commenced

with a will to proclaim the many advantages that would accrue to the city by holding an Exhibition within its limits, appealing by turns to the credulity, greed and rapacity of its merchants and citizens generally. Flaming posters, catalogues and prize lists were scattered far and wide over the province and neighboring States. Committees were organized to extract cash from the citizens and storekeepers generally, and the whole affair was under way. The grounds comprised some 35 acres, and already had one building on them, called the Crystal Palace, which, after being well shored and braced up to prevent its falling, was considered good enough to be the Main Building. The people themselves taking an active interest in the proposed show, for a time everything seemed to portend success and satisfaction. S. C. Stevenson, the Secretary of the Council of Arts and Manufactures, was appointed Secretary, and certainly worked well for the advancement of the interests of the Exhibition; but his hands were soon tied, and he was surrounded by a ravenous host of incompetents, whose relatives or friends had contributed something towards the furtherance of the object, and who brought such pressure to bear upon the Secretary that he was entirely unable to employ competent men, for most of those who had contributed to help along the expenses had done so with the express or implied understanding that they were either to have a place for themselves or their friends. The Exhibition was advertised to be open to the public on the 14th of September, but on that day, owing to incompetency of the officials in charge, nothing was in readiness, even in the first building. Exhibitors (some of them at least) had their spaces given away to other parties, and, at the last moment, when all was hurry,

bustle and confusion, chaos reigned supreme, and the
credulous public who paid their quarters were just so
much out. Three days afterwards the great Manitoba Exhibit was displayed, and comprised some sage grass, a few
sheafs of wheat, green tomatoes, sickly cabbages and half-
grown beets, with the explanatory note that the vegetables
were plucked before they were ripe. A few Indian wap-
pings, old wigwams, snow-shoes, canoes, and a worn-out
government ammunition waggon, were the attractions. The
cattle and stock did not reach the grounds until the 20th
inst., and the root and grain building was not open until
that time. The formal opening did not take place until
the 21st, when the Governor General officiated. The Judges
deserve great credit, and should now be quoted as experts.
One, a butcher, who had never wet a line, was a judge of
fishing tackle, and endeavored to please all by awarding a
prize to each exhibitor. A leather-merchant was one of
the judges of flour, and knew corn starch and pea meal
were composed of the same ingredients. A farmer, who
was one of the judges of race horses, awarded a prize to an
animal because the owner was his neighbor, whilst two of
the judges of wine (teetotalers) were earnestly endeavoring
to convince the balance of their number that the "Volnay"
and Moulin à Vent on Exhibition was a new-fangled
style of whiskey,—"they could tell by the smell." Rag
carpets, ready-made clothing, home-made quilts, rugs,
etc., were the chief attractions at the Provincial; but one
thing is certain; all exhibitors were satisfied, for the majority
either obtained medals or were recommended for diplomas.
No sight was so touching as to see Mr. Moses Morningstar stand arrayed like Solomon in his glory, before his
" clodings " exhibit, and to hear him in accents mild and

persuasive invite the visitors to "shust look ofer dot fine stock of goods, dem clodings wuz made by mine brudder in Nieu Yorick to be gif to de gafener general, but dey wuz a liddle too schmall in the back behind, und sell dem at less uf de first cost; just look at dem button holes und oxamine de qualidty uf de suit. Dem suit I schwear by Aaron who wuz Moses' big brudder get five diplomas und von golt metal at dis oxhibition. Dondt oxamine dat odder man's goots; he has got nodings oxcept half soled socks und delapidated suspenders und neck wear; he only get him a silver metal, und he haf to pay in cash de difference uf price for de bronze uf de silfver. Now, shentlemens, jusht ccme to my schtore down town, und I sell you goots for nodings, and credit you uf all de balance. Dake von uf my carts, und don'd forget it was Moses Morningstar, de clodier." The audacity of the few who have taken control of this thing is easily noticed, whilst their boldness in seizing was unequalled by "Tweed's" Aldermen, even in their palmiest days. The Legislature of the Province of Quebec, on various pretexts, granted thousands of dollars out of the public purse of the Province to assist in erecting the buildings, adorning the grounds, etc., etc. The City Council was prevailed upon to contribute some thousands more for a like purpose, whilst the individual citizens and storekeepers were solicited to contribute liberally according to their means, to which appeal they responded well, as the subscriptions aggregated some 10 or 12,000 dollars at each exhibition. Then after everything had been properly secured, the few who seem to carry the interests of Montreal in their vest pocket kindly took the management out of the hands of the people, and going to Parliament obtained a charter incorporating "The Permanent Exhibition," and placing the entire institution in their hands, *in trust.* A citizen wept when he saw Herman Schuffensnaffler sell the watch he had not the power to redeem, the citizens of Quebec sigh with regret when they see their fine Exhibition passing silently away, but the managers are enterprising, and it is stated that the various Governors of the different states are to be invited to the next fair and then shown off and exhibited to newly-arrived immigrants and citizens generally as real, live American Governors like so many prize cattle at so much per head. This is called kid-gloved handling.

Although the show was professedly open to the "*world*" one of the judges publicly expressed his determination of not looking at American goods at all, and at this remark some of the exhibitors became so disgusted as to remove their entire exhibit, and declined to show their goods, after all the expense they had entailed. So, taken all in all, the great Dominion Exhibition was far from being the success it was anticipated it would be, and it is to be hoped that the managers of the next will be men who will discountenance every attempt at imposition, and whose aim will be not only to make the show a success, but to thoroughly satisfy and please the people who are attracted there, and who contribute to its support.

VENNOR, THE PROPHET.

"Vennor's kerrect agin, and I'll tell you how 'twas," remarked a farmer journeying from Southampton : "Well, you see, I was looking in the almanax, and he said there was to be snow; well, pretty soon, she just came along, full pelt. You see them drifts? Well there is over sixteen feet in e'n, and on a level all you can see is the tops of the stakes and the ryder across; that means over seven feet snow. After

that says I to the wife, 'Vennor says that we're going to
have a cold spell, and I'll bet we git it,' says I, 'and I'm
going to watch out,' so I took the Kermometer, and set her
up on the porch. After a while the cold began to come
along, and that durned thing marked lower and lower till it
struck the last notch, and then bust the bottom and fell
through onto the porch. Well, you know Chippewa Sam what
works for me,—he come along in the morning, and thought
he found a silver or gold button or something, and went to
pick it up off'n the porch, and that little inside of the
Kermometer burnt his two forefingers and his thumb off
clean to the first joint before he could drap it. Cold! well
I should remark; and it ain't overly warm now." Another
gentleman well acquainted, and just from the West, said
that the Profit wuz an ould man who lived near Hell or
Halifax or Quebec, or some of them places, and wuz in league
wid another feller in the Rockies who had a kind uv a
way of fixing up the weather by a kind of a proceeding
between thimsilves; whilst another argued that he must be
a kind of a Yankee feller, for he was mighty lucky sometimes. Therefore, having my curiosity aroused, and being in
the city in which the Prophet now abides, I took an early
opportunity to look him up. I met him, and my whitened
beard dropped off with astonishment, my pale leathery
cheek resumed it roseate hue, and thus rudely was another
dream dispelled,—for the Prophet is as young as either you
or I. Of course I asked him all his secrets, and how it was
that he could forecast the changes of the weather with such
accuracy so long ahead, but, instead of receiving the reply
I expected from such a sage—"Why you see that certain
combustible elements having their consanguinity over certain elevated positions, whereby the storm cloud, forming ar

aqueous wave, lowers its impending influences over the subterraneous portions of the vasty deep, and consolidated vacuum is thus created, in the conglomerated mass of heteregeneous vapors that constitute a storm centre, and accumulate in the substratum of the ether that surrounds this planet"—he simply and modestly said : "I do not claim any special merit for my prognostications—they are merely the result of study ; and by steady appliance to the work in hand, with constant comparisons of other seasons, I have been enabled for some time ahead to forecast the probabilities of approaching seasons with a tolerable degree of success and accuracy, very satisfactory to both my friends and myself." Mr. Vennor claims that he makes a point of the following features, and maintains that, by proper application the changes in the weather may be foretold : the dryness or humidity of previous seasons, extremes of heat or cold, general direction of winds, time of commencement of spring and fall, with characteristics of mid-summer, aspect and intensity of first frosts, abundance or rarity of thunder storms, years of unusual meteoric displays, &c. Of course exactly how the Prophet does it is for the curious to find out, but no doubt many of our ambitious young men will be in the field, and prophesy with more or less degree of success, now that the *modus operandi* has been explained, but still there is room enough for all, and a little generally mixed-up weather won't do any harm, even if it does dampen the politicians and officials generally. -The Prophet, although a great naturalist and an authority on " Our Birds of Prey," or the " Eagles, Hawks and Owls of Canada," is not to be fooled by the habits of animals or the flights of birds ; he considers them something like the promises of an M. P. or head of a department—generally speaking, very.

uncertain—but relies more especially on scientific knowledge and his own past experience. He also states that young men who are about to enter into the prophesying business should bear in mind that, to understand the weather, they must be out in it and live in it: not for an hour or a week or so but for a number of years, say twenty-five or fifty for the average young man, although a very ambitious youth might experiment in the back-yard in his shirt sleeves until it rained, when he would be in a position to amply verify the fact that the aqueous fluid was wet, and thus would one item of knowledge be gained—and so would a cold.

Leaving the city, we wend our way to the Dominion Capital. There are several routes from Montreal to the City of Ottawa, viz.: by boat up the river, by the Q. M. O. & O. R. R., by the Grand Trunk to Prescott or Brockville, thence by St. L. & O. or the B. & O. R. R. direct to the city, but by far the most pleasant route in summer is by river. Taking the early morning train by the G. T. R. to Lachine, eight miles distant, or if you are healthy and strong, either walk or drive along the Lachine road from the city, and you will find it a pleasant recreation. The roadway is studded with houses and farms of both the most primitive as well as the entre modern styles, the orchards are numerous, and in season well filled, whilst the roads are in excellent condition for either a drive or walk. Arriving at Lachine, and whilst waiting for the boat at the Depôt landing, you most effectually dispel the illusion that all railroad officials are sordid, grasping, uncommunicative and unfriendly, for acquaintance once made with Mr. J. T. O'Flaherty, the Agent of the Grand Trunk, and a taste of his native juice, and you will have the pleasure to uncover a jolly, good-natured, rollicking gentleman, one of the old school, so rarely met with in these latter days, and who has become both popular and a favorite with all whom business or pleasure calls to Lachine. Almost opposite the town on the south side of the river is the village of Caughnawaga, and as we are now getting into the country where legends abound, it will be well to note the Caughnawaga Bell before we go on board.

CAUGHNAWAGA BELL.

Almost opposite Lachine, so named by La Salle as being the point from which he took his departure, on the south side of the river, is the village of Caughnawaga, where the mail boat takes on board the Indian pilot Baptiste, to assist in guiding the steamer through the wildest and most dangerous of all the rapids, the "Lachine," that commences just below the town. The village is composed of a few streets of log huts, but in contra-distinction to the poverty of the surroundings stands a massive stone church, in the belfry of which hang two bells, one a large and modern one; whilst the other is a small one of the last century, and is of itself the subject of an historical legend, in the manner of its acquirement. It seems that, in the year 1690, one Father Niccls, one of those Missionaries who were the first to set the example of Christianizing the heathen, who had made numerous converts from amongst the Indians of the Caughnawaga tribe, had persuaded his hearers to give him furs enough to erect his church, and when they were all converted, he convinced them that religion was not worth having unless they had a bell to their church; so they became enthusiastic in the cause of the bell, and, so to speak, passed round the hat, and contributed a goodly portion of the furs that they had secured from their season's hunt to purchase the bell for their ed   Of course the Indians did not know what a bell was, but believed it was a something that spoke in consecrated and angelic tones, and was a necessary adjunct to their new religion. They soon accumulated a considerable stock of furs, which were sent by Father Nicols to an ecclesiastical friend in Havre, France, who exchanged them for the article required, and no doubt divided the profits, and shipped the bell to Montreal. For some time the priest and his tribe of converts awaited its arrival, and it was thought at length that the vessel had foundered, but after a while the news reached them that it had been captured by an English man-of-war, taken to the port of Salem, Mass., and, further, that the bell was hung in a church at Deerfield, and rang in the interests of heretics instead of good Catholics. This intelligence, through the wise counselling of the priest, not only made the Indians mad, but aroused their savage resentment. The priest advised them that the bell, which had not yet received the sacrament of baptism, was a captive in the custody of heretics, and caused them to register a vow that the first opportunity that occurred should be taken for its recovery. Some years passed before a chance offered, but the time was not lost, for Father Nicols' converts were enthusiasts, and diligently employed in adding new converts to the cause of Christianity, and in religiously plying the tomahawk and scalping knife upon such of their unregenerate neighbors as refused to acknowledge the new faith. But in the year 1704 the Marquis de Vaudreuil, then Governor of Canada, wishing to kill as many Englishmen as possible by stealth and strategy, as well as open warfare, went to the meek and lowly follower and advocate of Christianity, as the diplomatic head of the tribe, and prayed for the aid of the

Caughnawagas to assist him to destroy his foes; but the holy father would only give his consent to lead a murdering and pillaging expedition upon the tacit understanding that the objective point should be the town of Deerfield. This condition, of course, was acceded to, and so the man of God assembled his savage converts, and with uplifted hands and stirring words informed them that the time for rescuing the bell had arrived, and appealed to them in the name of the Deity to rally, and march upon the crusade for its recovery. Like a second Gideon, he placed himself at their head, and his words and actions awoke enthusiasm in their savage hearts. Weapons were put in order, war paint donned, and in the middle of winter the savages, with their Christian pastor as a leader, departed to join the regulars of the Marquis at Fort Chambly. The French troops, unaccustomed to travelling through snowdrifts and to endure the hardships of winter warfare, were with difficulty restrained from mutiny, but the Indians, familiar with snowshoe travel, progressed almost as easily as if the season had been summer. At the head of his savage Christian legion marched Father Nicols on his errand of murder and pillage, whilst by his side a stalwart convert bore the banner of the cross as an offset. At night the Indians were cheered by the voice of their leader in *prayer and exhortation.* Arriving at the head of Lake Champlain, the expedition marched upon the ice, until the spot now occupied by the City of Burlington was reached, when it took its course by compass through the wilderness of Vermont for Deerfield. Considerable hardships were endured by the expedition, but Father Nicols, sustained by remarkable zeal, continued on, until the expedition, on the 29th of February, saw in the distance its destination, and

awaited the approach of night.some four miles from town.
At daylight De Rouville ordered his forces to advance. A
strong wind was blowing, encrusted with ice, which broke
beneath the weight of his men; he therefore adopted the
ruse of ordering the column to proceed a short distance
upon the run, then to halt suddenly, thus imitating the
sound of gusts of wind. The inhabitants of the town were
wholly unsuspicious of any movement against them, and
like the people of Laish of old, were wrapt in profound
slumber. Even the solitary sentinel was asleep, and the hard
snow piled nearly to the top of the stockades gave the
assaulting an easy means of ingress. Quickly and silently
they scaled the walls, and the sleeping sentinel was the
first to receive his death-blow from a tomahawk. The
surprise was complete, and no resistance was offered. Then
a terrible scene of massacre occurred; some few escaped,
numbers were slain, and about one hundred and twenty
made prisoners. The troops rioted amid the plunder, but
the Indians were after their bell. At the request of Father
Nicols, the commandant despatched a soldier to ring it. As
the first tones of the bell sounded on the cold morning air
and fell upon their ears, they reverently knelt, whilst the
priest solemnly returned thanks to God for their success,
and invoked a blessing on the murders they had committed.
What a sight! the ground strewn with the mangled and
mutilated corpses of the innocent slain; the trembling
captives mourning. the loss of relatives, friends and homes,
and fearing death and even worse at the hands of their barbarous captors; the savages seeking to do homage to an unknown God whose precepts commanded love and kindness,
but whom, through the doctrine and instruction of a pre-
ceptor they sought to serve by slaughter and cruelty. The

bell was removed from the belfry and hung upon cross poles in order to be transported, the buildings of the place fired, and the party retreated; the captives, men, women and children, were forced to keep up with the column, and when they dropped through exhaustion, or were unable to keep up, they were tomahawked before the view of the others, and their gory scalps added to those on the belts of their savage captors. By the time they arrived at Burlington Bay the Indians were thoroughly tired out with carrying the bell, whose weight their snowshoes would not sustain, so they found a likely spot and buried it. In the spring, upon their return, they found the bell had been undisturbed, and with joy the party bore it homeward, whilst those at Caughnawaga anxiously awaited its arrival, for those who had been on the expedition for its capture had described it in glowing terms. It was said that its tones were sweeter than those of the birds, clearer than the rippling melody of the river, and that it could be heard beyond the murmuring of the rapids. At length, whilst all were discussing the anticipated arrival, a novel sound was heard in the woods, and interest being awakened, a voice shouted "the bell! it is the bell!" when rushing to the edge of the clearing they met the returning expedition, at the head of which were yoked two snow-white oxen bearing the bell hung between them. Both bell and oxen were adorned with wreaths of leaves and wild flowers. The bell, after being closely examined and commented upon by the curious, was raised to its place in the belfry, and awoke with its tones the echoes of the St. Lawrence. The Indians for some time continued their rejoicings, but the sound of the bell fell upon the ears of the captives as the death knells of murdered relatives, and as a reminder of

destroyed and desolated homes, and which they despaired
of ever again beholding.   However, two years later, the
Governor of Massachusetts, together with the Governor of
Canada, succeeded in obtaining the release of the survivors,
some fifty-seven in number. Such is the history of the bell
of Caughnawaga, and it is believed to be strictly true in all
its particulars.

Embarking on the splendid saloon steamer "Prince
of Wales," under the command of Capt. H. W. Shepherd,
or the "Princess," Capt. A. Bowie, we commence to ascend
Lake St. Louis, passing Point Claire with its cottages and
vineyards, to the village of St. Anne's, a pleasant run of 18
miles. Here the steamer passes through a lock 45 feet wide
and 180 feet long to avoid a succession of rapids, with a
fall of but $3\frac{1}{2}$ feet, on the Ottawa river. The village is a
charming place of summer resort and situated at the south-
west end of the Island of Montreal, and is the place to
which the poet Moore dedicated his Canadian boat song.
Two miles west of St. Anne's, commences the Lake of the
Two Mountains, an expansion of the Ottawa, some 10
miles in length by 8 in width. From this lake a branch
called the Rivière des Prairies, North, or Back river, flows
toward the north-east, and forms a boundary to the Island
of Montreal, and forming the Sault au Recollet, down
which rapids most of the rafts from the Ottawa descend,
and in which current some years ago the Indians drowned
Father Nichols. The Indian village, that still contains a
small remnant of the once powerful Mohawks and Algon-
quins, is next passed, above which the river narrows to a
width of about a half mile for a short distance, then again
expanding it forms the Upper Lake of the Two Mountains
which lake and coast has both its legends and romances,

of which I note one from "Maple Leaves," by Dr. J. C. Le Moine.

THE GRAVE OF CADIEUX.

In ascending the Ottawa river one has to stop at the rock of the High Mountain situated in the middle of the Portage of the Seven Chutes, at the foot of the Island of the *Grand Calumet*—it is there lies Cadieux's tomb, surrounded by a wooden railing. Each time canoes pass the little rock the old voyageur relates to his younger companions the fate of the brave interpreter. Cadieux was a roving interpreter, brave, poetical, and of a romantic turn of mind, and was often employed by both the government and missionaries to interpret the various Indian dialects. He generally spent the summer hunting, and in winter would purchase furs for the traders. After a winter thus passed by Cadieux at the portage, where he and the other families had their wigwams, it was decided in May to wait for other Indian tribes who had furs for sale, and then all were to come to Montreal. Profound peace was supposed at the time to exist in the settlements. All of a sudden, one day a young Indian, roaming about close to the rapids, got up quite a scare by rushing back out of breath and shouting, Nathaouè! Nathaouè!! the Iroquois! the Iroquois!! There was in reality below the rapids of the Seven Falls a party of Iroquois warriors who had been christianized, and were then waiting to levy toll, and appropriate the canoes that generally descended at that season loaded with skins. Only one chance of escape presented itself to the minds of the affrighted ones, and that was to attempt to bring the canoe through the rapids, a project that had previously been considered hopeless. It was also thought.

necessary to station some parties in the woods, in order, by firing, to draw off the attention of the Iroquois from the desperate attempt to run the rapids, and thus prevent pursuit. Cadieux, being the ablest and most resolute, chose a young Algonquin warrior to accompany him in this perilous service; and it was agreed that when the interpreter and his comrade should have succeeded to inveigle the Iroquois into the woods, they would try a circuitous route and attempt to join their friends, who also were to send after them should they be too long absent. Cadieux and the young warrior started for the Iroquois encampment, agreeing that the sign for the canoes to break cover and start on their fearful race would be the firing of their guns. Soon the report of fire-arms was heard in the distance, and was followed by three or four others in quick succession. On went the frail birch canoes amidst the foam and rocks, flying like sea-birds over the boiling caldron. It was verily a race for life, the extraordinary and superhuman skill of the Redskins alone saving them from death in a thousand shapes. "I saw nothing during our passage over the rapids," said Cadieux's wife, a pious woman, "but the form of *a tall lady in white*, hovering over the canoes, and showing us the way." They had invoked St. Anne, the patron saint of the mariner. The canoes escaped with safety, and arrived at the Lake of Two Mountains, but it was not ascertained until some time after, from the Iroquois themselves, what had become of Cadieux and his devoted follower. It seems that Cadieux had quietly watched for the Iroquois at the portage, placing himself about an acre from his colleague, to allow the Iroquois to penetrate to the centre of the portage; he then quietly waited for the death-yell of one of them shot by his helpmate, and then fired with unerring aim. The war-whoop resounded, and the Iroquois, fancying they were attacked by a large party of the enemy, separated, and charged in different directions. It was supposed the young Algonquin fell in attempting to join Cadieux. For three days the aborigines searched the woods in order to find traces of the encampment, never thinking the enemy had attempted to descend the rapids; for three days and nights they searched for Cadieux, and those were sleepless times for the white man. Foiled in their object they returned to their canoes. Several days then elapsed, and, as no tidings of Cadieux came, a party was formed and sent to scour the woods: traces of the Iroquois were unmistakable, and indications of Cadieux's presence were found. At the *Portage des Sept Chutes* they noticed a small hut of branches which, apparently, had been abandoned; they passed it without search and continued their route, under the impression that Cadieux might have been compelled to ascend the Ottawa, and take refuge with the Indians of the Island. Two days later, the thirteenth after the skirmish, they noticed on repassing the hut, a small cross, at the head of a fresh grave on the surface. In it was found the corpse of Cadieux, half covered with green branches; his hands, clasping a sheet of birch bark (on which he had considerately written his own dirge), were laid over his chest. The opinion was, on reading the inscription on the bark, that exhaustion, hunger and anxiety had produced on the interpreter a species of hallucination called " *la folie de bois.*" He had doubtless lived on wild fruit and berries, not daring to light a fire, for fear of betraying his place of concealment. He had been growing weaker daily, and, when the relief party had passed the hut two days previously he

had recognized them as friends, but the sudden joy at a
prospect of a speedy deliverance had been so great that it
made him speechless and inanimate. Seeing his last hope
vanish as they passed him, and feeling his strength failing,
he scribbled his adieux to the living; and then prepared his
last resting-place. This done, and the cross erected, he laid
himself down for the sleep of death. Before laying down to
rest he embodied in verse his own dirge; this *chaunt* by
its simplicity is very attractive, being an expression of his
feelings to the objects which surround him, and his own
regret for quitting life, closing by an invocation to the
Virgin Mary. The bark on which the death-song was
written was afterwards brought to the post of the Lake of
the Two Mountains. The *voyageurs* have set it to a plaintive melody, and it runs thus:

> " Petit rocher de la Haute montagne,
> Je viens finir ici cette campagne.
> Ah ! doux échos ; entendez mes soupirs,
> En languissant je vais bientôt mourir.
>
> Petits oiseaux, vos douces harmonies,
> Quand vous chantez me rattachent à la vie ;
> Ah ! si j'avais des ailes comme vous,
> Je serais heureux avant qu'il fut deux jours.
>
> Seul en ces bois, que j'ai eu de soucies
> Pensant toujours à mes si chers amis ;
> Je demandais : Hélas ! sont-ils noyés ?
> Les Iroquois les auraient-ils tués ?   (finale)
>
> Un de ces jours, que m'étant éloigné
> En revenant je vis une fumée
> Je me suis dit.   Ah ! Grand Dieu, qu'est ceci
> Les Iroquois m'ont-ils pris mon logis.
>
> Je me suis mis en père à l'embassade
> Afin de voir se c'était embuscade
> Alors je vis trois visages français
> M'ont mis le cœur d'une trop grande joie.

Mes genoux plient, ma faible voix s'arrête
Je tombe......Hélas ! à partir ils s'apprêtent.
Je reste seul......Pas un qui me console
Quand la mort vient par un si grande désole.

Un loup hurlant vient près de ma cabane
Vour si mon feu n'avait plus de boucane,
Je lui ai dit : Retire-toi d'ici,
Car, par ma foi, je percerai ton habit.

Un noir corbeau volant à là aventure
Vient se percher tout près de ma toiture
Je lui ai dit : mangeur de chair humaine
Va-t'en chercher autre viande que mienne ;

Va-t'en là bas, dans ces bois et marais,
Tu trouveras plusiers corps Iroquois :
Tu trouveras des chairs, aussi des os ;
Va-t'en plus loin, laisse moi en repos.

Rossignolet, va dire à ma maîtresse
A mes enfants qu'un adieu je leur laisse
Que j'ai gardé mon amour et ma foi
Et désormais faut renoncer à moi.

C'est donc ici que le monde m'abandonne,
Mais j'ai secours en vous, Sauveur des hommes !
Très-Sainte Vierge, ah ! m'abandonnez pas,
Permettez-moi de mourir entre vos bras !

Passing Rigaud Mountain we arrive at Carillon ; rapids again occurring here, are overcome by means of a lock and canal 12 miles in length ; then by Grenville to l'Orignal ; thence 8 miles by waggon-road, and we arrive at the far-famed Caledonia Springs, noted from the earliest settlement of the country. It was these Springs formerly called " New-henee," that were spoken of by the untutored Gaspé Indians in terms of adoration and reverence to Jacques Cartier, upon his arrival at their camp, as the " life waters ; " and still further upon the Captain General's arrival at Quebec, the chief Donacona urged him forward to the Springs, whilst,

in the midst of winter, his crew and comrades were
suffering death and were the victims of disease, ice-locked
on board their ships in the St. Croix River. It was amid
the forests of this country that the Indian tribes placed
their dead, and the young warriors brought the ailing and
decrepid of their nation to partake of the healing waters,
and once more obtain the strength that was supposed to be
gone for ever. It is to these same life-giving waters that
many of the robust men of our present time owe the exube-
rance of their feelings and their strength. Once a trackless
wild and hard of access, now a most popular place of resort.
A magnificent hotel is erected near their site; a village
occupies the grounds that were formerly a forest entangled
by undergrowth; beautiful cottages now adorn the swards
that were once encumbered by wigwams and squatters'
tents, until, to-day, that which was a wilderness now blos-
soms as the rose, and what was once a barren waste is now
almost a second Eden. There are three springs in the
village, and all are the property of the proprietors of the
hotel, who, to benefit the entire community, have spared
no expense to form a comfortable residence for all who
may seek its waters, either in pursuit of health or merely
for a summer's recreation. The carbonated or Gas Spring
discharges some four gallons per minute; the spring is
far more effectual in its results than the waters of Europe—
the gas evolved being carburetted hydrogen, three hundred cubic inches per minute, pleasantly saline to the taste,
and its reaction distinctly alkaline.

The Saline Spring, which is distant from the Gas Spring
about 130 feet, is the one most generally sought for. It
was this spring that, during the terrible epidemic of the
year 1836-7, was accredited with restoring to normal

health the afflicted sufferers, both white and red, that camped about its waters. Its characteristics are slightly saline, evolving a small quantity of carburetted hydrogen, whilst its reaction is more strongly alkaline than the Gas Spring.

The White Sulphur Spring arises but a few feet from the Saline, discharges about four gallons per minute, is feebly sulphurous in both taste and odor. The efficacy of this spring in rheumatic and other affections is well attested, and the cures in proportion rival by far those of the famous German waters or the Hot Springs of Arkansas. The analysis comprising scientific figures, with which I will not bother the reader, therefore he cannot doubt their accuracy, comprise chloride of sodium, potassium, bromide of sodium, carbonate of lime, soda, magnesia, iron, iodide of sodium, sulphate of soda, potash, alumina, silica and carbonic acid. No well regulated visitor passing through this section of the country should fail to visit these Springs, and to carry away with him a proportion of that robust health that is here generally lying around loose, awaiting applicants from the busy, bustling world without. These Springs maintain the same flow and temperature at all seasons of the year, and the slightest change in their component parts has not been discovered since the Springs passed into the hands of the white settlers, but the season is short, extending but from the 1st June to 1st October.

LEGENDS OF THE OTTAWA.

The memory of the trip either up or down the Ottawa river is fraught with pleasing reminiscences : hardly a hill or headland that comes in sight but at one time was the scene of some of those fierce conflicts that were continually occurring between the Indians and the early French set-

HEROES OF VILLE-MARIE.

tlers. These legends, whether of victory or defeat, are invariably celebrated in song or verse. The attack on Daulac and his sixteen followers, by the Indians, in May, 1660, is made the subject of a delightful poem by Geo. Murray, which is well worth obtaining, and is of considerable length, although interesting throughout. A portion of the legend as rendered by Geo. Martin appears in " The Heroes of Ville Marie." The Indians had boasted that they would wipe the French from the face of the earth, and carry the white girls to their villages. Adam Daulac, or Dollard, Sieur des Ormeaux, was a young man, twenty-two years of age, fiery and impetuous, who had arrived in the colony some three years previous. Without enquiring to find out where the grievance of the Indians was located, he collected sixteen followers, whom he bound by an oath to help exterminate the Indians. They pledged themselves to neither give nor ask quarter; they then made their wills, confessed, and received the Sacraments, and started on their murderous errand, and erected a fort or stockade some fifty miles up the Ottawa river. The Indians had heard of their arrival and their determination, so they assembled in council, and decided that the invaders should perish. Their decision and subsequent attack on the French is thus described :

THE HEROES OF VILLE MARIE, MAY, 1660.

The doom is proclaimed! 'twas the Sachems that spoke,
And, rising, the calumet fiercely they broke ;
The war-dance is danced, and the war-song is sung,
And the warriors, full painted, their weapons have slung.

Each armed with his arquebuse, hatchet and knife,
How they hunger and thirst for the barbarous strife!
They have said it : *The Frenchman shall sleep with the slain,*
Maid, matron and babe—not a soul shall remain!

They have spoken, those braves of the Iroquois league,
Renowned for fierce courage and shrewdest intrigue.
Through the " Ottawa's " forest like panthers they tread,
As if stepping already o'er the pale-visaged dead.

Adam Dollard, defender of fair Ville Marie,
Has pondered and prayed o'er the savage decree,
And a desperate purpose is stamped on his brow,
And no one can slacken his ultimate vow.

  *   *   *   *   *

There are some—Oh how few!—in the bloom of their years,
Who have listened and pledged him and trampled their fears;
With hot hearts as brave as their sabres are keen,
They are mustered around him—his gallant *sixteen !*

  *   *   *   *   *

In a ready Redoubt, as by Providence meant,
They hastily fashion their evergreen tent,
And, here, in the forest, where " Uttawas " flows,
They prepare for the speedy descent of their foes.

  *   *   *   *   *

Hark! near, and still nearer, yell answers to yell,
All the forest is peopled with spectres of hell!
Not a tree but now looks as if changed to a fiend,
Not a rock but behind it a demon is screened.

From the loop-holed Redoubt their first volley they pour,
And Mohawks and Senecas sink in their gore ;
From musket and huge musketoon they have seen,
And heard—that our heroes count just *seventeen.*

Then dire is the rage of the shame-smitten crew,
When they find that the Pale-faces number so few ;
Again and again comes the stormy attack,
And still, like pierced griffins, the pagans fall back.

Day and night, night and day, till the tenth set of the sun,
No trophy the maddened assailants have won,
Though their fleet-footed runners have hurried from far,
Half a thousand tried allies—their whirlwinds of war.

Onondagas, Cayugas, Oneidas, are there,
Some howling for vengeance, some wild with despair ;
Once again, with a hurricane rush and a shout,
Like a deluge of lightning, they storm the Redoubt.

  *   *   *   *   *

In a moment, 'tis over! flash blending with flash,
As sword-blades and tomahawks bloodily clash ;
" *Vive le Canadá,*" Dollard exultingly cried,
Then, with cross to his lips, like a martyr he died.

And his faithful companions, his chivalrous band,
With their gallant young captain, passed out of the land.
Draw a veil, pallid muse, o'er the finishing scene,
And crown with fresh garlands the brave seventeen.

        *   *   *   *   *

  Nearing Ottawa we pass at Edinburgh, a South Eastern suburb of the city, the Rideau Falls (the Curtain) formed by the waters of the Rideau river emptying into the Ottawa. The Falls were at one time an interesting feature in the scenery of the river, and were a filmy, cloudy fall of some 30 feet, attracting much notice—being seen to advantage from the deck of the steamer, but of late business encroachments have made of the Falls a useful auxiliary instead of an ornament, by damming the current, and using it as a motive power for the saw mills that line its banks, and forcing the river to discharge the bulk of its waters into the canal, so the scenery, as nature finished it, exists only in the minds of old-time residents, and early visitors. Arriving at the City of Ottawa, navigation is at an end until after the Chaudière Falls (the Boiling Pot) is passed. These falls are formed by a series of rapids, which commence in the Ottawa river, six miles above the city, and are the most interesting feature in it. The greatest height of the falls is about 40 feet, whilst every variety of form is presented : the volume of water descending in vast dark masses (the color of the water of the river being something like that of a tan pit) in graceful cascades, or in tumbling, struggling spray; they have been well described as a hundred rivers struggling for a passage, the grandest sight being that of the lost Chaudière, where an immense body of water is quietly sucked down and disappears under ground.

> I see thy waters boil,
> As if all Hades did burn,
> And Satan's imps, with ardor hot,
> Were thrusting wood beneath the pot.

In the autumn and part of the winter the rocks around the Chaudière become entirely bare, and expose to view a cliff-like mass of shale, allowing a near approach for the contemplation of the enormous power of the seething waters which, with the slides, log runs, etc., is the real means of the commercial prosperity of the city. Some thirty mills are in operation around its base, and not one use steam as a motive power. At Aylmer, nine miles above the falls, situated at the foot of Chaudière lake, an expansion of the Upper Ottawa, navigation is again resumed to Arnprior, at which place occur falls of some twelve feet, and thence to Pembroke, a lumbering town, 100 miles above the city, and which ranks as a town of some importance on the upper Ottawa. The region around stands unrivalled as a timber district, but, even with its apparant vastness of resource, the finest of the timber, both red and white pine, maple and ash, is rapidly being thinned out, revealing only a sandy and seemingly sterile soil, fit but for the cultivation of root crops. The length of the Ottawa river is about 780 miles, and is computed to drain a territory of fully 40,000 square miles.

OTTAWA.

The city of Ottawa, the seat of the Imperial Government, situated on the banks of the Ottawa river, just below

Chaudière Falls, was formerly called By-town, being named after a Col. By, chief of Staff of Royal Engineers, engaged in the construction of the Rideau canal, from Kingston to Ottawa, but the citizens becoming ashamed either of the name of the Colonel, or the unaristocratic affix to their city, in the year 1855 petitioned Parliament to change its name to the present one of Ottawa. The city, like that of Quebec, is divided into Upper and Lower town. Across the Suspension bridge is the thriving town of Hull, formerly Slab Town, the store house for lumber prior to its shipment. Slides are erected on each side of the river for the passage of timber in order to avoid the great fall, and the sight of the cribs of timber darting down these slides is a pleasing one. The present population of the city is 27,412, and is divided into two classes,—Government officials, politicians, and lumber dealers, raftsmen, or connected in some way with the lumber interest.

The Parliamentary houses, situated on Barrack Hill and overlooking the river, are a splendid block of buildings, in the Italian Gothic style of architecture, and cost the people of the Dominion the sum of $4,041,914.37 in their erection. The buildings are in three blocks, the right and left wings being used as department and ministerial offices. In the eastern half of the centre block is the Senate Chamber of the Dominion, having a membership of 77 persons, and employing a clerical force of 84 ; whilst the Commons, occupying the other section of the centre block, has a membership of 206, being M.P.'s in contradistinction to the M. P. P.'s of the Provincial Legislatures. The arduous duties of these servants of the public, for the last session at least, seem to have consisted in a strenuous defence of themselves as individuals, against accusations of jobbery, bribery and other small

PARLIAMENT HOUSES, OTTAWA.

corrupt practices, although it is stated that those who
voted for the Syndicate are free from such accusations,
being financially too well heeled and too high priced; but
when such accusations for such paltry sums as $250 are
earnestly entertained against a Dominion M.P., what
then can be the price of a Provincial M.P.P. The total
revenue derived by the Dominion Government is estimated
at some $52,585,501.62, which enormous revenue is
annually expended in governing the 4,000,000 of population. The salaries alone of the Governor General with
the nine Lieut.-Governors of the Province amount to
the sum of $683,967.94, whilst the contingent expenses,
hack hire, ice, stationery, etc., etc., amount to $177,202.91,
not a bad showing for ten men—an expenditure of
$861,170.85, with house rent and other little etceteras
free; but still the Canadians are a hard set to govern, and
probably the officials deserve the cash, although with all
the resources of the Government it is all they can do to
keep the people from earnest inquiry as to where the
money goes, but its *protegés* are numerous, and are
composed of relatives and friends of the Government of
Great Britain, Army officers out of commission, with quite
an array of clergy who are trying their hand in a new
country, and who must be provided for. Justice is administered throughout the Dominion at an expense to the
people of some $577,896.58. The cash goes out in
quantity to all supporters of the Government, $489,327.29
is set apart for the Indians; how they get it will be shown
as we get out into the territory. Widows of clergy-
men are allowed $10,949.37; Geological Survey costs
$52,933.97; subsidies are granted to the amount of
$398,876.76, whilst the allowance for the volunteer

service is $777,698.90, the show for which latter expenditure is like that offered to Napoleon the 3rd, all on paper, whilst miscellaneous fees and favoritism are credited with costing $101,602.15.

The visit to Great Britain in 1880 of various ministers, finally resulted, upon their return to Ottawa, upon the preparation and final passing of the Bill creating and contracting for the building of the Canadian Pacific Railroad, but it was only after years of disputations, heart-burnings and numerous disappointments, that the construction of the road was at last determined upon, but the fact is stated, that even now the line has been commenced without accurate survey, or estimates having been prepared, therefore it becomes a firm belief with many of its well-wishers that the difficulties of the road that are inevitable cannot be slightly overcome. The Canadian Goverment binds itself to a pro-cash grant per mile for each mile completed. So long, then, as the Government's credit is good, and the cash be forthcoming, so long will the C.P.R. boom, and if eventually the line is completed the total money grant will be $25,000,000, and the total land grant 25 million acres. The Government paying but a *pro rata*, it matters little whether the whole line is completed or not. The expenditures for surveys alone on account of this road from 1871 to 1877 amounted, to $3,136,615, of which the London Engineers with their numerous *protegés* and favorites are supposed to have received the lion's share. The people naturally inquiring what has been done for the sum of over $3,000,000 taken from the pockets of a half starved community, were answered oh! ah! and consoled by the assertion, that the work was all classified substantially as follows:

1st. Pleasure trip over the ground, 1st season.

2nd. Pleasure trip with surveyor and Government preacher as guest, who neither eat pemmican, or drink alkali water, 2nd season.

3rd. Pleasure trip to revise the last with a few friends.

4th. Pleasure **trip** with some parties who must be conciliated.

5th. Cash trips with laborers for locations.

6th. Cash trips for adepts to revise locations which are now mostly changed.

, Such is a synopsis of the work accomplished for an expenditure of three millions of money, but as regards those who entrust their money to the enterprise the results should be known for a certainty or foreseen as far as possible instead of trusting to a chance that if not propitious may bring ruin and beggary to thousands. The formation of the Company was one of the understandings with which the people of British Columbia joined the Confederation, for by the construction of the road it will bring the people of that Province into direct communication with the Atlantic Seaboard. The route of the road, so far as at present can be ascertained, will be from Montreal to Callender, Lake Nipissing, about 350 miles; to Thunder Bay, 650 miles; thence to Lake of the Woods, Manitoba, 220 miles, which forms beyond that point a connecting line with the present one from Winnipeg. Through Winnipeg to Brandon, below Rapid City, 275 miles; from thence through the fertile belt to the foot of the Rocky Mountains, 800 miles; thence across the Rockies, it is supposed, by Kicking Horse Pass (Yellowhead, and Kootenay Passes, having been disapproved of, after all the expense of survey), 300 miles; thence to Port Moody by Kamloops, Lytton and Yale, 250 miles; making the total number of miles 2,915, of

which about 845 are constructed and 2,070 yet to be built.
There is no doubt but that when the spurs of the Rockies;
are reached, that engineering difficulties will arise that will:
be almost insurmountable, and with the drawbacks of the
climate superhuman efforts will have to be made before
the line can even hope to be a permanent one; but once'
over the Mountains and into British Columbia, passing
the Lake Kamloops to the shores of Port Moody, the line
will be of great benefit to the people of the Pacific coast,:
and a portion may be managed so as to pay its own
working expenses. It is stated that, as the credit of
the Government wanes, we shall hear far more of,
annexation, or independence, as a mode of escape
from the mountain of debt now being piled up. It is
calculated when the engagements to the Syndicate are
paid the total debt of the Dominion will amount to
$203,397,680, which is certainly pretty good for a popula-
tion of 4,000,000 ; and, estimating the increase at 18 per:
cent., each individual will find himself generously provided
with a burden of $54.27 to wipe out for the benefit of the
C.P.R. and the Government generally. As the colored.
gentleman remarked " wen de intrust begins to go out de·
kentry jus look out, fur sumthing will hev to drap."
The Hon. Edw. Blake, whilst admitting the existence of
considerable prairie lands along the route, also avers that
there are 515 miles in the territory unfit for cultivation,
whilst in the Eastern section some 500 miles is wholly:
unfit for habitation. Labouchere most bitterly condemns·
the enterprise, so it remains yet to be seen whether the road
will be pushed through to completion and ultimate success,·
for it is thought that, even should the road become an·
accomplished fact, results would be anything but

CHAUDIERE FALLS.

satisfactory to the investor and returns from the small amount of Pacific territory to be drained would have to be something enormous to even pay expenses, much less interest on capital and wear and tear of machinery and plant. The N. P., or National Policy of Sir John A. Macdonald and his party, comes in for a good deal of controversy at present. Its advocates point with pride to the results of the policy of protection in the United States and of industries fostered and nourished by its protecting influences. The Opposition contend that, whilst it may be of benefit to a country with a climate and a soil that can raise such a diversity of products as not only to supply the actual wants, but also all the artificial requirements of its people, protection will never amount to much in Canada, for the simple reason that there is but little to protect either in staple industries or minerals. It is true that the Canadians have an almost boundless continent from the banks of the St. Lawrence clear up to the North Pole itself, but the only inhabitants of those high regions, the bears, wolves and seals, do not appear to care a cent whether they are protected by the N. P. or not

PUBLIC OFFICERS.

Right Hon. Sir John A. MacDonald, K.C.B., Premier and Minister of the Interior, was born in Scotland in the year 1815, and educated in Kingston, Ont.; he is therefore (1882) 67 years of age; has a half-Jewish, half-Scotch cast of countenance, his face wrinkled and tough-looking, but not unpleasant to gaze upon. In manner he is genial, and has constantly a smile for all who approach. In speech he is cool, collected, and a trifle hesitating, sarcastic, humorous, and sometimes witty in his remarks, quick to grasp a subject, forcible in his criticisms, a man whose exterior gives no signs of the passions ruling within. After being called to the Bar, in 1836 (note page 42 old edition), he was created a Queen's Counsel, and from the year 1847 his public

RT. HON. SIR JOHN A. MACDONALD, K.C.B.

official life may be said to have begun. From that on he became a power in political circles, and held various offices until 1867; in 1871 he was appointed one of Her Majesty's High Joint Commissioners who sat at Geneva on the arbitration of the famous Alabama Claims, by which award the American Government received some $15,000,000 of

British money. He received the degree (Honorary) from
Oxford of D.C.L. (1861); he is also LL.D. of Queen's
University. He was created K.C.B. (civil) by Her Majesty
in 1867; he was K.G.C. of Spain, 1872, and was also
appointed a member of Her Majesty's Most Honorable Privy
Council in 1872; sat for Kingston in the Canada Assembly
from 1844 until the Union, in 1867. Returned to Commons
in 1867, and again in '72, '74, '78 and '82. He has taken
part in many important public measures, and, like the late
Disraeli of England, is quick to grasp and use every opportunity that presents itself; he manages comfortably on a
salary of $8,000 per annum and other perquisites.

The Hon. Edward Blake, leader of the Opposition, is,
intellectually speaking, the peer of Canadian statesmen. He
was born in Upper Canada in the year 1832, and received
a thorough University education. As a speaker he is
clear, concise and apt, evidently possessing great oratori-
cal powers, and from his leadership great things are expected
by his party. The differences between the Liberals, of whom
he is the chief, and the Conservatives are to a great extent of
an historical character—the Conservative party being the
legitimate offspring of the old "Family Compact" which
ruled the country at its own sweet will in the early times
of the British *régime*. The "Family Compact" consisted
of the scapegoat representatives of broken-down British
squires, packed off to the colonies to be got rid of, and of a
few sharp men who saw where a good thing was to be got
and wanted to keep it to themselves. For many years the
country suffered the oligarchical rule of the "Family
Compact" until a Reform party arose in opposition to it and
rebellion resulted. The "Family Compact," although
broken up, spread itself into a Conservative party; and the

MARQUIS OF LORNE.

Reformers, flushed with their first success, pushed on the battle still further around such questions as the abolition of the feudal system of seigniorial tenure, the granting of municipal privileges, extending the franchise, purifying the election law, abolishing the unjust clergy reserves, etc.—Whilst these questions were foremost in the public mind many hard battles were fought, and although in the end the object of the Reformers was gained on all these questions, yet they could not be claimed as party triumphs. When popular clamor could no longer be resisted, the wily leaders of the Conservatives were wont to yield their principles to the expediency of the hour, and adopt the measures their opponents had been endeavoring to pass. As a consequence the Conservatives have had by far the longest terms of office, being only ousted when occasionally some act of more than ordinary official corruption has aroused the dormant electorate. It is now held by numerous supporters of the party in power that the next few years will bring about a crisis in Canadian Government; and, as the present party remain in power until that time, they will either be permanent or leave the country in such a state that it will take generations to redeem it. Nothing is more noticeable in Canadian politics than the absence of individuality or individual independence, either in thought or action; to be a party machine and to be used and despised, to be driven like dogs and then kicked is the height, seemingly, of their aspirations, whilst even the papers who seemingly wish to cultivate and assist in gaining a hearing for independent expression are started with the full purpose of betraying into other hands the unfortunate dupes who may be honestly endeavoring to give expression to their thoughts. No wonder the rulers feel secure, and openly despise and denounce the vulgar horde who clothed them with power. The member wears his kid gloves, whilst the stolen tribute trots the cattle up to vote.

The Princess Louise, wife of the Governor General, accompanied by her brother, Prince Leopold and suite, left for England during the summer of 1880 on a visit, to recruit her health, returning in 1882, thinking, no doubt, that a continued residence here was hardly desirable. It was expected at first that her husband, the Marquis of Lorne, would have accompanied her; but from politic reasons he made a tour of the Lower Provinces instead. Possibly the Marquis feels that he can enjoy himself with more freedom in the Dominion than he can at the Court of St. James, for the Londoners assert that the Marquis is not over anxious to reside amongst them, and his stay in their city on the occasion of his visits was certainly very limited. The Marquis of Lorne is a fair skinned, blue eyed, light haired, little gentleman, good-natured, and just diffident enough to be led by the politicians, and to accept the Governorship of the Dominion, so as to be out of the way of his royal relations, and comes of an old and noble family. As a matter of interest I give a synopsis of the history of the family, so far as can be at present ascertained.

MARQUIS OF LORNE.

His Excellency the Right Honorable John George Edward Henry Douglas Sutherland Campbell, Marquis of Lorne, Governor General and Commander in Chief of the Dominion of Canada. According to the historian Hogg: "It seems very evident that the ancestors of the present Marquis

PRINCESS LOUISE.

formed one of the primitive branches of the roving or stranger tribes of visitants to Scotland of the Irish or at least Celtic races. The first traces of the house are recorded in the Statutes of Alexander 1st in the thirteenth century, but their real start is ascribed to Sir Colin Campbell as far back as the year 1293. It is stated that the origin of the Campbells has never been fully and satisfactorily settled, but it is accredited that one of the first of the name married the heiress of O'Duin and thus became Lord of Lochow, in the District of Argyll. Still later another Campbell was one of the supporters of King Robert Bruce, and for his loyalty and friendship to his cause the King bestowed on Neil Campbell the hand of his sister, the Lady Mary, in marriage. This was a lucky stroke of policy, for the matrimonial alliance marked the commencement of a new era in the history and fortunes of the Campbells; henceforward their advancement, both political and social, was rapid and substantial, for the intermarriage with the Bruces gave fortune and fame and lands extending nearly into the heart of Athol, also the hereditary sheriffdom of Argyll. The head of the Campbells was summoned to Parliament in the year 1445, and was styled Lord Campbell, but titles being the aspiration of the family, on the accession of James II. that monarch raised Colin, the grandson of Duncan, to the dignity of Earl of Argyll in the year 1457, at which period the Lorne estates came into possession of the Campbells. Colin afterwards served in public life under the rule of James III. and James IV., and his great ambition and success in acquiring lands and properties gave birth to the by-word, "the greed of the Campbells;" it is also stated that his generation were men of ability," skillful in detecting and using opportunities." During the war with Charles 1st of England Archibald, the eighth Earl and first Marquis of Argyll, was a bitter opponent of that unfortunate monarch, and actively contended for civil and religious freedom on account of finding that the English King had promised to Lord Antrim the estates of Kintyre, which had been recently accorded to the house of Argyll, but the opposition to the English King finally cost him his head and the confiscation of his lands. In the year 1661 his son Duncan finding that opposition did not pay, became intensely loyal, and shortly afterwards, in 1663, was rewarded for his adherence by having the immense estates restored to him by the Crown with the title of his Grandfather, the Earl of Argyll. The next Earl managed also to get into disfavor with his King, so on the 30th of June, 1685, in the Castle of Edinburgh, he also parted with his head to please his royal master, but upon the accession of King William of Orange the Campbells were again brought forward, and John was an acknowledged favorite, so in June, 1701, he was created the Duke of Argyll, on whose title all true and devout Scotchmen are said to constantly invoke the blessing of the Lord, presumably on account of the scratching post question. In the year 1747 the then Duke of Argyll was called to part with several important privileges and rank, of power of life and death over all around him, and it is no doubt partly to the unlimited power wielded sometimes with extreme cruelty — by the chiefs that some of the present Scottish race, although shielded under a thin garb of sanctity, still show on every occasion the results of the training of their forefathers, for such stories as that of Janet telling the husband to ascend the gallows tree "like a man, to please the laird," and the constant fear that they were liable to be strung up to a tree for refusing to plunder or to fight at the command of the lords of the soil, made the average clansman very willing to do such acts, which were then classed as " devotion to the chief," " romantic fidelity," and such names and phrases to cover the baseness of their operations and their chief's unhappy ambition and quarrels. From that time the title descended through brothers and younger sons until 1823, when his Grace the present Duke of Argyll was born, and who since maturity has held several high and influential positions under Her Majesty's Government, and for the edification of those of my readers who love to roll a genuine high-toned title under their tongue, I give the honors of the house in full. His Grace is Duke and Earl of Argyll, Marquis of Lorne and Kintyre, Earl of Campbell and Cowal, Viscount of Lochow and Glenilla, Baron Campbell and Baron of Lorne, Inverary, Mull, Morvin and Tiry in the peerage of Scotland, and Baron of Sundridge and Hamilton in the peerage of Great Britain. He is Knight of the Thistle, a Privy Councillor (1853), Lord Lieutenant and Hereditary Sheriff of the County of Argyll, Hereditary Master of the Queen's Household, Keeper of the Great Seal, one of Her Majesty's State Councillors for Scotland, Admiral of the Western Isles, Keeper of Dunoon Castle, and of Dunnstaffnage and Carrick, Chancellor of the University of St. Andrews (1851), a sometime Lord Rector of the University of Glasgow (1854), and President of the Royal Society of Edinburgh (1861), LL.D., Cambridge (1862), a Trustee of the British Museum and holder of various political offices. The arms of the house are described thus :

Arms, Quarterly; first and fourth, Girony of eight pieces or and sable; second and third argent, a Galley or Lymphad, sails furled up, for the Lordship of Lorne.

Crest: A Boar's head, Coupeed, or.

Supporters: Two Lions.

Motto, *vix ea nostra voco* (I scarcely call all this my own).

The Duke John added *ne obliviscaris* (forget not), get more. Badge Myrtle.

The present Marquis was born in London in the year 1845, and is about three years the senior of his royal wife. He now manages to rule the Dominion on a salary of $48,666.66 per annum, with house rent and other little etceteras free.

In the interregnum, caused by change or absence, the Government is administered by General Sir Patrick L. Macdougall, who is also Commander in Chief of the Forces in Canada, an old and experienced British Army officer but not necessarily a statesman of renown.

The Princess Louise, Marchioness of Lorne, is a lady of medium height, with a good-natured face, and, were she not a princess, would be just the sort of lovable home wife to make a man happy. Although not possessed of a style of beauty equal to her royal sister-in-law, the Princess Alexandra, still she has that pleasant cast of countenance that marks so distinctively the children of Queen Victoria. H.R.H. The Princess Louise Caroline Alberta is the fourth daughter of Her Majesty Queen Victoria; she is talented and accomplished, and has developed a natural talent in the studies of drawing, painting and sculpture, fond of reading, with decided literary tastes. Was married to the Marquis of Lorne at Windsor Castle, near London, on the 21st March, 1871, which alliance at the time was thought to be very condescending on the part of Royalty. She is the eighth Princess of whom we have record who married a subject, the others

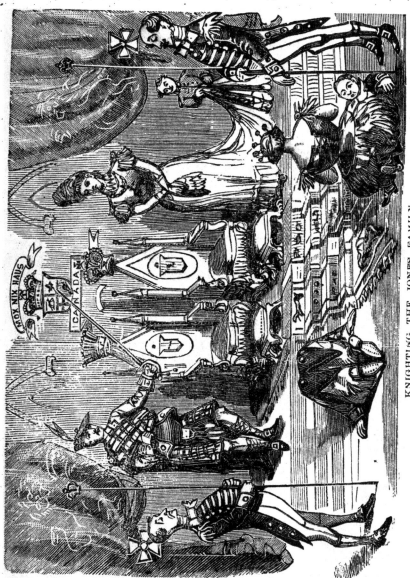

KNIGHTING THE JONES FAMILY.

being Eleanor, the third daughter of King John; Isabella, the eldest daughter of Edward III; Cecilia, third daughter of Edward IV; Annie and Catherine, also daughter of Edward IV; Mary Tudor, third daughter of Henry VIII, a beautiful and accomplished princess, was the last who openly married a subject, but in two other instances princesses have allied themselves to persons below them in rank, and so popular did this style of secret marriage become that in 1792 The Royal Marriage Act, which forbade any of the Royal Family contracting marriage without the royal sanction whilst under the age of twenty-five years, was enacted to put a stop to this sort of thing, as alliances with subjects were becoming too common and monotonous; but in the alliance of H.R.H. with the Marquis, on the 21st March, 1871, all loyal subjects of the Queen were rejoiced, as it removed another barrier in the approach to Royalty.

Of course, Ottawa being the residence of semi-royalty, European manners were to come in vogue. The Palace being the Rideau Hall, court etiquette must be followed and nobles and titled gentry created, but how to work over the raw material of Canada into blue-blooded aristocrats was a difficult problem to solve, so to the tailors, dressmakers and leaders of opinion of the Capital the Canadians are indebted for some of the absurd and ridiculous fashions now considered *au fait* at the Court of Ottawa. During this administration low-necked dresses, short sleeves, or doctors' certificates, were first instituted as costume for the ladies at receptions, and in this latitude it is especially appropriate and becoming: fancy Mrs. J. Muggins Jones, weighing 905 or 509 lbs., the wife of a retired eating-house keeper, after months of earnest supplication, solicitation, and fees innumerable, to ushers, secretaries, and understrappers generally, has at last the wish of her heart and prayer of her life answered, for she and Mr. J. Muggins Jones are to be presented at Court. On the day appointed for the presentation, the happy pair drive to the Vice-Regal residence in their own carriage, adorned with the newly-emblazoned family coat of arms—*une saucisse, deux pommes de terre, assiette, couteau et fourchette à la cross-wise*, probably. Notice the happy smile that illumines the countenance of Mrs. J. M. J. as the footman alights from his post on the box with the coachman, and opens the door of the carriage for her ladyship to descend; then behold her, after being assisted to alight, take the arm of her lord, and with stately tread mount the steps to the Gubernatorial mansion; then, handing her wrap to the first high watcher of the door bell, she takes her place in a line with others for the presentation. Poor Jones all this time feels ill at ease, he gazes on his brogans, and wonders if No. 16 feet are the usual size admitted to Court; he gets himself into a profuse perspiration in attempting to draw a No. 9 glove over a hand like the hand of Providence, covered with warts and freckles; finally the kid gives way, and he feels like reliev-ing his mind in good old home style, but is silently admon-ished by his wife, so he occupies the balance of his time in endeavoring to remember the instructions in the book as to how to accomplish the *recherche* court bow, but he can re-member everything but that and his prayers. The hearts of himself and spouse are in a flutter, and each moment rise higher and higher in their throats. At last their names are called, and they are ushered into the Vice-Regal presence. Then behold the couple, at the zenith of their ambition. Madame Jones, like the Queen of Sheba or an immense lager bier barrel, attired in a beautiful blue silk, cut bias in the

back, and low-necked to the waist, short-sleeved in front:
warm with excitement, perspiration and grease oozing
from every pore, and a smile of gratified ambition upon her
face.   Her better half in his dress suit of black broadcloth
trying to look unconcerned, but missing it every time, with
great beads of perspiration on his brow, his hands convul-
sively either clutching his watch-chain or hunting for the
pocket-handkerchief he dropped in the ante-room.   There
the couple stand, presented at court, monuments of gratified
ambition, silent, stupid, but grateful and satisfied plumb
down to their boot heels.   Jones is soon brought to his
senses by the usher of the red bamboo tapping him on the
head to remind him of his obeisance.   All at once he
remembers his court bow, and, in attempting to execute it,
bends too low, and goes sprawling on all fours.   His
spouse, noticing her lord's discomfiture, endeavors to
rectify it by placing her hand upon her heart and
dropping a courtesy, but for such a mountain of flesh
to expand something must give way, so, whilst attempting to courtsey, buttons from the back of the beautiful
blue silk fly in every direction, whilst a lace in her
elegant corsets snapped like a whip, and in attempting
to back out from the Vice-Regal presence she overturned
a page who was approaching with a wrap, and sitting
down upon him flattened him out like a pancake on Shrove
Tuesday; but the ordeal was passed, the presentation
was over, and the Joneses returned to their family mansion, feeling that they were no longer of the lower
orders, and already began to despise the "vulgah horde"
who had never been presented at court.   What mattered
the cold and consequent fever that laid that amiable and
aspiring woman up for the next two months, or the at-

tack of rheumatism that confined Jones himself to the
house, had they not attained the highest pinnacle of their
ambition, and was not Jones when he went to his old sausage factory to collect the rents looked upon with awe and
reverence when his exploits became known to the common
people; in fact, the Joneses were daily becoming more con-
scious of their greatness and superiority. It is stated that
several new orders of knighthood will be introduced at
court next season, and will be conferred on the worthy ones,
i.e., those who pay at extremely low prices for cash, and
soon our ears will become familiar with such sounds as
Juke Moses Abram Isaacs Threebal, Lord Squeezem
Banker Smith, Sir Charcuterie Francis, Rt. Hon. Cent per
Cent Grabal, etc. It is also rumored that on the return of
Royalty the court ladies themselves are to become exclusive and distinctive, and no doubt we shall soon hear of
orders amongst the fair sex that will outshine in dignity
any honors the sterner relatives can acquire or assume.
In order to uphold the anticipated magnificence of the
Court and imbue the commonalty with a due appreciation
of its dignity, it will soon be necessary for the Government
of the Dominion to follow the example of the Province of
Quebec and go to France to borrow a few more millions
at 5 or 8 per cent., and then levy a tax for interest.

Outside of political circles the city is a pleasant one in
which to dwell. Hotels are numerous and well kept, the
New Russell being one of the finest in the Dominion. Under
the management of Mr. James A. Gouin it has become as
popular an institution as any on the continent. The hotel
is admirably situted, whilst its cuisine is as fine as that
afforded by the boasted hotels of the Pacific coast, for both
the products of the Arctic and equator contribute to its board,

whilst the stranger or visitor will find to his surprise that he could not have fallen into more pleasant and agreeable hands.

The Windsor is also a noted hostelry, and economical in its charges.

The trade in lumber at Ottawa is something enormous, whilst the demand is yearly increasing, and affords employment in the timber districts during the winter season to a vast number of men.

CITY OF OTTAWA.

Leaving Ottawa by the Government Railroad, the Q. M. O. & O., now the Canada Pacific, we have a pleasant run of 115 miles to Montreal. This road, which was built and controlled by the Government, cost some $13,000,000 in its construction, and extends from Ottawa to Quebec, a distance of 293 miles. The roadbed is an excellent one, its appointments well kept, and its service regular; but for some years the road was run at a loss, being altogether in the hands of scheming politicians. Lately, however, the Western Section, that extending from Montreal to Ottawa, was sold to the C. P. R. to form part of the system of that road ; the Eastern Section is still in the hands of the Provincial Parliament.

Leaving the cars at Hochelaga, the present Montreal terminus, we hasten to the Jacques Cartier wharf to take the boat for Quebec—distance by river some 180 miles. The steamer Quebec, Capt Robert Nelson, and Montreal, Capt Burns, perform a daily service between the two cities, and, so far as the captains can control matters, are pleasant boats to travel on. The steamers are large and commodious, and well patronized by visitors and tourists. Leaving Montreal, St. Helen's Island with its recreation grounds, and the Fort with its breast works, are soon left behind. then comes Longueuil, the South shore terminus of the S. E. R. R., a company who, by the way, have shown considerable enterprise and vitality of late in securing a good portion of the forwarding traffic, and who anticipate excavating a tunnel under the St. Lawrence in the near future. Further down stream a number of low islands are passed, one of which. Isle Gros Bois, is quite a place of resort during the summer season.

The French village of Var nnes is next sighted. At this place are mineral springs of the usual class. The town consists of a number of houses and cottages, clustered about a double-spired, tin-plated church, a sight common along the banks of the lower St Lawrence. At about sixteen miles from Montreal the mouth of the northern branch of the Ottawa River is passed, numerous small islands concealing it in part ; then for a stretch of several miles the St. Lawrence widens considerably, the stream being from two

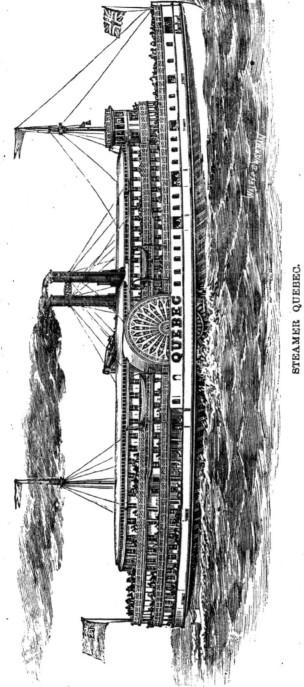

STEAMER QUEBEC.

to four miles in width, and presents a grand appearance like the Mississippi during the June rise, but before reaching Sorel, forty-five miles below Montreal, the river contracts to about one mile in width with more elevated banks. The Richelieu River, draining from Lake Champlain, along whose banks are located quite a numerous agricultural population, enters the St. Lawrence at Sorel. The town, an old-fashioned one, is one of the oldest settled towns in Canada, having been founded in the year 1618, and was formerly the seat of government of the French Governors. It is populated chiefly by French Canadians, with but few English-speaking inhabitants.

Leaving Sorel several more small islands are passed, and the steamer soon enters Lake St. Peter, an expansion of the St. Lawrence. The lake is some twenty-five miles in length and from twelve to fifteen miles in width, shallow but with a dredged channel, now averaging about eighteen feet at ordinary low water, thereby admitting the ocean fleet to Montreal.

Trois Rivières, the next stopping-place, forty-five miles from Sorel and eighty above Quebec, is also an old and important town, advantageously situated at the mouth of the River St. Maurice; numerous vessels load here with timber for Europe. From Three Rivers to Quebec the scenery from the river is beautiful and grand: the eye never becomes weary of gazing on the ever-changing and varied aspects of the banks of the St. Lawrence. The hills and hillocks, many of them replete with historical interest, the seemingly cosy little French towns and their clean white cottages along the banks are tastefully laid out and admirably situated, and during the summer seem to nestle in a forest of verdure; but once ashore, and the dream is soon

dispelled, for, with the exception of a narrow strip of
bottom land along the St. Lawrence, we find the country
at the back of the hills barren, generally unproductive and
unfit either for agriculture or mining purposes,—like the
Dead Sea fruit—pleasant to the eye but ashes in the grasp.
Then we pass through elevated banks to a bold headland
called *Point aux Trembles*, passing numerous residences
that in their present surroundings looked really picturesque.
The population of this portion are, with few exceptions,
French, and the churches of the Roman Catholic denomination. Cap Rouge, 8 miles above Quebec, is next passed;
rounding which we come into full view of Point Levis and
the citadel. Wolfe's Cove, two miles above the city,
commemorates the spot where the General landed with the
English army in 1759, to participate in the fight on the
Plains of Abraham. From this point we are soon landed
at the old wharf in Lower Town, which skirts the base of
the rocky promontory on which is located the quaint old
city of Quebec.

QUEBEC.

On arrival at the ancient city the stranger somehow feels
that he is on historical ground and amid old associations. It
was here the adventurous Jacques Cartier, after planting a
cross at Gaspé and ascending the St. Lawrence, passing in
safety the gloomy gorge of the Saguenay, that he wintered
during the winter of 1535-6, in the River St. Charles, by
him called St. Croix. The panorama that greeted the bold
navigator on his first appearance at the foot of Cape
Diamond is thus described : " A mighty promontory, rugged
and bare, thrust its scarped front into the surging current.
Here, clothed in the majesty of solitude, breathing the

stern poetry of the wilderness, arose the cliffs now rich with heroic memories, where the fiery Count Frontenac cast defiance at his foes, where Wolfe, Montcalm and Montgomery fell,—as yet all was a nameless barbarism, and a cluster of wigwams held the site of the rock-built city of Quebec. Its name was Stadacona, and it owned the sway of the Royal Donacona. But Cartier and his adventurers were soon besieged by the rigors of a Canadian winter, the rocks, the shores, the pine trees, the solid floor of the river, all alike were blanketed in snow; the drifts rose far above the sides of their ships, and a frosty armor four inches thick encased the bulwarks, and, to make matters worse, the scurvy broke out amongst the crew, and numbers of them died, leaving but a few in health. At last the terrible winter broke up, and Cartier and his comrades, having had enough of Canada for one season, and feeling considerably homesick, took the first opportunity to return, in order to give the other boys a chance to explore, so, after setting his men to gather a number of crystals, which he fondly imagined were diamonds, and also collecting a quantity of glittering mica, that he thought gold, he stole or kidnapped the two Indian chiefs, Tuigaragny and Donacona, with their effects, to exhibit on his arrival as specimens of the natural productions of "New France," as Canada was then called, planted the emblem of Christianity, and sailed away, arriving under the walls of St. Malo, 16th July, 1536. Regarding Donacona and his Tribesmen so basely kidnapped by Cartier, excellent care had been taken of their souls, as also of their furs and other trappings, which were taken for their passage across. In due time they had both been baptized, and soon reaped the benefit of the rite, since they both died within a year or two, to the great detriment of the next expedition.

The next explorer, in the person of Jean François de la
Roque, Sieur de Roberval, a nobleman of Picardy, came in
state with the following honors attached (on parchment):
Lord of Norembega, Viceroy and Lieut. General in Canada,
Hochelaga, Saguenay, Newfoundland, Belle Isle, Carpunt,
Labrador, the Great Bay, and Baccalaos. He also got a good
cash grant from the French Treasury, with which he equipped
five vessels, and to Cartier was given the post of Captain
General, and a divy of the spoils. On again arriving at
Quebec the savages anxiously enquired for their kidnappe
chiefs, then the nobleman, like Jeremiah of old, was
diplomatic, and lied like a trooper, telling the savages that,
although Donacona was dead, the others had married in
France, and were living in state like great lords. This
season, like the first, was a hard one on these pioneers.
In the year 1542 Roberval, with three ships and two
hundred colonists, made the first attempt at settlement
on the heights of Cap Rouge; here all the colonists were
housed under one roof, like one of the experimental communities of recent days, officers, soldiers, nobles, artisans,
laborers and convicts, with the women and children with
whom lay the future of New France. This first
attempt at a settlement soon proved a failure, and the
Canadians annals from 1542 to 1608 offer a perfect blank, no
Europeans having remained behind. On the third of July,
1608, a group of French artificers, 28 in number, under the
command of Captain Samuel de Champlain, were engaged
(on the site where 82 years afterwards, in 1690, was built,
to commemorate a French victory, the church of Notre Dame
de la Victoire) in the construction of an " habitation," and
thus laid the foundation of the future " city of Quebec."
They next proceeded to clear lands for gardens, and, although

BREAK NECK STAIRS, QUEBEC.

suffering terrible hardships during their first winters, soon obtained a substantial foothold. In the following spring the colony was augmented by Marias and Pontgravé with a number of new settlers. In 1615 the Recollet Fathers, members of the order of St. Francis, arrived at Quebec. In 1616 the peltry trade with the savages had assumed considerable proportions, and the gains from that trade served to erect substantial dwellings and churches. The colony thus founded continued to flourish until the year 1689, when a Frenchman named DeCallier originated a daring plan, in which he proposed that France should make herself mistress of New York and Virginia by purchase, treaty or force, offering to conduct, in order to effect the desired result, thirteen hundred soldiers and three hundred Canadians to Fort Orange on the Hudson and Manhattan (New York), in order to capture those posts by sudden assault. The conquest, he argued, would make the King of France master of one of the finest seaports in America, open at all seasons to navigation of all kinds, and of a region possessing a fine climate and fertile lands, which the English themselves had conquered from the "Dutch." The French King and his ministers approved of the plans submitted, and the breaking out of the war between France and England shortly afterwards prepared for the city of Champlain the thrilling scenes which were afterwards enacted in Quebec upon the return of Count de Frontenac in 1689. The year following a Quebecer named de Portneuf started with 50 French Canadians and 60 Indians to attack and capture the stations on the Bay of Casco, near where Portland, Maine, now stands, which stations surrendered after a slight resistance. The scenes of blood, midnight pillage and destruction by the Montreal band at Schenectady and by the Three Rivers.

band at Salmon Falls, with the barbarism and atrocities committed by the Quebec band and their Indian allies, have already passed into history, and led to a terrible retaliation by the English, who, after a series of disastrous defeats and few victories, succeeded in capturing the City of Quebec after the decisive battle on the Plains of Abraham, on the 13th September, 1759, a victory which cost the lives of the victorious Wolfe and the gallant, brave but vanquished Marquis de Montcalm, thus bringing the city under English rule.   For a while afterwards the bitterness of feeling between the French and English-speaking communities entirely placed a barrier to the progress of the city, but as the younger generations grew up, and a new population poured in, new suburbs were added, and now the city comprises Quebec within, Quebec without, Lower Town, St Rochs and St. Sauveur, and numbers about 40,000 people, Quebec within being entirely walled in—a city within a fortress.   The public buildings are numerous and substantial, and along the St. Louis, St. Johns and Montmorenci roads are many residences and mansions that will contrast favorably with those on the outskirts of London itself.   The citizens generally are sociable and democratic in' their tendencies, and are certainly, taken as a body, the most conscientious of any in the Dominion; they have several institutions of benefit to the community, such as the Museums, Historical Society, Hospital, also a Y. M. C. A. Rooms and various Catholic religious institutions.   The shipping business is but of short duration, the season lasting but from May until the middle of November, and consists almost exclusively of the export of timber and logs, in which an immense trade is transacted every season. The monetary value of the exports of lumber from Quebec alone during the season of 1880 amounted to $900,000.

The City of Quebec, whose name is derived from an old Algonquin term meaning "take care of the rock," is situated on the upper bank of the St. Lawrence, at the point where it is joined by the St. Charles, about 400 miles from the gulf; it bears about 46°49′ N. lat. and 71°16′ W. long. The citadel has often been called the Gibraltar of America; it is approached both by a winding pathway and a stairway up the side of the rock from Dufferin Terrace. Inside the fortress may be compared to a town in itself. The officers' quarters overlook the St. Lawrence, whilst the soldiers are located under the ramparts. The armories, magazines and warlike implements make considerable show in time of peace, but the day of their usefulness may perhaps be past, through the introduction of the numerous inventions of modern times. There is, however, one consolation, which also makes it a source of pride to the citizens, and that is its usefulness to the whole community, for at all times the fortress is continually undergoing repairs, and no sooner does one portion obtain the necessary improvement or patching than another part gives way, thus affording employment to the otherwise idle labor of the city, whilst the officers and garrison support to a great extent the traders and storekeepers; the citadel itself crowns the highest point of Cape Diamond, at an elevation of some 350 feet above the river, and presents an almost perpendicular front towards the water. The city is built from the water's edge along the foot of these cliffs, in the angle formed by the junction of the St. Lawrence and St. Charles rivers, and ascends upwards to the walls of the citadel, being divided into Lower and Upper Town—the one being enclosed within the walls, and the

other skirting the narrow strip at the foot of the cliffs. To
pass from one portion of the town to the other the visitor
has either to take the anscenseur or hydraulic inclined
railway (for which the charge is but 3 cents, and which
saves the passenger over 500 per cent. in fuel and energetic
language alone) to the top; or visitors, to enjoy themselves
in the city, should be double-jointed in the knees or wind
their way through steep and narrow streets, with still nar-
rower alleys and flights of steep steps both to the right and
left of them, until they reach the line of the fortifications,
which line stretches nearly across the peninsula in the
west, and runs along a ridge between the upper and lower
parts of the city.

Dufferin Terrace (named after a former governor)
commands a picturesque view, having the lower part of
the city in the foreground, and the shores and waters
of the St. Lawrence, with the Island of Orleans extending
far in the distance. The public garden off the terrace
contains a shaft erected to the joint memories of Wolfe and
Montcalm: it is a Corinthian shaft, mounted on a square base,
and is some 65 feet in height, but the inhabitants have so
disfigured the side on which Wolfe's name was engraved
as to render the former inscription almost illegible. Both
from the terrace and the esplanade most delightful views
of the surrounding country and river scenery are obtained
and enjoyed, and during the evenings of the summer
season, whilst the military band discourses its music, the
terrace is thronged with citizens and visitors. The new
Provincial Parliament buildings are an elegant and imposing
pile, built at a cost to the people of $1,250,000 (the old
Parliament house was destroyed by fire in 1853). Being
the capital of the Province the Legislature meet here to

MONTMORENCI FALLS.

enact laws for the government of the Province of Quebec with its 1,359,027 inhabitants. This being one of the larger provinces its Lieut.-Governor receives a salary of some $9,999.96 annually, together with a free residence in the governmental mansion at Spencer Wood, a short distance from the city. Some little stir has been created from the fact that during the last season the Lieut.-Governor sent in his little bill in addition to his salary for the amount of $15,243, which he claims to have spent in carriage hire at Quebec and Montreal, hotel fare whilst visiting, the Brass band for his reception, and the uniform for his aide de camp, etc. The House has a membership of 68, who represent the different districts, and were paid $500 per session, which amount on their last assemblage they raised to $800. Now that the people are beginning to count the cost of these petty Provincial legislatures and notice the evils they perpetuate, breeds a feeling of discontent, and starts a more thorough enquiry, so of late the Government has been most freely censured; and as numerous members seek to promote misrule for their own advantage, thus rearing and endeavoring to uphold a government not at all parental and protective in their dealings with the people, so each succeeding year.finds the idea of abolishing these local parliaments more and more in favor with the people at large. The entire debt of the Province of Quebec is some $18,500,000; but this season they are contracting another loan of $1,500,000, so as to call it the even twenty millions. Its total receipts and revenue amount to $7,504,497.85, whilst its cost of legislation, etc., foots up $7,212,129.17. The cost of legislation in the Province amounts to 13 6-10 cents per head, per annum of the entire population, so no wonder the people are awaking to the fact that they need a tremendous amount

of governing. Of late years the city has been the scene of
several most disastrous and destructive fires, still she never
seems to profit by past experience, but goes on rebuilding
her dwellings and appealing for aid in the same old style,
paying up her debts and enriching her churches from the
charity bestowed by the world on her citizens.   Although
of late a law has been enacted to prevent the erection of
wooden buildings within the city limits, still the majority
are but slightly better, being for the most part wooden erec-
tions with a shell work of brick or thin coating of stone.
The Court House, City Hall and Marine Hospital are fine
public buildings. The Lunatic Asylum (and no well regulated Canadian city is complete without one or two; it
almost seems that one-third of the people endeavor to keep
the other two either within the walls of a jail or in the
asylum) is situated at Beauport, 3 miles from the city. The
Asylum is an extensive building and enclosed in its grounds
of some 200 acres, and is the recipient of an annual grant
from the Provincial Legislature of $120,794.83.   The Ex-
change Institute, Historical Society (presided over by Dr. J.
L. Lemoine, Author, Customs Officer, etc.), the Library
Association and Advocates Library, are all institutions of
interest. The city contains a R. C. Cathedral and numerous
R. C. churches, the bulk of the population inclining to that
faith. The English or Episcopal Cathedral is an edifice 135
feet by 75, and will seat from 3,000 to 4,000 people if it is
ever fortunate enough to obtain them.   Notre Dame de la
Victoire, a stone structure, was erected in 1690.   Trinity
Church, also of stone, is of date 1824, whilst Baptists,
Congregational, Methodists and Presbyterians, although of
later dates, are represented.   Hotels are numerous, the St.
Louis and Russell taking the lead; there are also several

nunneries, the Hotel Dieu being the principal, and also used as an Hospital, the Nuns acting as nurses and also as teachers, the religious institutions being numerous and conducted on the routine plan. The population being mostly French, that language, or rather a *patois*, is spoken in all circles; in fact it has become a popular saying, that there is no chance for 'a man to live in Quebec who parlés Anglaise. The wharves along the river from the Custom House to the Allan's Dock are substantial and well built; vessels and steamships of the heaviest burthen and deepest draught of water come up to the river front. The harbor between the city and the Island of Orleans, formerly called Isle Bacchus from the numerous wild grapes it produced, is a large and commodious one, the depth of its waters being about 160 feet. The tide rises from 16 to 18 feet at neaps, and from 24 to 30 during the spring.

The Plains of Abraham, the old battlefield and scene of the struggle between Wolfe and Montcalm, lies on the top of the hill, or rather on the side of the highest rise, a short distance southwest of the citadel. A monument was here erected with the inscription "*Here fell Wolfe victorious,*" which inscription the Frenchmen have kindly obliterated, in order to remove, if possible, disagreeable reminiscences, so the representatives of each nation now live together in peace and harmony, willing at any time to assist in exterminating each other, in the cause of religion, politics, or on any pretext whatsoever, either simple or complex.

In the year 1775 Quebec was invaded by the forces of General Montgomery and the Englishman Arnold. Landing at Point Levis, a night attack was determined upon by the American General, for from the 1st of December the city had been invested, and several attacks made but without

success, but the night attack was hoped to ensure the
surrender of the fortress.   The attempt was duly made by
General Montgomery approaching from the southern and
Arnold from the northern side of Lower Town.   Both
attacks were impetuous and made with great courage, but
both failed.   In the southern attack, made from where the
Allan's wharf is now located, General Montgomery and
nearly all his personal staff were killed. A tablet has been
placed on the rock about 50 feet above the road, near the
spot where the General and his two aides-de-camp fell.
On the tablet is the inscription, " Here fell Montgomery,
December 31, 1775," whilst on the St. Louis road a candy
store makes capital by advertising the fact that the
General's body lay in that house four days.   In the attack
from the northern portion General Arnold was wounded,
and, with most of his followers, taken prisoners.   The British
being well fortified behind the rocks and ambuscades their
loss was comparatively slight, and the Americans being in
full view had to bear the brunt; however they did not
give up the attempt to reduce Quebec, but renewed the
attack the following year, since which time the Ancient
Capital has been free from military threatenings.

It was my privilege, whilst in this city, to see a party
planted in style, under the auspices and according to the rules
of the English Cathedral. In the State in which I was raised
the planting is done mighty quiet like, but here it was a
different thing entirely. A surveyor, a Government official,
had recently handed in his checks away up in the woods
somewhere, and when his relatives got hold of his carcass
they resolved to give him a good send-off, so they published
the fact of his demise, and it was soon rumored around that
he was a Government official, and very rich, so the citizens

turned out in force, as if for a gala day : women and children
in their best lined the streets, and clambered around
the palings of the Cathedral, and occasionally a young Miss
would murmur, " Ma, just isn't it lovely ? " and Ma would
respond, " Perfectly elegant, dear ; and such fine weather
too." About the time the crowds were thickest around the
church the strains of music were heard in the distance, and
soon a band at the head of the procession appeared, lending
quite a charm to the proceedings, and putting the spectators
in excellent good humor. The procession consisted of quite
a number of men in their Sunday black, with stove-pipe hats
and sashes of various colors, either hung over their shoulders
or tied around their waists, beating anything seen lately,
even in electioneering for Governor ; then the waggon containing the *departed* , and following came hacks, traps and
drays, in fact, it was quite a wholesale turn out. As they
approached the gates the band ceased, and the crowds made
way right and left for the candidate ; then six of the boys,
with new gloves and long sashes, unlocked the door and
hauled the lately *translated* out feet foremost, and as they
went up the steps were met by the two clerks in white
gowns with black hoods, and those two were in such a
hurry to earn their ten spot apiece that they commenced
to read the document before the man's feet were on a level
with the doorway. As soon as they ended the procession
formed again, the band struck up a lively tune, and hurried
him up to the boneyard and planted him in style. It was
the generally expressed opinion of the crowd that it was
the best and most stylish send-off they had seen in six
months, and, as a gentleman remarked, "When Quebec
takes a notion to do a thing up handsome she can, you may
rely ; " and each of the throng wished he was a Government

official and rich, so that some time he might give his friends such a treat.

We also availed ourselves of the opportunity to witness the celebration at the Hotel Dieu on the first Friday in October, the anniversary of " Le Crucifix outrage," occasion for which impressive ceremonies was brought about as follows: The inscription of the day was the cabalistic letters " I.N.R.I."—*Jesus Nazerence Rex Judearorem*. In the year 1742 one of the soldiers belonging to the garrison at the citadel, in order to acquire either fame or cash, or perhaps both, played off as a sorcerer, and of course was looked upon with superstitious awe by his comrades and the natives generally. Finding that he had got a fair start, he obtained a good-sized crucifix, and covered the cross and figure with tar and feathers, coal oil or some other inflammable material, placed it in a conspicuous position in the market place and set it on fire, pretending, whilst reading passages of Scripture and incantations, to be working his diabolical arts. The mob started with horror at his audacity, and the priests cried sacrilege, so of course the soldier was promptly arrested, tried, convicted and sentenced to make public reparation, and afterwards to serve three years in the galleys for his short-lived notoriety. So he was led by the public executioner with a cord around his neck, bare-headed and bare-footed, wearing only a long shirt, and having a placard on his breast and back on which was inscribed the legend, " Desecrator of Holy Things," *Profanateur des choses Saintes* ; he was then marched in front of the parish church in Montreal, and being thrown upon his knees he made the *amende honorable* to God, to the King and to justice for profaning the image of Jesus Christ ; he was then taken to each cross-road and there publicly scourged, after which castigation he was placed in prison, and finally sent to France to work out his sentence, all of which punishment he calculated and endured, preferring the galleys of " *La Belle* France " to a residence in Quebec. In consequence of the act of this soldier the Pope ordered that public veneration of the relic should occur on the first Friday in each October, so that, if that old vagabond of a soldier happens to be drifting around in the

WOLFE'S MONUMENT.

spirit, and enters the Hotel Dieu during these ceremonies, he will thank his lucky stars that he is not again in the flesh on such occasions.

Opposite to the City of Quebec is Point Levis, a town of some 10,000 inhabitants, and terminus of the Grand Trunk Railroad. It is here the emigrants are landed on arrival in the Dominion, and from this point the cattle are shipped on the outward-bound steamers. The point was named after a French Jew, Henri De Levis, Duc de Venta-

dour, who claimed to be a lineal descendant of the Israelite
Jacob (who beat his brother on the blessing and pottage
question), and who was just as ready to swindle his
brethren as that hoary-headed old Patriarch. The historian
informs us that in a chapel belonging to the family a
painting was exposed representing the Holy Virgin and a
member of the Levi family, with his hat in his hand. Two
inscriptions explained the scene : " Couvrez vous, mon cou-
sin," said the Virgin. " C'est mon plaisir, ma cousine,"
replied the descendant of Levi. Like the Jews of old and
the present, the Levis seemed to have grabbed for all within
reach, and at one time owned the most considerable portion
of the entire town.

The Chaudière Falls, nine miles from Point Levis, are fine
natural falls and often visited ; they are some 130 feet in
height, whilst the cataract itself is a fierce and noisy one, and
can be heard some distance. The station at Chaudière
Curve, or junction of the G.T.R., is in close proximity to the
Falls.

From Quebec a delightful trip can be made by the Steamer
Miramichi, now commanded by Captain Bouchette. This
vessel, formerly one of the old blockade runners, is now
regularly engaged in the Gulf trade, and makes fortnightly
trips to Pictou, Nova Scotia and Charlottetown, P.E.I.,
calling at the Gulf Ports en route. The accommodation on
board is all that can be desired, whilst the courtesy of the
officers is such that is not experienced by every-day
travellers in other portions of the river and lakes.

Eight miles below the city of Quebec are situated the Falls
of Montmorenci. The road leading to the falls is a good one
to drive over ; crossing River St. Charles several fine residences are passed on the route to Beauport, which village is

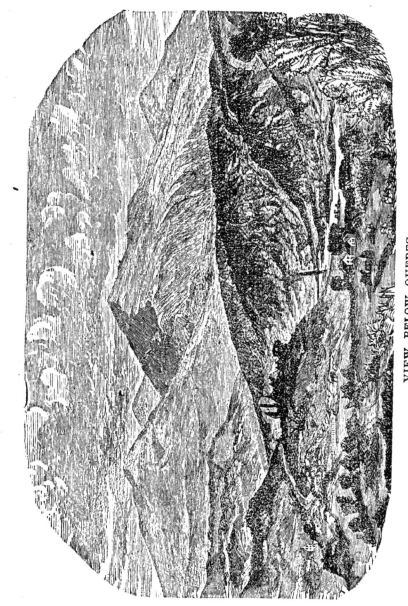

VIEW BELOW QUEBEC.

only unlike the ordinary French Canadian settlements from the fact of its having a church with *three* spires and a cluster of whitewashed cottages surrounding it. Along the road at intervals are passed monuments adorned with a cross, where in summer are frequently found persons kneeling and performing their devotions, and in turn soliciting charity at the hands of the passer-by. Arriving at the Falls you find a pretty little river but sixty feet wide, but the water tumbles to a depth of 240 feet before it reaches the St. Lawrence. Some of the professors have gone into ecstasies over these miniature cataracts, and assert that : "The river at some distance seems suspended in the air in a sheet of billowy foam, and, contrasted as it is with the dark waters into which it falls, makes it an object of the highest interest : the sheet of foam which first breaks over the ridge is more and more divided as it plunges, and is dashed against the successive layers of rock, which it completely veils from view ; the spray, becomes very delicate and abundant from top to bottom, hanging over and revolving around the torrent until it becomes lighter and more evanescent than the whitest fleecy clouds of summer, constituting the most airy and sumptuous drapery that can be imagined, yet, like the drapery of some of the Grecian statues, which, while it veils, exhibits more forcibly the form beneath,—this does not hide, but exalts the effects produced by this noble cataract." There is an opinion that cannot fail to please—it is so truthful that it is worthy to be quoted as the opinion of a Presbyterian preacher drawing government pay. In the winter the Falls become a scene of life and rare sport, and the feature that is then added may be considered its finest. The spray gradually freezes, and at length, forms a regular cone of one hundred feet or·

upward in height, immediately at the foot of the cataract, and down this cone come with the speed of the wind the various tabogganing parties that concentrate there to enjoy the sport. In the city the Snow Shoe Clubs make this the limit of their peregrinations, and during an assemblage at the cone all is mirth, festivity and joyousness, the sleighs returning with their happy occupants present a scene of mirth and seeming happiness in the midst of dreary, desolate and chill surroundings. The natural steps in the vicinity of the falls are also objects of interest, whilst generally the whole historical incidents that happened along its banks, with the victories and repulses that were met, both by the Indians, the French and English, render it almost classic ground.

Sixteen miles down the river we come to the Falls of Ste. Anne, near which is situated the chapel of Ste. Anne de Beaupré, where modern miracles are supposed to be worked, and where ferns from the grotto and pictures of the Saint are sold at low prices, C.O.D. The Falls are situated at the junction of the Ste. Anne river with the St. Lawrence, amidst wild and varied scenery.

THE SAGUENAY RIVER.

The Saguenay, one of the largest tributaries, enters the St. Lawrence river six miles below Tadousac, 115 miles from Quebec. The river is the outlet of Lake St. John, and is some 140 miles in length, an excellent stream for ship navigation, and vessels of the largest size ascend the entire distance. The stream itself is a grim, gloomy and peculiar one; its rough and uncouth surroundings, together with its eternal gloom, seem to impress the visitor with wonder and amazement, and make him wish he was home. Once seen few care to gaze upon its beauties again. The ascent of the river is made almost in stillness, only the monotonous plash, plash of the steamer's paddles, with the hoarse escape of steam ever and anon, re-echoing amidst the savage wildness, seems but to make the silence more impressive. Nature itself seems wearied out, and cast her huge bare cliffs around promiscuously, with hardly an effort to cover their cold, bleak and desolate sides with the scantiest verdure; and it is with a sigh of relief that the traveller emerges from its sullen gloom. It is wild without the' least variety, and grand even in its solitude and seeming desolation, whilst so dreary and monotonous becomes the constant gazing on towering black walls of rock that any change to thoughts savoring of life is eagerly grasped. Over 300 years ago Jacques Cartier landed at its mouth and rested at Tadousac, and the first mention we have of the Saguenay is one which well befits its savage aspect, for Cartier sent a boat and crew to explore its rocky chasm, which were never more heard of. (He was a wise man was Cartier, and did not believe in doing himself what others could do for him.) At the mouth of the river the water varies in depth from fifty to seventy-five feet, but once between its walls of rock the depth is never less than 500 feet, sometimes as high as 750 feet. On either side, at a distance of about a mile, the cliffs rise up straight, dark, and weather-scarred, varying in perpendicular from 1,200 feet to 1,600 feet,—such is its character from its source until it joins the St. Lawrence. On the right bank the cliffs are poorly mantled here and there with stunted pines and scrub timber, but on the left there is scarcely a sign of life or verdure, and the rocks stick up bare and rugged in the gloomy atmosphere like the bones of an old world after a terrible volcanic disturbance. Lake St. John, the head water of the river, is some forty miles in length, fringed with heavy timber and a level sandy country. Its waters are clear, and contain numbers of small fish. Eleven rivers flow into the lake, and yet it has but the one outlet for its immense body of water.

There is a curtain fall of some two hundred and thirty-six feet, called by the Indians " Oueat Chouan," flowing into the lake, and so conspicuous as to be visible for some miles distant; there are several towns along the Saguenay, and from which large quantities of timber are annually exported. A few miles below the southern fall in the river is Chicoutimi, which is the head of tide water, and to which point vessels of the largest class ascend for lumber. Ha! Ha! Bay, some sixty miles from the St. Lawrence, is a fine spread of water after emerging from the gorge of the Lower Saguenay; it is said the name was given to the bay, in an ecstasy of delight by a party of explorers, who were astonished to find open water after such dismal realities. At two places, St. Marguerite and between Capes Trinity and Eternity, where smaller tributaries help swell the deep black stream, a breach occurs in the wall of rocks as if some giant hand had torn them forcibly back and left them strewn and baffled of their power, in uncouth lumps over the valleys beyond, but these are the only openings, from the silent gloom of this dead river. Than these two dreadful headlands nothing can be imagined more grand or impressive; the rugged character of the river is partly softened, and bears an aspect akin to the canons of the Sierra Nevada in freshet time; the land wears a look of life and wild luxuriance which, though not rich, seems so in comparison with the previous awful barrenness. Cape

Trinity is thickly clothed with fir and beech, mingled in a color contrast, which is pleasant and attractive to the eye, especially when the rocks show out amongst them with their little cascades and waterfalls like strips of silver shining in the sun. But Cape Eternity is the very reverse of this and well becomes its name. It is one tremendous cliff of limestone, more than 1,500 feet high, and inclining forward more than 200 feet, and seeming as if at any moment it would fall down and overwhelm the deep black stream which flows so cold, deep and motionless below. Companionship becomes a necessity in a solitude like that encountered on the Saguenay, if only to relieve the mind of the feeling of loneliness and desolation that seems to oppress all who venture up this stern, grim, watery chasm, for the idea of mirth abroad seems like a schoolboy's idea of fun in a graveyard at midnight.

Statue Point is another attraction, where, at about 1,000 feet above the water, a huge rough Gothic arch gives entrance to a cave. Before the entrance to this black aperture a gigantic rock once stood; some winters ago it gave way, and the monstrous block of granite came crashing through the ice of the Saguenay, and left bare to view the entrance to the cavern it had guarded, perhaps for ages. The Tableau Rock is a cliff of dark limestone, some 600 feet high by 300 wide, straight, and almost as smooth as a mirror. At different points of the ascent steam is shut off, and the best views presented to the traveller, and plenty of time is allowed by the captain for a thorough study of the various aspects of the scenery. In times past the Marguerite and other tributaries, together with the Saguenay, bore an excellent reputation for salmon fishing, but in this respect these rivers are becoming beautifully less each succeeding year: all the really productive streams where fishing is a sport, or even can be made a pastime, are leased to private parties or individuals, so that the enthusiastic disciple of Izaak Walton who expects to find good fishing along the rivers of Lower Canada will return considerably enlightened with regard to Canadian fishing. At Tadousac the Government have one of their fish-breeding establishments, and it is said there are so many officials who have to be supplied, and so many friends in Parliament who watch with interest the venture, that it takes all the larger size fish to supply the want of those who advocate the institution. The small fry, from one inch to an inch and a half long, are turned adrift at the mouths of the rivers to which they are consigned, where they at once become food for sea-trout, king-fishers, ducks, gulls, &c. This is now the sixth year that these fish-breeding operations have been established, and it is estimated that for every full-growth salmon distributed to the rivers it must have cost the Government some $75 each fish. One thing is certain, and to which fisherman and habitants all agree in opinion, that since the Government has taken to making laws and regulations as to fish and fishing, the fishing has been getting worse. An Indian was asked if he could give any reason for the gradual decrease of salmon in the Saguenay district, and his reply was: "They try make salmon at Tadousac—God not like that, salmon not like that, salmon go away." In ten days fishing on the "Marguerite" five salmon were seen in and out of the water, and each with the unmistakeable mark of the net around its neck; therefore the best way to go salmon fishing on these rivers is to go to sleep or read and smoke and hire an Indian to capture or catch you the fish needed. The sea-trout fishing

ROCHE PERCE, GASPE.

in the Saguenay district is getting worse and worse every year. The Bergeronne is mostly reserved by the Government for the *preservation* of sea-trout; so by the time the habitants and the Government net have closed their operations there are but few left to be either preserved or destroyed.

There are several delightful legends connected with the Saguenay and the Lower St. Lawrence published at Quebec, and in the French language, that will amply repay the time and labor spent in the translation. *L'Ornithologie du Canada, Soirées Canadiennes, Historical Works of Marmette,* and *Maple Leaves,* by Dr. Le Moine, are all very entertaining.

L'ISLET-AU MASSACRE.

Not far from Bic Harbor there lies a small island to which there is attached quite an interesting legend. For over 200 years it has been known as l'Islet au Massacre. Tradition and history furnish the details of the scene of blood by which it gained its name. It is related that some 200 Micmac Indians, being about to remove further up the country to better hunting-grounds and more peaceful neighbors, camped on this island for the night, lit their fires in a cavern amid the rocks, and placed therein their wives and children. Apparently no place could be better adapted for their safety and security from outside foes, the cavern reaching some distance back in the lofty rocks which bound the coast. The canoes were drawn high up on the beach, their evening meal was ended, the pipe of peace indulged in, stories were related of the spoils of the chase further west, and at last, wearied and tired, in fancied peace and security, these warriors with their wives and children

were sunk in profound slumber, quietly awaiting 'the
return of the morrow's sun to resume their journey.   The
Micmacs slept, but their lynx-eyed enemies, the Iroquois
were wide awake, and had scented out their prey.   Silently
approaching the Island, in their birch bark canoes, they
came, until a considerable number were congregated to
compass the destruction of the slumbering foe.   Parties
were dispatched in all directions, and came back laden
with birch bark, faggots, and other light and combustible materials, and, when all was prepared and
in readiness, the Iroquois noiselessly surrounded the
cavern, and piled the faggots high above its mouth,
whilst the sleepers were still dreaming inside.   They
then applied the torch, and gave their double yell, their
fiendish and well-known war-whoop.   In terror the Micmacs awoke and seized their arms, resolving to sell their
lives dearly, and to defend to the last their squaws and
loved ones, but the scorching flames and suffocating heat
leave them but one alternative, that of rushing out from
their lurking place, it was their only mode of escape from
death most horrible.   Wild despair nerved their hearts, and
with one desperate resolve men, women and children
crowd through the narrow passage amidst the scorching
flames, but the human hyenas are on the watch, and as the
terror-stricken ones rush forth a shower of poisoned arrows
mow them down.   The Iroquois warrior, gloating on his
victory, flourishes his tomahawk with a yell of triumph and
deadly hate, and soon the silence of death pervades the
narrow abode.   The time from the attack until morning
was then spent by the victors in securing the trophies—the
scalps of their victims, and history mentions that but five
out of the whole company of two hundred escaped with their

lives. This dark deed, still vivid by tradition, is often made the subject of remark by the Restigouche settlers, and until a few decades ago the blanched and mouldering bones of the Micmacs could be seen strewn over the grotto. This deed is mentioned in Jacques Cartier's Second Voyage, Ch. IX., and is the subject of a legend in the *Soirées Canadiennes*.

The student of psychology whilst rambling on the island of the lower St. Lawrence, or up the silent Saguenay, will meet with numberless places where deeds of darkness were perpetrated, in such modes as to still chain the restless wandering spirit to the things of earth and its wild abode, whilst here no doubt those disturbed and restless spirits are still meandering about the places from whence they departed and are possibly endeavoring by all the means within their power to make known through some medium in *rapport* with themselves the terrible history of the deeds of their time. Many are the tales told by sailors and others, which, although laughed at, cannot be scientifically or reasonably explained away—the various apparitions of restless spirits that still linger or visit those gloomy rocks, and of the plaintive sounds and doleful cries uttered by the *Braillard de la Magdeleine*, so that the secrets so long silent may yet be revealed to those who are sufficiently versed with the workings of the so-called supernatural to pursue and hold converse with the troubled spirits who have gone before.

ST. LAWRENCE LEGENDS.

Below Cape Désespoir is a treacherous ledge called Red Island Reef, formerly an object of dread to all inbound vessels. One of the first who suffered from its presence was Emery de Caen, who in 1629 got his vessel aground

on the reef whilst attempting to weather Pointe aux Allou-
ettes.   A singular disaster and shipwreck occurred in September, 1846, that of the brigantine " Gaspé Packet."
The vessel was owned and commanded by a Capt. Brulette, an eccentric old sea dog, who for forty years had
scanned every creek and shore from Gaspé to Quebec.
He was a good seaman and a careful navigator, and was
also master of a perverse habit of swearing at his crew on
any and every occasion; it was stated that when anything

GASPÉ PACKET.

" riled the old man " he would stand on the quarter-deck
and " cuss " a blue streak, until the peak and throat hal-
yards both gave way, and sometimes he would storm and
rave so much as to loosen the main backstay, and for hours
afterwards the smell of brimstone could be plainly dis-
cerned by those whose duty called them aft.   The Captain
himself was an enthusiast, he believed in the principles of
Neal Dow, and enforced them most rigorously amongst his
crew.   It was an affecting sight, and one to be remembered, to see this old pirate, on a winter's night, when the

rigging was stiff with ice, with beaming countenance, clad in his overcoats and oilskins, with two or three second mate's nips of real old stingo underneath his vest, stationed by the galley door, with a kettle of hot tea, dishing it out by the dipperful to poor shivering Jack as he came down from aloft, almost benumbed from shortening sail on a winter's night, and who would tremblingly remark that it was a d——d poor apology for seven water grog ; and, after ministering to the wants of his sailors, the good-natured captain would return to his cabin, take a " nightcap," and then " turn in." As a consequence of the enforcement of cold water principles amongst his crew, and of destroying the grog himself, he was continually changing his men, and those who were continually fed upon such diet had neither nerve nor courage, but were composed chiefly of the most ignorant and superstitious class. So one day he shipped a fresh crew of hands, and left Gaspé with a full cargo. A brisk easterly wind, gradually freshening into a gale, made the old brigantine bowl the knots off lively. It was the 20th of September, and the equinox was not far off for the wind continued to increase. The mate on passing Percé Rock had noticed the wild fowl clustering and screaming as the old brigantine scudded by, and he observed to the captain that it was a sure presage of the coming storm. The gale increasing, it soon became necessary to shorten sail ; the mainsail and foretopsail were double reefed accordingly, and things were made as snug as possible. The night was dark, but it being a following wind, it was merely necessary to head the vessel for Quebec, and it was calculated forty-eight hours more would see her at her berth. A drizzly rain soon set in, and unmistakable signs of the coming storm were observed ; drifting clouds and the piercing cry

of the petrel bade the old mariner beware—it was the
equinoctial gale, which came howling over the great deep.
Soon the sharp voice of the commander was heard ordering
one of his tea-fed sailors to go out on the bowsprit, and
clew down some of the tackle and canvas that had worked
loose: after some fruitless efforts the sailor came aboard,
and stated he could not perform his task on account of
the violence of the wind.

The venerable skipper "cussed" him for a while, and
ordering him to take the wheel went forward to make all
snug himself. Whilst so engaged, and bending over the
bowsprit, the brig took a green sea clean to her foremast,
and the next minute the skipper was seen on the crest of
a billow, uttering loud cries for help. The "Gaspé Packet"
was hove to, and an attempt made to lower a boat, but it
was swamped and broke adrift. Carried onward by the
storm went the old brigantine, leaving her commander to
his fate, and soon despair seemed to take possession of the
minds of all on board, for old "Brulette" had ever been
the soul and ruler of the "Gaspé Packet," always being
able to enforce his commands either by an oath or a belay-
ing pin, and the Jacks knew him so well that they never
thought or stopped to think for themselves. The mate was
so awestruck by the catastrophe as to well-nigh lose his
reason. He retired helplessly to the cabin to pray : a sailor
was placed at the wheel, and once more the vessel headed
for Quebec. In addition to being well grounded in Brulette's
temperance principles, his crew were very superstitious,
and totally devoid of that self-reliance and nautical knowledge for which the Canadian caboteurs are so conspicuous,
for no sooner had darkness set in on the troubled waters
than down came the steersman, and at his heels the cook,

vowing by all that was sacred that a black object, which they were certain was the captain's ghost, had passed over the brig. One sailor alone, who had brought his own grog aboard in his chest, seems to have been free from these vain fears, but he was a new hand and not familiar with the coast: he was bewildered by the rain and darkness, and allowed the "Gaspé Packet" to take her own course, merely keeping her head straight. Some time had thus passed, during which the vessel had shipped some heavy seas, which swept the deck and poured profusely into the cabin, where the mate and the rest of the crew were engaged in prayer, then, without a moment's warning, a terrific crash was heard, and the foremast went by the board, the vessel had struck on Red Island Reef, the roar of the surf and the dim outline of the land soon revealed that fact. At this moment the slight hope which still lingered in the breasts of the crew seemed to have fled. The brig had not been stranded many moments when a huge wave inundated the cabin: the intrepid steersman rushed below, and heard the voices of his shipmates begging him to join in a vow to *La Bonne Ste. Anne,* the patron saint of the mariners. Some of the affrighted hands even went so far as to promise their next year's wages, which they could safely do now that the skipper was gone, but the Saint was not to be conciliated, and had evidently heard such promises before, for she refused to help or even aid them for less than *spot cash;* so whatever the brave seaman thought at that moment of the Saint, he evidently considered it his duty to do his utmost to help himself, and knowing the vessel would go to pieces in a few minutes, he seized one of the hatches, lashed himself to it, and watching for a coming wave he dived over the side of the ship. He drifted with the ebb and back again with the flood tide the whole night, and was picked up in the morning near the south shore of the St. Lawrence, and he alone of the entire crew of the "Gaspé Packet" escaped to tell the tale of terror and shipwreck.

Gaspé, on Gaspé Basin, was at one time quite a noted port, being the rendezvous for the fishing fleet of the entire coast, beside considerable timber business being transacted. Now, since the consolidation, the harbor seems to have lost its charms somewhat, and although there are delightful legends connected with its coast, and former piratical and citizen wreckers, passing visitors do not seem to care about remaining to acquaint themselves with its mode of life, or to explore the scenery or its surroundings. There are several large firms who still employ numerous hands and fit out quite a fleet of fishing boats, the industry alone assisting materially to support the business of the town. The country itself is unattractive enough, being for the most part unproductive sands and rock, although interspersed at intervals with patches of seeming fertility ; but the inhabitants generally, being Norwegians or Swedes, and trade having fallen off considerably, the attractions for settlers are not very numerous. Although food, in the shape of black bread, molasses, fish and pork, seems plenty and to spare in each family, and freely shared with the stranger, still, if confined to the one article of diet for a few years, a man is apt to become weary of life and sigh for release, although the "boys" assert " it's good enough, so long's there's plenty." It is stated that quite a number of rich veins of lead and copper have been discovered in this vicinity, and that there are every indications of a valuable deposit of these metals, so possibly at some future time the minerals and oil with which it is believed the country

abounds may become a source of wealth to this people. There are already a few lead mines some little distance off that are said to be worked to an advantage, and to yield a profit to their owners.

From Gaspé the coast presents several features of interest. The rock or headland west of the bay terminates in a perpendicular cliff overhanging a column of rock, which is known as the "Old Woman." The shore, after leaving, presents a long low line of red sandstone, worn and indentedi nto all manner of shapes by the action of the winds and waves. The various rocks and islands now passed present to the beholder some peculiar configurations, the result of the continual wear and action upon them by the sea.

HALIFAX.

Keeping well to the north and east of the Magdalen Islands, around St. Paul and Cape Breton Islands, then to the southward and westward, we soon come in sight of the light off Halifax harbor—the city lying well back on the hill, almost in the bight of the bay or inner harbor. The harbor of Halifax affords a splendid anchorage, and is used by the British as the naval station for their North Atlantic squadron, and also a coaling depot for homeward-bound steamships. As a military station it was formerly well garrisoned, but of late the soldiers stationed have not been very numerous. It was found by the authorities that after an enfeebling service in the West Indies or India, the bracing atmosphere of Nova Scotia and Quebec was of immense benefit to the men, and therefore took advantage of the situation offered

to locate their military and naval posts. It was in the
city of Halifax that the famous Fishery Award Commission
brought itself into notoriety, and whose actions and practices
may yet foment bad blood amongst the citizens of two
great nations. The City of Halifax, the capital of Nova
Scotia, is situated on an eminence, and is connected with
the interior and northern ports by rail, which makes the
circuit of the inner harbor; it lies in about the same latitude
as Bordeaux, France, 44° 30′ N., but, unlike the latter
city, has not the soothing influences of the Gulf Stream to
moderate its winters and render pleasant the summer
months. The city at present contains some 45,000 inhabitants, and, being the shipping terminus of the Intercolonial R. R., is striving to become the winter port of the
Dominion, but as yet several obstacles seem to arise that
will have to be dispelled before the wish is realized : petty
and sectional jealousies will have to be dissipated, energy
and enterprise must be evinced, elevators erected, and
public opinion so enlisted as to make the port a trade
centre, and a port for commerce. At present both Boston
and Portland monopolize a large proportion of trade through
the enterprising spirit of their merchants that might
otherwise have been diverted for the benefit of Nova Scotia,
and it is doubtful that, were the subsidy that is now granted
to the " Allans " revoked, whether the vessels of that line
would ever call at the port. Approaching from the sea the
view is a fine one, but the country around is poor, comprising rocks and sandy stretches, and clothed with a
verdure of scrub pine, with very little arable or agricultural
lands, therefore the inducements held out to settlers to
reside in its immediate neighborhood are neither very great
nor very promising,

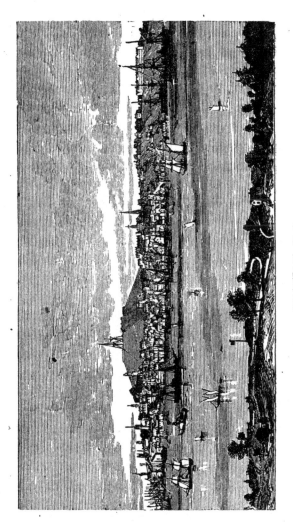

HALIFAX, N. S,

·· On entering the port of Halifax from the ocean the view of the land is very gratifying to the eye, through the outer harbor or bay, which will afford good anchorage to the navies of several nations.   The sail is delightful—a naval review would no doubt be a very pleasant sight to witness in its waters ; thence through the inner harbor, and·once landed through the depot, you find the streets of the city narrow, dingy-looking thoroughfares, lined with apparently dilapidated dwellings, reminding one somewhat of the older French portions of Quebec or Montreal, although on the rise are several blocks of business houses, well built, and faced with granite, that would reflect credit upon business architecture of ·any city further west.   The city of Halifax numbers some 36,000 people, whilst the entire Province of Nova Scotia contains a population of 440,672.   Her Lieut. Governor receives but $9,000 per annum, and her legislators are paid by the session.   The barracks for the use of the garrison are a substantial and well-built block of buildings, said to be but seldom excelled even in Europe— another result of Great Britain's foresight for her soldiers who have passed through so many vicissitudes in her service ; by the time of their transfer to this point, they are well-drilled, cool and patient, and of the right material to render good service in case of need, therefore it pays to keep them in good health.   The banks, court house and cathedrals are fine structures.   The City Hall and Hospital comprise the public buildings.   The people complain some of the publicity of the assertion by their neighbors of New Brunswick, viz., "That the Nova Scotians are blue-noses, and that they and the Cape Bretons pry the sun up with a handspike." Whilst they acknowledge the soft impeachment that their noses may at times be blue, still they indignantly deny, that they have ever interfered with the habits of the sun, and I for one believe their assertion, for, if the glorious orb of day had to rely on the Nova Scotians for an early start, he would have to omit many a day's work in the course of the year. The Nova Scotia R.R. Co. do considerable local business, transporting the general products of the country by their passenger trains to the coast. Freights are mostly composed of truck and car loads of bricks and ice, of which products of skill and nature immense quantities are annually shipped; the supply of material being considered by the natives exhaustless, it must be a source of permanent wealth. It is needless to state that the breaking open of freight cars and the appropriation of property whilst *in transitu* is a crime of very infrequent occurrence, if not entirely unknown throughout the Province. The cost of keeping the prisoners of the province in the Halifax Penitentiary amounts to $24,807.83 annually, whilst the revenue derived from the inmates of the institution is but $6,122.14. It seems there is no fishing worthy of the name in Nova Scotia, although numerous schooners are fitted out from her ports, but they find their best markets elsewhere, and the ignorance of the people respecting their neighbors of the adjoining Provinces is something remarkable. The country from Halifax to Windsor is yet as nature made it: scrub timber, a mass of boulders, and bare rocks. Lakes abound, and on several of them companies have established ice houses, with railways complete, for exporting ice to the States and elsewhere. Some miles inland the country changes, the rocks are softer, and include shales, sandstone, limestone, and beds of clay, and in this portion the country is cleared and well cultivated. The tide at Halifax rises but four feet, whilst at Windsor, where the current has to

turn a point, the tide rises some 40 feet. In wider parts of
the Bay some 30 feet is the average, but in the Bay of
Minas the water sometimes rises as high as 75 feet.   In
some parts of the Bay are whirlpools that are considered
dangerous, and where the stream runs over 9 miles an hour,
and the sight is astonishing to notice what a few moments
before seemed to be a harbor of mud covered with rushing
turbulent waters.   About high-water mark the shores are
strewn with boulders of coarse granites and other rocks
foreign to these districts.   In winter the Bay of Fundy
freezes, and the great tides pack the ice until it looks
like the boulders on the   shores.   No doubt   the ice
moves the granite boulders and cuts into the grooved
banks like a saw.   Ice marks abound in the district,
and even at the summit level of 550 feet are discernible.   There is an entire absence of high mountains,
and local glaciers could not be accounted for on that hypo-
thesis, but the marks on the highest tops correspond in
direction with marks on the sea level twenty miles away.
The boulder clay contains fragments of sandstone, and the
coal measures lie to the N. 50 E. in Cape Breton and N.
W. in New Brunswick and Nova Scotia.

The hills range in altitude from 800 to 1,000 feet above
the sea level, and extend almost due east and west from
Truro to a total length of about 100 miles, and average
from ten to twelve miles in breadth.

The prevailing geological formations in the Cobequid
Hills are granite, porphyry, and clay slate in the upper
portions ; above the shores of the bay, limas, and on the
northern side red sandstone and the coal measures.   The
range is claimed to abound in minerals, a large vein of
specular iron ore occurs close to the line. No doubt, in the

future, the region will attract the attention of capitalists. Stellarton is the centre of a rich coal district. Iron ore is also found here in large quantities, and a furnace is in operation. The Albion mines have been worked some fifty years, and a few miles away are the Drummond, Acadia and Black Diamond mines. New Glasgow is some three miles from Stellarton, and situated in one of the richest mineral terri‑ tories on the continent; it also has an extensive ship-building trade, some of the largest vessels hailing from Nova Scotia having been built here. A track some five miles long is laid from the mine to Abercrombie Point in South Pictou, from which place the coal is shipped. The best mines on the northern coast being those in the vicinity of Pictou and New Glasgow. In the former place are not only found excellent mines of coal, but valuable quarries of building stone have been the means of producing a finely‑ settled country in its neighborhood, and its trade is considerable in stone, lumber, coal and fish, whilst that of New Glasgow is assuming considerable importance. Brigs and schooners from all portions of the American coast resort to Pictou, and the exports of this little town have at times amounted to considerable. The population is much the same class of men that are found amongst the " Geordies " or in Wigan and Swansea, but are not as intelligent and energetic as the miners of Pennsylvania, probably because they are fewer in number and more under control; but churches are numerous, therefore a continued residence amongst them would be the only means of ascertaining correctly their ideas and their ambitions.

In this district, as generally throughout Nova Scotia, the Scotch element predominates.

Opposite the town, the harbor extends and branches into

East, the West and Middle rivers, several mines and the town of New Glasgow being situated on the East river, boats also run up the others. Naturally one of the attractions whilst

JACQUES CARTIER.

here is to go "down in a coal mine, underneath the ground," which can be done by taking the steamer that runs regularly to the mines, and then making known your intentions to the foreman, who can generally find some one to *chaperone* you for a small consideration; then, if you are under the guidance of an old miner, he will conduct you to the mouth of the pit and bid you step into the cage or swinging bucket, then, with a "lower away" to the engineer, you commence to descend, and every once in a while hear the wire rope or chain crack above your head, which somehow makes you feel a little nervous about dropping into the black abyss, seemingly so far below. On arriving at the level, some hundreds of feet below the surface, you are taken in charge by a guide with a grimy face and blackened clothes, who, with a bull's-eye lantern attached to his cap, leads the way, and somehow or other, here in the darkness and groping your way through those flickering lights, you begin to think that at some sharp turning you may come suddenly in contact with His Satanic Majesty himself; and, when you remember the horrors the preacher depicted and the unpleasant odor of the brimstone, the feeling comes over you that you wish you had not come and would like to go home. Some of the miners on the lower levels work in such cramped-up positions that on arriving at the surface it is found almost impossible to straighten, and after a few years' service the acquired form of the body has become the most natural and comfortable position. The mines are worked daily, and during the busy season by additional gangs at night, the day gang returning to the surface each shift, but the horses are left constantly below to perform the work of hauling from place to place, as new levels are found and new veins struck. The vocation of a miner is alive with peril and fraught with danger, but the men themselves are a venturesome, jovial set, generally speaking, who view very lightly the hardships they undergo,

and even the numerous accidents are soon obliterated and
forgotten as soon as the danger is past. The explosion and
flooding of the mines and the recent Stellarton disaster are
already becoming to be quoted as a happening of the long
ago.

Twenty-four miles north-east from the City of Halifax
stands the grand old Mount Uniake, a basaltic deposit
whose rugged aspect gives but few signs of the mineral
wealth embodied in its formation. Its crystalized rock is
permeated with seams and veins of gold, silver, and other
minerals, copper that represent the wealth of the world at
large, and will in no distant period become the means of
attracting thousands to its vicinity, for, being in close
proximity to the city, and connecting with a series of hills
of easy ascent, no difficulty will be experienced in trans-
portation ; whilst further to the north, beyond the hills, the
soil becomes prolific, and is well watered and admirably
adapted to agriculture and the sustenance of a mining
population. Some of the hills scattered over this portion
of Nova Scotia produce a remarkable variation of the
magnetic needle, thereby indicating the presence of a body
of magnetic ore, and are supposed to be wonderfully rich
in precious metals ; but further north volcanic forces have
in the long distant past produced extraordinary results :
limestone, granite and trap-rock are heaped in a confused
mass, presenting a surface at once rough and rugged, and
which will take both enterprise and capital to thoroughly
explore and lay bare their riches. Being easy of access
and close to a port of entry, with the continued improvements in stamping and quartz crushing machinery, Mount
Uniake offers to the investor unequalled inducements to
develop her resources. Mr. Henry Hogan of Montreal,

and also an extensive stockholder in the De Lery gold mine in the Province of Quebec, is also the owner of a claim on Mount Uniake, comprising some 18 acres in extent area,

MOUNT UNIAKE.

21 specimens of which upon being assayed through the ordinary fire assay produce the following results : over 1½ ounces virgin gold to the ton, being a production of over 30 dollars per ton near the surface lode, and continually becomes richer as the vein is worked. Some three

barrels of the ore have been already sent to Boston, U. S., which has shown a result of 3¼ ounces to the ton of quartz, say about 67 dollars per ton. As improved machinery is employed, the mine is expected to yield on an average over 3 ounces per ton.

But to return back again to the Capital (which report has it is situated just three miles from H——, but that libel was evidently circulated by an early settler in disparagement of the country), gazing over the waters of its harbors to those of the deep, broad and restless blue Atlantic beyond, silently meditating, and oh ! the many scenes and memories of years gone by that come rushing to the mind ; episodes that transpired upon its waters that at times were productive of terror, at others of delight. The waters, now so placid and tranquil, seem hardly a part of the same ocean that gave us such a terrible experience on the night of the 18th of October, 1858, when the homeward-bound Australian "Royal Charter" met her fate off Puffin Island, or the angry seas that rolled over the monster "Great Eastern" 600 miles westward of Cape Clear, or those over which our swift blockaders were chased whilst making the South Carolinian port, each trip being fraught with danger and death both from cannon on the surface and chains and torpedoes below. The waters now so still, with scarcely a cat's paw to disturb their glassy serenity, seem as if repenting of their boisterous actions and alluring fogs, when the noble "Atlantic" with her living freight went head on to the bleak and sombre rocks to her destruction, and the loss of nearly 500 human lives. The terrible strength and fury of its wild waters when once aroused is never obliterated from the memory of those whose callings require them to brave its fury whilst in its

passionate moods. The first trip of the good steamship
" Minnesota," in the fall of 1872, comes vividly before
me : the fourteen days' combat with the winds and sea in
the Bay of Biscay ; the death of the quarter-master at the
wheel, with his ribs crushed in by the cruel spokes ; the in-
juring of the sailors ; the burials at sea, in the height of the
gale ; and, after escaping the perils of the ocean, the fire that
caught among the coals from combustion, and at the criti-
cal time the break-down of machinery on Christmas day,
whilst still 300 miles eastward of Havana ; the bending of
the stanchions under the cotton deck ; and the sliding of the
cargo of railroad iron, that momentarily threatened
destruction to over 200 souls on board, and the prayer of
thankfulness and sense of relief experienced when The Hole
in the Wall and Great Isaacs were first sighted. The heart-
felt eulogies that were passed upon those gallant officers and
true seamen, Captains Hamlin and Johnstone, are memories
that time cannot obliterate whilst the ocean remains to be
contemplated. And still another experience comes before the
mental vision : not of calm seas and hidden dangers, but
when mighty Boreas assumed full sway, and compelled
affrighted mortals to do him homage and acknowledge his
sceptre. The hurricanes experienced in the spring of
1876, when the barometer, even for the " roaring forties," was
unusually low, the highest pressure being 28.80. The
hurricane is thus alluded to by a fellow-voyager : At two
o'clock on the morning of Feb. 11, the barometer, which
had been stationary, unusually low, commenced suddenly
falling, and the wind that had been blowing a gale from
the north-west suddenly veered to the south-west, and
by six a.m. was blowing a gale from that quarter ; at nine
the gale increased to a hurricane, and the sea, " cross and

angry," · literally ran mountains. high. · The ship was
" hove to ". with her head on, but the force of the wind was
tremendous; hailstones struck with such violence as to
indent the woodwork where they fell; it was impossible at
times for any human being to stand on deck, except under
the lee of some of the houses or bulwarks, the waves making a clean sweep of the ship, and carrying with them
everything that was not well bound down. At twelve
next noon, after hours of painful anxiety, the hurricane was
at its height, and a heavy double sea struck the ship, completely submerging her and burying her deep in the foam.
There was a moment of suspense as the feeling that the
vessel was settling down came over one, but a gentle throb
from the engines gave signs that she was yet rising; the
officer on the bridge found himself standing in the midst of
the boiling foam, with the feeling that the ship was gone
from under him, and as he clung to the iron rails the storm
canvas was swept away, and the iron stanchions bent
like wire. As the ship righted, the damage was ascertained.
The chart room, officers' rooms, surgery, with all the deck
houses, were entirely swept away, timbers were smashed,
and the trim, staunch ship wore the appearance of having
passed through a fire. The gallant Captain Sadler with his
chief and second officers had a narrow escape with their
lives; whilst everything belonging to them was swept away
by the sea; heavy seas were shipped afterwards, but the
force of the hurricane was spent, so, with a succession of
south-easterly gales, the good ship made the port of New
York. Such are some of the dangers encountered by those
who tempt the moods of Neptune, but on days like this the
mind easily drifts away off, on the dark blue waters of
the Gulf of Mexico or over the light green of the coral

reefs, amongst the West Indies, around the Florida coasts, or skirting the " ever-faithful Isle," but such reveries are soon dispelled when we notice the practical, every-day life, indulged in by the fishermen who make this port their start-ing-point ; and surely a cod-fisher's life is not to be envied, for it is generally laborious work and heavy risks. The manner of their occupation usually followed is this : the owner of the schooner, who is often the captain also, hires a crew of from thirteen to fifteen men to work on "*sheeres*," that is, so many parts of the profits for the owners, so many for the captain, and a divide amongst the crew of the remain-der. After shipping, a day or two is occupied in fitting out, mending sails, setting running and fixing standing gear, and getting the vessel ship-shape. The cook is sometimes sent up town to lay in stores, and generally after ordering the provisions down takes a parting glass and returns next day, and sometimes under escort, to the great relief of those who were anxiously waiting for eight bells and grub time ; then sails are bent, decks washed off, touches of paint here and there, ends of lines whipped, ropes coiled down, and standing gear properly seized ; a jigger all around, and, with a fair wind, the fisherman stands out for the offing. Now he finds where the discomfort begins : with a crew of from thir-teen to fifteen or sixteen men, for one half to be below in the narrow limits of the cuddy, and in bad weather with the hatches closed, is something stifling, whilst on deck it is a continual drench. The first day out and our fisherman is transformed into something approaching a farmer, with a hoe in one hand, and a bucket hard-bye. The crew are all searching the shore for bait in the shape of clams, and in the course of a day or so enough have been dug up to serve for the trip. From the baiting-grounds to the " Georges

Banks " the time is generally occupied in mending line, splicing in hooks, improvising trolls and other tackle necessary. Then, on arrival at the fishing grounds, the kedge is dropped, and the crew are patiently seated on deck with their feet under the rail, in the wet, the chill and the fog, patiently tending their lines and chawing terbaccer, and as fast as the fish are hooked throwing them into the " well." At times in the midnight watch, when all seems so peaceful and serene, some huge monster of an ocean steamer comes along and crushes over the poor fisherman without ever feeling the shock or stopping her engines, and from fancied security he is hurried into a watery grave. Lucky he deems himself if in a week or two the " well " is full, and they make back for a market with a successful catch, and obtain a fair amount of cash to recompense them for their labor, still, year by year, does the fisherman have to venture further and further from the coasts in the quest of good grounds, until now the favorite localities are some thousand miles from the shores of America.

Nova Scotia, New Brunswick and Prince Edward Island, the three provinces that comprise the Eastern portion of the Dominion, contain in the aggregate some 750,000 inhabitants, hardly a sufficient number to populate a fourth-rate city. Still these provinces have three mimic houses of Parliament, with all the attendant dignity and paraphernalia ; two houses of Representatives, and three Lieutenant Governors ; in fact, if the strangers do not meet over five officials out of a possible six inhabitants or acquaintances it is quite a subject of remark, and speculation is rife about the vacancy that is thought about to occur. But this muchly-governed little country brings to mind very forcibly the Mississippian's opinion of "Louisiana's Government," that it was nothing but a two-bit arrangement all around! From Halifax to St. John, New Brunswick, is but a distance of 276 miles : here, as in Nova Scotia, Neal Dow's principles are *formally* enforced, and the only way for the bibulously-inclined to satisfy his longings.is to "go to de docter," as the colored gentleman advised his questioner, "why, boss, de only way what you kin git relieved of dem. ere cramps is to go de drug-store man, fur dere is a female samintery (seminary) near town, and de probation laws is a gwine here." So after paying heavily for a prescription, and imbibing some of the meanest concoctions of spirits and extracts, you fancy that the scriptural injunction was altogether wrong and astray, or at all events.not adapted for.these provinces, when it recommended to "give strong drink to him that is ready to perish, and wine to they that be of heavy heart." Of course throughout this barren unproductive region should anything be taken that would make glad the heart of man, it would possibly deplete his purse, and, as the opportunity would in all probability never again occur for him to obtain another nickel or a dime.it would be the height of folly to waste or expend that amount on a pleasure that was but momentary, for, as a friend remarked, "I feel pretty bad to-day, I have been reckless, and another ten cents has gone to the devil."

PRINCE EDWARD ISLAND.

From Halifax to Pictou is some seventy miles over a rocky, hilly, and generally unproductive, country; and from this coal region to Charlottetown is but fifty-five miles, whilst means of communication between the two ports is kept up regularly during the season by steamer. Charlottetown is the

capital and principal port of Prince Edward Island, and
contains 11,435 inhabitants. The Island is some one
hundred and thirty miles in length and thirty-four
miles in its greatest breadth, averaging eighteen miles;
it is divided into three counties, Kings, Queens and
Prince, and contains a population of 103,871. It is
an excellent farming country, and its soil is very fertile. Its
coasts on all sides are very much indented by inlets from the
sea, several of which form good harbors. The Island itself
lies between 46° and 47° N. lat., and between 62° and
64° 30' W. Long. The Island is situated in the southern
portion of the Gulf of St. Lawrence, and is separated from
the mainland by the Strait of Northumberland; and from
Cape Tormentine in New Brunswick to Cape Traverse in
P. E. I. is but a distance of nine miles. It seems there
were several claimants, from John Cabot down, who asserted
that they were the first discoverers of the Island; but,
as possession was nine points of the law, in the year
1523 one Verazzani, in the employ of the French
Government, planted, as was usual in those days, the
emblem of Christianity on its soil, and claimed the whole
region round about for the King of France, although no
attempt for the settlement of the Island was made until
the year 1663. In that year a French naval officer obtained
a grant of the Island from the company of New France
for the purpose of establishing fisheries along its coast,
somewhat after the style of our modern M.P.'s obtaining
North West lands for the purpose of stock-raising, farming,
distilling, etc., etc., to benefit the country at large. In the
year 1713, and after a war of over two years' duration,
between France and England, the Treaty of Utrecht was
entered into, and the Island began to be a settled Province,.

and Port Joy, now Charlottetown, was first founded by the
French; and it is claimed that in the year 1728 the population of the Island was about 300, and at the time of the
Treaty of Fontainbleau, in the year 1763, the French had
peopled the Island to the number of some 8000. In
that year the Island was placed under the jurisdiction of
the Governor of Nova Scotia, who had it surveyed. and
divided into sixty-seven townships or lots of some 20,000
acres each, which divisions still exist. At that time the
British were intent upon extending their territory and
planting colonies, so they started to give or grant to settlers,
upon certain conditions, this fertile little Island; but so
numerous were the applicants that they organized a lottery,
and the Island, in the shape of prizes, was awarded to some
sixty-seven lucky ones, or numbers. Of course as a high-
toned moral and Christian nation, she would not countenance such a proceeding at this day. The grants were issued
through Lord Campbell, Governor of Nova Scotia. Two
lots of 20,000 acres each were bestowed upon fishing companies, and one lot of 6000 acres was reserved for the
King, thereby showing that he was not very ambitious of
owning much stock on this side of the Atlantic. In 1770
the British Government, having no use for an Island so far
from its shores, made a separate Province of it, and
allowed the Islanders to govern themselves, first appointing
a governor to keep them in the traces. During the
American war of independence this Island was often visited
by privateers, *lettres du Marque,* and other vessels in
American service, and at times their visits were not without interest, especially in the vicinity of Charlottetown, for
not only the Americans, but the Nova Scotians cast a
longing eye in the vicinity of the Island, and at one time

laid plans for its capture, but they fell through. · On the north-western and west by southern portions of the Islands are extensive sand bars that make it dangerous for a mariner to approach in too close a proximity to its shores. The country has its mimic Upper and Lower Houses of Parliament, officers, civil, State, and ecclesiastic, with its Lieut-Governor—who receives but $5,000 for his important services—judges, justices and other civic dignitaries too numerous to mention, who administer public affairs with an amount of dignity that is at once ludicrous and amusing, and it is certainly a problem for the new arrival to solve how so many officials exist when, apparently, there are no private citizens to support them, but I suppose they were all in the lobster factories or out fishing. An appropriation of $2,000 is also made for the benefit of the Indians resident on the Island. The Island is a good place to spend a few weeks and on little cash, but for a permanent residence and have to work for a living the "Good Lord deliver us!" In many of the harbors on both the northern and southern coasts are finely-fitted yachts belonging to residents, and it seems strange that regattas that have Charlottetown or Summerside for a terminal point are not more freely indulged in by Portland, Boston and New York. Good deer-sea fishing can be enjoyed at almost any point off its shores, and the summer traveller will certainly find it to his advantage to hurry through the Upper Provinces and spend a few pleasant weeks in this vicinity.

To the northward of P. E. I. are situated the Magdalen Islands, some seven in number; they are inhabited chiefly by fishermen and those engaged in fishing and coaling interests, so although their homes seem bleak and desolate, still they enjoy in a comparative degree a sense of independence, and a freedom from the cares, tricks and tribulations of this designing universe, as to render them far happier in their poverty than many of their favored countrymen further west. Icebergs and islands of ice are frequently met with in crossing the Gulf of St. Lawrence in summer months, which are thought to have descended from the regions of Hudson's Bay or Davis Straits, whence they have been detached or severed from the main body by the violence of the storms that occur in those latitudes, and passing by the coasts of Labrador are carried by the indraught of the current into the straits of Belle Isle, thence through the Gulf into the open sea. Summer visitors to these latitudes will find both health and strength derived from the trip, whilst in the middle of July or August they will have ample opportunity for wearing winter clothing and donning their overcoats at night.

NEW BRUNSWICK.

The City of St. John, the commercial depôt of the Bay of Fundy, is situated on the Harbor and at the mouth of the river of the same name, and distant from Halifax some 276 miles, and is also the chief business town in the Province of New Brunswick, containing at present some 26,188 inhabitants, being a decrease during the year 1881 of 2,627 people, and is built upon a rocky peninsula of very uneven ground, sloping from a central ridge. A great deal of labor has been employed, and capital expended, in cutting down the hills, and leveling the streets. The principal wharves, docks and warehouses extend to the north and around the head of the basin, to within a short distance of the Falls, some five miles up the St. John River. The whole shore is lined with timber ponds, booms and ship yards, which receive the timber floated down the river.

The harbor of St. John is a safe one, but not very spacious or commodious, especially at low water. From its shallowness, and the strength of the current, large ships generally enter the harbor on the top of the flood tide. The tides rise some twenty-six feet, and, therefore, great facilities are afforded for repairing and launching vessels : for during the ebb the shores and a number of docks are left dry, but during the flood the harbor is easy of access for the largest ships, but a strong free wind is necessary to enable sailing vessels to enter without the aid of a tow-boat. The approaches and the shoals are well marked and buoyed ; the beacon on the bar is crowned by a good light, whilst on Partridge Island, at the entrance to the harbor, there is a fine light-house, battery, signal station, and hospital. The trade of the city consists mostly in the export of timber, shipbuilding, and the prominent industry of Nova Scotia, the Israelitish occupation of making brick. The whole district of St. John is rocky and broken, and viewed from any of the eminences the scenery is bold and picturesque : the river at low water dashing forward in columns of spray rushes through a narrow gorge into the harbor, and covers the surface of the water with wreaths of foam. The whole basin of the river seems to be covered with ships, steamboats, and small craft. Its buildings are substantial, and compare favorably with any in the provinces, whilst with the people there is a kind of don't-care-a-cent, independent air, that is certainly refreshing, in relief to the manners of some of the cities in Upper Canada.

The Province of New Brunswick is chiefly noted in history from the eternal quarrelling and fighting amongst its early settlers to obtain possession and a foothold for their respective governments. Until the year 1784 the colony of New Brunswick formed a portion of Acadia or New France, and was considered a part of Nova Scotia. During the reign of Henry IV. a speculator named De Monts made the third attempt at colonization in the province; he received from his sovereign almost unlimited powers and privileges, titles and patents of nobility that covered fourteen skins of parchment, and which took him three days to read in order to discover how great a man he really was. His commission embraced all the territory from the 40th to the 46th degree north latitude, or from Hudson's Bay to Virginia; and he had the monopoly of the fur trade over all that tract of country then called New France. Those old kings and potentates of Europe certainly did things up in style when they liked to encourage a favorite, and were as liberal as our Parliament to the Syndicate in giving away that which they hardly owned, but, at any rate, had no use for.

De Monts was a Protestant, so he at once borrowed all the cash he could from his friends to further his enterprise (history does not state that he ever returned it, or even gave his note for it), got permission to give his religion a fair show, on condition of his providing a few Catholic missionaries for the conversion of the natives, and to open up trade; so, having plenty of Christianity, as a kind of a cheap stock-in-trade, he set sail, and on the 16th day of May, 1604, he arrived at Rossignol (now Liverpool). At this place he found one Rossignol, whose name the harbor had received, trading with the Indians, and at once asked

the poor fellow to show his license, and Rossignol never
having heard of such an instrument or knowing what its
virtues were, or even who had authority to issue such a
thing, spoke out truthfully, and said that he had one all
right, but he left it at home, for his wife to make a bed
quilt out of; whereupon De Monts informed the trader
that he was afraid he was prevaricating, for nobody had
authority to issue such things except De Monts the Great.
He therefore immediately seized the vessel and goods of
the trader *for lying,* and by their sale enabled himself to
carry out the Christian colony scheme, which, otherwise,
would have failed. He then sailed along the coast to the
westward, and captured four more French vessels that
were engaged in trade, and whose captains were
unacquainted with the license question, so with the results
of the spoils captured from contraband trade he had accumulated quite a little pile, and planted colonies right
along the coast; had the country surveyed, discovered
a vein of iron ore, sent home specimens and word to his
friends that he had "struck it rich" " on a silver mine."
His friends in the Old Country suddenly found out that
they loved him immensely, and began to look up anecdotes
concerning his progenitors and the status of their own
relationship, and numbers of them found life unendurable
so far away, so they longed to be near their friend and in
the vicinity of the *silver mine;* but after their arrival they
found he was mistaken in the quality of the material, for
the silver proved to be the shining specular iron, yet found
on Digby Neck. Then his relatives suddenly lost their
affection and all wanted "to go home," but De Monts quietly
left them in his new colony and went home himself, and
afterwards returned, bringing several more colonists and

also a *respectable* lawyer by the name of L'Escarbot, who soon quieted the murmurings of the former lot by informing them that, if they returned, they would be sent to the galleys, so he advised them to devote their energies to the introduction of agriculture and the importation of domestic animals. There is but little doubt that it was from acts of violence committed by such characters as De Monts, Cartier, Poutrincourt and others, who were the first voyagers to America, upon the natives, that they were induced to cherish that spirit of retaliation that was afterwards so terribly manifested upon whole villages of European settlers, when neither sex nor age was spared from the tomahawk and scalping knife. In the year 1625, Charles I. renewed a patent formerly granted by James I., in the year 1621, to Sir William Alexander, in which he gave away "all the country from the St. Croix to the St. Lawrence," including "the whole course of the St. Lawrence to the Gulf of California," which included the whole of Canada and the chief part of the United States. An order of Baronets were created to hold jurisdiction over the country, and they solemnly assembled on the castle hill of Edinburgh, Scotland, to take legal possession and rule over a world unknown. Another instance of the bounty of a liberal monarch. Some of the Baronets never even visited their possessions that had been so freely bestowed, but those who did come found the French already in possession, and not in the least disposed to give up their possessions peaceably. From that on at different times there was nothing but periodic quarrelling and fighting between the French and English settlers, but the French, with the aid of the priests, got a little ahead, for they offered a premium for their men to marry with the Micmacs and other tribes of

Indians, and by a Frenchman marrying a squaw, and an Indian a French woman, they made their interests mutual, and gained a savage ally in time of war, and also produced a tribe of mongrels who reside in the Province to this day. During the 17th century barbarities of the most horrible description were practised upon the rival settlers, and when they could find no rivals to practice on they turned upon their own countrymen, after the style of "Charnisé," of Penobscot, besieging Madame La Tour, on the St. John, but that woman fought him gallantly, and it was not until after several attacks in different years that he was enabled to subdue the brave little Dame.

The Province of New Brunswick extends nearly North and South, and lies between 45° 5' and 48° 20' N. lat., and between 63° 50' and 68° W. long., forming an irregular square between Nova Scotia and Quebec. On the north it is bounded by the Bay Chaleurs and the Gulf of St. Lawrence, which separate it from Gaspé; north-west by the Restigouche river; on the east it extends to the Gulf; a Peninsula joins it to Nova Scotia on the south-east, and it is separated from that Province on the south by the Bay of Fundy; on the west it meets the State of Maine. It contains some 26,000 square miles, and is probably the richest in minerals of the Lower Provinces; it has a population of 321,233, whose indebtedness per head amounted in 1880 to the sum of $17.77. There is a great diversity in the appearance of the Province: the lands on the whole northern coast slope gradually down beneath the sea; the water is generally shallow, and along the ocean border there are banks of sand and shingle. The water in all the river channels is deep enough to admit the largest ships. On the northern side or coast of Gaspé the

shores frequently present bold over-hanging cliffs.   Along'
the coast of the Bay of Fundy there is a tract of hilly.
country, but few of which attain any considerable degree
of elevation. The scenery is wild and picturesque ; bold cliffs
and rugged precipices, deep valleys, the quiet lake, and the
dashing waterfall are often presented at a single view ; the
forests in summer time appear like green waves rising above
each other.   The north-eastern side from Bay Verte to
Bathurst presents a low and level surface, unbroken by
hills.   Marshes, bottom lands and peat bogs are peculiar to
this tract, and extend in a S. W. direction to the river St.
John ; this is the region of the New Brunswick coal fields,
covering an area of some 5,000 square miles. ˉ The Grand
Falls of St. John are only surpassed by the cataract of Niagara, and are some 200 miles from the mouth of the river.
Having its waters considerably increased by its numerous
branches, the river sweeps through the country, and expands
itself into a beautiful basin just above the cataract, but the
basin is suddenly contracted, and the river turning to the
south rushes into a deep rocky gorge only 250 feet wide ; the
water falls into the gorge from the front and from each
side, and the river makes a leap of 58 feet over a perpendicular cliff.   In the mist is seen the rainbow, and clouds
of white spray float over the cataract, whilst the noise of
the water pouring over the rocks reminds one of Niagara
itself. The entire fall of the river at this point is some 116
feet.   In the freshets of the spring the broken ice for many
miles drifts down the river, and in the shallow water close
up and collect in enormous masses, forming what is called
an "ice jam," and the pent-up water extends far and wide,
causing a freshet that sweeps away cattle, buildings and
everything within its reach : logs, trees and dwellings are

borne along, and aid in forming the obstruction, whilst the inhabitants themselves, having reached higher ground, form interesting groups as washed-out families.

The surface of New Brunswick presents a confusion of heterogeneous substances, but it will be found upon inspection that not only the rocks but the soils succeed each other in regular rotation or strata: the rock itself is first seen protruding through the soil or rising into mountain ranges, yet the action of heat, frost, moisture, and other meteoric agents are constantly reducing the flinty mass, and forming a fertile soil which, if not retained on the table lands and slopes, is carried by the torrents down to the valleys to render them more favorable for agricultural purposes; then come boulders and, succeeding these, extensive beds of gravel, sand and clay, above which the soil, varying in thickness, and differing only from the general deposit beneath in being reduced to a finer state, and by containing remains of the vegetation that once flourished upon it. The soil derived from trap rock contains much potash, and almost always produces hard wood, such as beech, birch, maple, oak, ash and butternut. Granite and syenite soil are also favorable to those growths, but where there is a sufficient depth of earth, and the land is sandy, white and red pine grow to a large size; but, owing to the incursions and raids made upon the timber of the province, in the course of a few years the supply will be thoroughly exhausted. The people of New Brunswick claim that their vegetables are the finest produced in America, and they certainly have some grounds for that belief, although they have competitors in both Nova Scotia, Cape Breton and Prince Edward Island; but their potatoes are as near perfection as can' be found, and are both so delicious in flavor and mealy to look upon that they would make the heart of an Irishman rejoice. Apples, turnips and hen fruit (or eggs) are produced in great varieties. Many may disparage the statements concerning the product of the fowl, but it is so—there are over sixteen varieties of aigs produced in this Province.

The climate differs but little from the Province of Lower Canada; frost is seen some seven months in the year. In the summer twilight is seen after nine o'clock in the evening, whilst daybreak occurs at two in the morning. The aurora borealis is very brilliant at all seasons. The break-up usually occurs during April, and by May the weather becomes settled. It is still in tradition that, after the wizard was expelled from the Isle of Man, he came to New Brunswick and brought with him his art of covering the country with a fog in order to delude and befog his enemies. The climate is a healthy one, and without a doctor can get hold of a genuine Old Country patient, or invent some new disease, he has a hard row to weed to get a living. Most of the practitioners generally board around like a school-master, and look out for chances, such as broken legs and accidents to lumbermen or river drivers.

One of the industries, like that of Quebec, is the making of maple sugar, from which occupation considerable revenue is derived by the inhabitants. During the months of March and April a vast quantity of sugar is made in the province; the trees are numerous and in good seasons will yield from three to five pounds of sugar per tree; the quality is good when properly made, whilst the process is extremely simple. As soon as the sap commences rising, in the spring, the tree is tapped by boring a hole with an inch auger, four inches deep; a small spile is then inserted, through which the sap flows to the tub or pail beneath. The sugar, although sweet, has a certain disagreeable woody taste to those who have been accustomed to the products of the cane, and it takes some little time before it is fancied for every-day use. On the lands of many of the seigniories in the Lower Provinces are regular sugar farms, producing a sure revenue at very slight cost. The trees run best when the days are warm and the nights frosty. The juice at present is evaporated in a very primitive way, that of boiling in deep kettles. There is room here for the introduction of some of the southern evaporators and boiling pans, although to get them adopted would be a work of time. It might become a source of profit, and quite health-giving, for a company to form in order to invite young Englishmen and Americans from the cities to take a trip to the Province, in order to shoot moose, carriboo and deer, or trap for bear and beaver. There was a real Virginian deer seen here in 1818, and the skins of the other animals are valuable when obtained. Fishing, both lake and river, can be indulged in, with considerable success. Salmon are plentiful in most rivers, and rise freely at a proper fly, and will afford the angler admirable sport. Trout are numerous in almost all streams, and are taken by the children, with a baited hook, fastened to a piece of twine on the end of a light pole. The best fly to fish with is the red hackle, and the weight of the fish is from a half pound to six pounds. The Tobique, Aroostook, Miramichi, Nepisiquit, Upsalquitch, and Restigouche are the best rivers for sport. The fisheries of New Brunswick, and especially those on the Restigouche, have already become the subject of considerable talk and comment—the authority arrogated to himself by the River

Warden being almost absolute in his district, and only equalled by his insatiate greed. Being at once River Warden, with a good salary, Hatchery Inspector (also with salary) paymaster for the district (small remuneration) his opportunities were many and varied; but amongst them all this overburdened official manages to exist through the fisheries department, and is happily saved and providentially spared to become the means of assisting his immediate relatives, for his expenses show that he pays one son several hundred dollars for procuring trout ova, and another a large amount for catching parent salmon, the class usually sold to sportsmen and tourists. No wonder the sportsman, after paying toll for the privilege of fishing a portion of the stream or pool, always finds at the end of the stay that the salmon are caught in another portion just a little "higher up," and are exultantly exhibited by those who know the ropes.—Moral for amateurs: always stand in with the Inspector and you will catch salmon. Salt-water fisheries have always been a source of revenue and income to the Province, but, through the enterprise and energy of the Americans, the "Brunswickers" are being rapidly crowded out, and their industry monopolized—mackerel, herring, gaspereau and cod being the chief kinds sought, and this industry alone gives employment to some thousands of men. The boats employed are well fitted, staunch and sea-worthy, and on leaving are filled to the hatches with salt, empties and provisions. Along the deck are empty puncheons and casks, whilst for each man six mackerel lines, completely fitted, are attached to the stanchions in the bulwarks. The hooks used are about the size of salmon hooks, with a jig or bright piece of metal, which in the water resembles the sepia. Nets are sometimes

SHOOTING THE RAPIDS.

used. When in with a "school" of mackerel or other fish, pork, old rags, red shirts, and other materials, are thrown into a bait mill and ground up, the inside of the mill containing a revolving set of sharp knives, and the product, upon being turned out, is something like putrid sausage meat— this is called poheegàn or squash—and, when signs are on, a hogshead of this mixture is thrown overboard, and the mackerel rise in shoals, covering at times the surface of the water for miles, and for hours afterwards all hands are actively employed in hooking, jigging and drawing in the fish. Then, all of a sudden, as if by magic, the fish disappear, and the vessel has to move to new grounds. The Americans have got the science of fishing down so fine that they can come into the ports of the provinces, and sell fish, at a profit to themselves, at less figures than a native can afford to catch them for. The inhabitants of the coasts and islands engage in the different employments of agriculture, fishing and lumbering, therefore they cannot devote their attention entirely to one pursuit.

In conclusion, I would advise the traveller to devote some time in exploration of the Province, for he will find it both an interesting and instructive pursuit.

Leaving St. John we take the cars of the Intercolonial R.R. for the return to Quebec. This road is a Government one, built as a military necessity, and at present is run at a serious loss; its working expenses, being an excess over the revenue produced, in one year amounted to $716,083.53. Eighty-nine miles lands us in Moncton, the head-quarters of the railway and junction with the main line on to Halifax. The town numbers some 5000, and is situated on the Petit-codiac River. The shops being located here, it is, like Hamilton, a railroad town, but has a good surrounding country.

Taking refreshments at Moncton we rush onward through a level and uninteresting country, passing Newcastle, seventy-eight miles away, and situated on the bank of the Miramichi River, one of the largest rivers in the Province, it being some 220 miles in length, whilst at its mouth it attains a width of nine miles. Thence on to Bathurst, some forty-four miles. The country is undulating, the vegetation good, the soil being a sandy loam, and the scenery attractive. The town is the usual stopping-place for young anglers about to be initiated into the mysteries of salmon-fishing in the Province of New Brunswick. On again past Campbellton, Metapedia on the boundary between Quebec and New Brunswick, through the Morrisey rock tunnel, 300 feet long, and the only tunnel through rock in the country until those through the Selkirk Range are constructed. Crossing the famous bridges over the Restigouche and Millstream we run up the Metapedia Valley past the Notre Dame mountains, and come to a halt at Rimouski, a town of about 1500 inhabitants, the station at which the English mails are landed and taken on board the mail steamships. The country about here is terribly afflicted with mosquitoes, and at every stopping-place these ubiquitous insects pour into the car in countless myriads.

Leaving Rimouski, sixty-six miles lands us at Rivière du Loup, thence 126 miles brings us to Chaudière Junction, seven miles from Quebec, at which place we connect with the Grand Trunk Railroad—this section being under the management of Mr. Gregory; thence 100 miles to Richmond, a town of 1500 inhabitants, and situated on the St. Francis River, seventy-five miles S. W. from where it joins the St. Lawrence. It is from here downwards that the logs are gathered in drives, and at certain seasons

a boom of logs blocks up the river for miles, covering the
entire surface of the water and rendering it impossible for
even a skiff to ascend. At Richmond is the junction of the
road through the Eastern Townships, which follows the St.
Francis River to Sherbrooke, situated on the St. Francis and
Magog Rivers, and the best business town between Montreal and the Line. The rapids on the Magog River, within
a half mile of the town, fall a distance of 119 feet, thus
furnishing unlimited power to the various industries
located along its banks. The town contains about 5000
people, and is mainly supported by manufacturing and
milling interests. Some attempts are being made to introduce the cultivation of beets for the purpose of making
sugar, and a factory is now being erected. Between this
place and Island Pond, on the borders of Vermont, is
Coaticooke, a dull, uninteresting little town of probably,
1000 inhabitants. The scenery around the Pond is
delightful and attractive, the ranges of green hills forming
a circlet around a pond of clear water of some seven miles in
length and two in breadth, in the centre of which, at short
distances from each other, lie three small islands covered
with verdure, as with a carpet, that assist materially in
making the town a favorite place of resort for boating and
fishing parties.

But back again, through Richmond, we resume the
route to Montreal, some seventy-six miles distant,
passing the French town of St. Hyacinthe, a thriving place of
nearly 8000 inhabitants and situated on the Yamaska
River, forty miles above its outlet in Lake St. Peter;
next comes Mont Belœil, a conglomeration of three
hills on the summit, in the centre of which is an
excellent lake of the purest water, derived from the

fall of snow during the winter. The hotel situated on the mountain is a favorite resort for Montrealers during the heated term. Thence, in less than an hour, once more we are landed at St. Lambert, so before crossing the bridge we take the cars of the G. T. R. and Central Vermont, making a pleasant run through a level and uninteresting portion of the country to St. Johns, twenty-seven miles distant. The town contains about 4000 inhabitants, is well situated on the St. Johns or Richelieu River, but a few miles distant from the head of Lake Champlain. The community surrounding are farmers, and the town is a prosperous one. Twenty-three miles further south we come to the pretty little village of Rouse's Point, situated within the boundary lines of the State of New York and on the northern edge of Lake Champlain. The town is a pretty one, and has been built up in part by the industries that have located near the Line. The printing establishment of John Lovell & Sons has probably contributed as much to the success of the towns in the N. E. portion of the State as any other industry. At present the hotels are good, business fair, and the town rapidly growing in favor with summer visitors. A neat little paper, *The Sun*, is published, under the editorship of W. S. Phillips. Five railroads centre at the Point, so its prosperity as a railroad town is no doubt assured.

Returning by express, a short run of an hour and a half lands us again in Montreal, at the famed St. Lawrence Hall. It was on our return we met the Ex-President of the Southern Confederacy busily employed in finishing the details connected with the issuing of his work on the "Rise and Fall of the Southern Confederacy." In person Jefferson Davis is yet remarkable—a venerable gentleman,

whose inexpressible benignity of countenance and cour-
teousness of demeanor cannot readily be forgotten by those
who have had the pleasure of meeting him. Although in
his seventy-third year, with his hair of snowy whiteness, in
health and looks he appears younger and more vivacious than
he did sixteen years ago; his form, though fragile, is still
erect, his bearing still courtly and dignified, with that frank
and genial way so noticeable amongst the old-time Southern
gentlemen, and whose simple nature has endeared him to
every Southern heart, and won respect and friendship even
from his enemies; whilst his friends have proved their
devotion to the cause and their chieftain by the sacrifice
of their lives, and his countrywomen have had a noble
example set them in Mrs. Dorsey, who donated her entire
estate, and thus provided the Ex-Chief with his beautiful
home at Beavoir, Mississippi. In Canada he still has many
professing friends, but, should they be again tried, would
probably repeat the war record of professing friendship
and sympathy for one side whilst money could be gained,
but selling their countrymen, relations and friends to
whoever would buy for a few paltry dollars, thus following out their scriptural principles of being all things to all
men, and at the same time making money.

From Montreal we take a run north of the St. Lawrence on the branches of the Q. M. O. & O., passing St.
Vincent de Paul, a village of some 2500 inhabitants, with
its Penitentiary and its 350 unfortunate inmates, who produce a revenue to the Province of some $3,459.02, against a
cost to the country of $88,826.35; thence through the sand
dunes to Joliette, a French Canadian town of some 8000
inhabitants, at which point the gentlemanly bailiff wished
us to take note of the intense respect that the population

had for "process of law." A storekeeper was sick in bed, and a creditor in the city of Montreal, thinking he might die, ran in a seizure before judgment. The proprietor having been found, the bailiff announced : "*Excusez-moi, il est malheureux et bien pénible, j'ai une saisie a pratiqué sur vos biens, meubles et effets.*" "*Sacré*," exclaimed the merchant, "I have no notice, I was not even sue, ze note is not due, and I am getting well, my property is large, why you not wait to see if I die ?" "That makes no difference, I must seize," replied the bailiff. "*Merci, bon*, ze law is just, help yourself," replied the merchant, and thus do country traders pay the expenses of city sharp practice.

Cutting again over a sandy and, in spots, entirely barren country, through the little villages of St. Sophie and New Glasgow to St. Annes, soon we are again in the city, thankful to the powers that our lot was not cast at birth in this portion of our great continent. Leaving the city for the West the most pleasant and agreeable route, for a short distance at least, is to take the boat from the city ascending through the canals. The passengers being comparatively few in number, the time occupied in the ascent as far as Kingston, 172 miles, being two days, the time is most agreeably spent. During the day the refreshing breeze keeps everything cool and acquaintances are formed, whilst in the evening the saloons are put in trim ; the officers and passengers assemble, music and singing are indulged in, and the company upon its final separation remember with feelings of pleasure the few happy moments enjoyed whilst journeying up the Great St. Lawrence, moments that are only equalled on the continent by the delightful journeys up the glorious Mississippi, so parting from the famous "Algerian" with its genial Captain, John Towerwell, at Kingston, drive a short distance out of town to the Depôt, and take the Grand Trunk cars, thence rapidly passing Belleville and Cobourg, in a few hours are landed once more in Toronto. The section of the country at Cobourg, Port Hope and Whitby is well supplied with railroads running some hundreds of miles north, penetrating into the free grant lands of Ontario, and even reaching into the Parry Sound and Muskoka Districts, the latter being the district to which the Oka Indians, of the Ottawa, have been recently removed by the Seminary, as the land which was brought into cultivation by them is now becoming marketable and therefore of value. From Toronto a three hours run by the Northern Railway brings us to the town of Barrie, situated on the westerly armlet of Lake Simcoe. Orillia, Beaverton, Jackson's Point, and Belle Ewart, are all resorts situated on the side of the Lake, which is a pretty sheet of water, and studded, as these northern lakes generally are, with small rocky islands. It is about 40 miles long from north to south and some 25 miles wide; its waters are elevated some 474 feet above Lake Ontario and 134 feet above Lake Huron, the surplus waters emptying through the Severn River into Georgian Bay, an inlet of Lake Huron. There are several villages and steamboat landings around its shores, together with numerous Indian villages and reservations. The trip through the lake, whether by pleasure steamer or canoe, is a delightful one, if you bring your own provisions and go through safely, whilst good sport in the way of fishing can be obtained. From Barrie to Collingwood is about an hour's ride by the Northern R. R., and we find ourselves in a bustling little town of some 2000 inhabitants; the terminus of the Lake Superior Line of Steamers. The town is located at the

head of an indentation of the Georgian Bay, formerly
called Nottawassaga Bay, from whence steamers ply
regularly during the season to Parry Sound and the
Archipelago, Mackinac, Green Bay, Chicago, Sault Ste.
Marie, Duluth and various other ports on the Upper Lakes.
Collingwood is situated some 94 miles north of Toronto,
and it was expected at one time that it would become one
of the most important shipping points on the Northern
coast. Vast quantities of fish are taken in the bay, and find
a ready market in the cities to the south. The fish generally
taken on the north shore comprise white fish, herring,
pickerel, salmon trout, maskalonge and some other varieties.   There are several lines of propellers and also one
regular ocean class steamer, the "Campagna" (formerly a
British transport for the Cape of Good Hope), running in
the "Superior" trade, so taking the propeller, or, as they
call them, an upper cabin steamer, we set sail, avoiding as
far as possible the open waters of Lake Huron, and steam
away through the sheltered waters of the Georgian Bay,
through the North Manitoulin channel between the Grand
Manitoulin Island (Great Spirit or Sacred Island) through
Heywood Sound, and passing La Cloche Island, a little mass
of uncultivable rock, we pick our way through the mazes
of seemingly intricate channels and pass numerous islands,
on none of which we would care to reside.   We sight next
Cockburn Island, belonging still to Canada, then we pass
Drummond Island, belonging to the State of Michigan,
thence pass a group of rocky islets. Still keeping along the
North channel we pass St. Joseph's Island, a tolerably fertile
island which may in time supply some of the miners with
its fort and lighthouse, whilst on the opposite shore is the
little mining village of Bruce Mines, built upon the bare

SAULT STE. MARIE, FROM THE MICHIGAN SHORE.

rocks, whose population depend for their supplies upon the visits of the steamers. The Bruce mines are probably the oldest worked to pay on the lake; they are situated at the most north-western extremity of Lake Huron, and almost at the mouth of the river flowing from Superior, in long. 84° W. and lat. 46° 19′ N., about 700 miles from Montreal. The rocks on which the town is built contain strata of different kinds of copper ore, but the copper of the Bruce mines is generally a sulphuret in compact dioritic rock; there is also a formation of amygdaloid quartzite or glittering mica quartz. Near the Bruce mines is the Wellington location, which has been partially worked, and not far again from those mines copper is found in Copper Arbor, at which place a vein comes out from the lake and extends several feet on dry land, but is soon cut off and no further trace has been so far found; still, there is no doubt but that the mass of rock that constitutes the borders of the lake has been subject more or less to a severe electro-magnetic action, and the veins in many parts exposed.

Passing Encampment and Sugar Islands, "though any other name would sound as sweet," we wind our way up St. Mary's River, passing occasionally a farm on the Michigan side, and see at times an Indian hut on the reservation on the Canadian side, and soon we arrive at foot of the rapids of the Sault Ste. Marie. These are a series of rapids with no specific fall of any height, that rush wildly over the rocks for some three-quarters of mile. With skillful men, and avoiding the main volume of water and heaviest of the current, a canoe properly manned with a couple of good Half-breeds or residents can force its way throughout the entire length of the rapids, but in the center the waters

rush down with seemingly great velocity and fury, breaking, and sending a huge combing over the rocks. To overcome these falls a ship canal has been built on the Michigan shore. The canal is 5,694 feet in length, its bed is 64
feet wide at the bottom and 100 feet in width at water
level, and 115 at the top of its banks; the locks are 350
feet in length by 70 feet in width, and will accommodate
steamboats of 2,000 tons. The sides of the canal are strongly
walled with stone throughout its entire length, the lock
walls being 10 feet thick at the bottom. The construction
of the canal cost the United States nearly one million of
dollars.

Passing the town of St. Mary's we had the pleasure of meeting one genial acquaintance at least in the
person of Frank J. Hughes, of Algoma, as genial, as jovial
a gentleman as any who reside along the Lakes. Thence
we enter into Whitefish Bay and into the broad waters of
Lake Superior, the largest as well as the deepest of these
inland seas, whose length is 460 miles and whose breadth
is 170 miles, its depth 798 feet, some 627 feet above the
sea, and nearly 200 feet below the level of the Atlantic
Ocean.

Still skirting, the aspect of the North or Canadian
shore from Sault Ste. Marie to Prince Arthur's Landing is
cold, barren and desolate, the very realization of despair
to the farmer or cultivator, being, as far as the eye can
penetrate, nothing but a conglomeration of worthless
rock, relieved at intervals by other rock, containing
minerals, such as lead, copper, iron, copper sulphates, with
occasionally signs of both gold and silver. The rock itself
has been so named by explorers as to confound, if possible,
so in contra-distinction to the worthless Jurassic,

Cambrian, Carboniferous, Devonian, &c., of Europe, here are applied to formations such as Huronian, Sillery, Laurentine and Richelieu. But, as an illustration how the really productive regions are held in reserve, and how thoroughly the regions around have been explored by special parties and made to subserve the interests of capital: Sir Hugh Allan, Andrew Allan (Government subsidy monopolists), Ryan, McDonald, Edmondson and others, have been possessors of various claims, even before 1856, in the valuable region northward of the Batchewa-wanong Bay at a place called Mamains, at which point works were located and claims founded, and which, like the territory owned by the H. B. Co., were kept as secret as possible from all outside. The copper at Mamains contains silver and also traces of gold, and is by far the richest on the Lake shore. If, as is stated, the axiom maintains that money makes money, then the " Allans " should be especially congratulated, for, having subsidies granted, first on one side of the Atlantic and then on the other, with cash allowed to forward their every scheme, no wonder that they have become connected with every interest in the Dominion of Canada, that has the making of money for its ultimate object; but if Scripture might be allowed to intrude in these barren regions the question might be asked, " What shall it profit, if, etc., etc. ? " A number of localities were formerly explored and worked to some extent on Michipicoten Island, but they were abandoned prior to the year 1856. The Quebec and Lake Superior Mining Association commenced operations in 1846 at the *Pointe aux Mines* on a vein that was said at the time to be two feet wide and rich in sulphate of copper. An adit was driven 200 feet, three shafts were sunk, and the ten fathom

or sixty-six foot level was commenced.   About this time
it was discovered that the cash of the stockholders was
sunk also, so, after expending upwards of £30,000, or
$150,000, it was opportunely discovered that there was
no ore to smelt, so the works were abandoned, and the
stockholders the happy recipients of another lesson in
investments.   There is no doubt in the minds of Geologists
that, in the conglomeration of rock that abounds in inter-
minable stretches towards the watersheds and frozen north,
native copper exists not only in veins, but, in the
different rocks of greywacke, red sandstone, etc. ; but the
fact of so little legislation aiding the development of
minerals (except amongst the monopolist class) but little
energy is evinced.   Should charts be published showing
the nature of the soil—of which there is but little—and
the character of the metalliferous strata, affording all
possible information with respect to the localities, so that
in time, even if in the far future, the existence of mineral
wealth may become known to the world at large, and thus
assist to develop the resources of the country.   On the
South, or United States side of the Lake, the mining
interests have been tolerably well protected and aided by
the General Government.   In that country, geological
charts are published from year to year, and may be found
in use with the departments at Ottawa, as a source of
information, but in the States they are attainable by all,
together with scientific works   containing researches
especially aiding in the development of the mines of the
country.   But for a number of years it has been apparent
to the most casual observer that the Canadian Government
gave very little aid to the development of its minerals,
but, possibly in the future, the need will be seen by even

THUNDER CAPE, LAKE SUPERIOR.

cash-absorbing politicians and the time will arrive for the interests of the country to outweigh the obstructions of monopolists. At *La Pointe aux Mines* the sandstone is of staly structure, inclining towards the south-west and crossed by lines from west to east. The veins are of a quartz nature, and are often crystalized; sometimes they even consist of agates or jaspers. In these rocks are found the veins of zinc that are known as ferriferous zinc; whilst at Mica Bay, Cape Choyer, near River Michipicoten and *A la Chienne,* are to be found various kinds of rock, such as sandstone, traprock, greywacke and schistose sandstone. These rocks no doubt will in the near future become a medium of trade, but for the present are worthless to a community not having for its object the permanent settlement and building up of the country. The island of Michipicoten is probably the most prolific in minerals on the Canadian side, but, as the claims are taken up mostly by those in the ring, the only way for the observing emigrant will be to anticipate the advice of the Sage of Chautauqua and go west between the prairie and the mountain, for the islands of Michipicoten and Mamains are about the only places that can present an inducement to the miner, and they certainly possess some of the characteristics of mineral wealth. At intervals numerous species of rock containing native copper can be found upon the islands in every state from molecules to pieces of several pounds in weight. The rocks, too, are softer than those upon the main land, and are consequently more easily worked.

But, whilst disserting on the coast and possibilities, we are still steaming onwards, and soon come in sight of Thunder Cape at the entrance to the bay of that

name: The Cape need hardly be described, it has been
" done " so often ; let us say a cliff of limestone white and
weather-scarred, with a narrow beach of pebbles skirting its
base, on whose summit the Indians supposed that thunder
clouds arose.   But, rounding up under the lee of Fort
William, or Prince Arthur's Landing, we bid good-bye to the
Steamer and its pleasant and numerous occupants, the
roaches.   Then embarking on the cars of the Canada Pacific
R.R. we commence our journey for Winnipeg, distant some
433 miles.   The country west for a considerable distance
toward Selkirk is mountainous, rocky and broken, abounding in lakes, water courses and ravines, unfit for cultivation, with heavy fillings, broad cuts and high trestles.
The original estimate of the cost for this portion of the
road was some .$14,705,000, but it is stated that already
nearly $2,000,000 in addition has been expended, and
the end is not yet; so, after jolting and jogging for
weary hours over a road that undoubtedly has no
equal, hungry, dirty, dry and careworn, we arrive at
Selkirk, twenty-three miles from the city of Winnipeg, a
name that has been ringing in our ears for weeks and
which when once reached we had hoped would prove our
Eldorado, but on arrival at Selkirk we still find that we are
23 miles yet from our destination, so contenting ourselves
we run the other hour or so, and crossing from St. Boniface
we arrive in the city of our hopes, but alas ! how trans-
parent.

WINNIPEG.

The City of " Winnipeg " (signifying muddy or tur-
bid water) was formerly the location of the Upper Fort
Garry, one of the Depôts of the H. B. Co. as a trading

post and for the storage of their goods. It is now the capital of the Province of Manitoba, and is located on a swampy promontory nearly opposite to the confluence of the Assiniboine and Red Rivers, where the former joins the Red River of the North, whose waters flow from south to north, entering Lake Winnipeg beyond Selkirk to the northward of the city. Between the years of 1811 and 1816, Lord Selkirk made an attempt at colonizing a few Scotch settlers, but for all those old chieftains held absolute power over the members of their clans, it was too close to American institutions to prove a success, and after the H. B. Co. located they kept it merely a trading post, it being against their interest to allow settlers to locate or the country to be developed, but some twelve or thirteen years ago the vicinity began to take on a seemingly new life, for the Scotch settlers are now considerable, their farms being mostly west of the Red River, whilst the Canadians and French half-breeds occupy the eastern or St. Boniface side. Here they have quite a town with a cathedral, a nunnery and other religious edifices. The population of the city is at present some 15,000, and partakes of the nature of new frontier settlements generally, for, being built in anticipation, speculation is rife amongst its citizens, one of the chief aspirations seemingly being to sell out and go further for the long wished for Eldorado. The country around is low and swampy, and subject to overflows and inundations on the rising of the river or the break up in the spring, but as improvements and good drainage is accomplished it may be rendered possibly more clean and yet more healthy city. The water is poor, and brackish to the taste. Two Artesian wells are sunk, that supply some 120 gallons per hour, so when numerous others are sunk water enough can be had for all practical purposes. Main street, the principal thoroughfare, is 132 feet in width, well lined with seemingly substantial buildings, stores, and business houses ; the other streets laid out at angles range from sixty-six to ninety-nine feet in width and make fine thoroughfares, whilst for the information of intending visitors I would say, leave all your good clothes at home and take only buckskin, jeans and cowhide boots, you will find the hint profitable. Since the contract for the building of the Railroad has been signed, a new impetus has been given to the city, merchants have crowded in, stores have opened, labor has thronged the city, and numerous branches of banks and business houses from the older Provinces have been established in its midst. One of the great drawbacks to the settlement of these cities and towns is the terrible system of monopoly sought to be established, that will in time result in serfdom far more dire in its effects than ever perpetrated at the South, the West Indies, Russia, or on a limited scale that now existing amongst the fishermen on the island of Anticosti. The manner in which the merchant is closed out and competition stopped is simply this : A merchant from the older Provinces or the mother country has been induced to locate. After purchasing his lot, erecting his store, bringing over a large stock of such goods and wares as are required by the residents and the community generally, he opens up for business with great *éclat* and large hopes for his future business prosperity. Shortly he is visited by a farmer who orders his provisions, hardware and common necessaries, etc., etc., amounting in the aggregate to a respectable sum, say $800. Then comes the settlement. " What are the terms?" asks the farmer.

"Cash, or interest at three months," replies the merchant. "I sell my goods low and must realize as soon as possible, for I pay cash." "Then," says the farmer, "I own a ¼ section in range 4, district 8, township 3, there are my deeds and the land and property is all paid for; my crops are not yet in the ground, and it will be next season before I can pay you." So the farmer goes to the Hudson Bay Co., they look up the lot sold by themselves, make the farmer pay for a mortgagé and give him all the credit he wants, the object being to keep him in debt from season to season. The question may be asked, why the merchant does not make other arrangements so as to allow the farmer as good a credit, but I would answer, that were he plucky enough for that, then other influences would be brought to bear, and finally he would find, like Paul, it was no use in kicking against the pricks. Then again ten per cent. per month on call loans, and a squeeze by the banks when they have the upper hand, is no small joke to a merchant of family who has his little all invested in the stock he is trying to dispose of honestly in the way of trade. Thus the merchant is ruined, reduced, or returns discontented, the farmer becomes indebted, in difficulties, and in time a serf, so it is by these means that God's chosen few seek to bring forward the millenium, and who will eventually live off of the labor of the lower strata.

From Winnipeg both upon the banks of the Assiniboine West and the Red River, both north and south-east, towns have been located and have sprung up with rapidity. Although on the latter river south of Winnipeg the lands are seemingly rich and alluvial, and under different climatic influences would undoubtedly be most productive, still a residence on its banks even in summer is hardly agreeable. Capt. Butler in his work gives his experience which can hardly be improved upon or surpassed, and, therefore, we quote his own words whilst journeying along its banks and over the adjacent prairies. In approximating the time to reach a given spot the remark was made that it would be reached in a given time "if the mosquitoes let us travel." The observation was at once conceded to be some stupendous joke of the driver's in order to intimidate, but he adds, "the wind, which was very light, was blowing from the north-east; a small cloud appeared which rapidly increased in size, the wind soon dying away altogether, and there came upon us, brought apparently by the cloud, dense swarms of mosquitoes humming and buzzing along with us, and covering our faces and heads with their sharp stinging bites. They seemed to come with us, after us, and against us, from above, from below, in volumes that ever increased. Meantime the cloud assumed large proportions, occupying the whole west, and was moving on towards the north; presently from out of the dark heavens streamed liquid fire, and long peals of thunder rolled away over the gloomy prairies. So sudden appeared the change that one could scarce realize that only a little while before the stars had been shining so brightly upon the ocean of grass. At length the bright flashes came nearer and nearer, the thunder rolled louder and louder, and the mosquitoes seemed to have made up their minds that to achieve the maximum of torture in the minimum of time was the sole end and aim of their existence: the pony showed many signs of agony, the dog howled with pain, so nothing remained but to unhitch and lie down; so putting the oil

cloth over the cart and covering with a blanket they crept
inside, whilst the storm was at its height. When the crash
came the fire seemed to pour out from the clouds; during
three hours the lightning seemed to run like a river of
flame, sometimes a stream would descend and, dividing
into two branches, would pour down on the prairie two
distinct channels of fire, whilst the rain came down in
drenching torrents, and the lightning flashed with angry
fury over the long corn-like grass, beaten flat by the rain
torrent." The following night, whilst still on the prairie,
wading through the rank sedge grass, he was hardly more
fortunate, for he adds: "As soon as the sun had dipped
beneath the sea of verdure an ominous sound caused me
to gallop on with increased haste. The pony seemed to
know the significance of that sound much better than its
rider. He no longer lagged nor needed the spur or whip
to urge him to faster exertion, for darker and denser than
on the previous night there rose around us vast numbers
of mosquitoes—choking masses of biting insects, no mere
cloud, thicker and denser in one place than another, but
one huge wall of never-ending insects, filling nostrils, ears
and eyes. Where they came from I cannot tell—the prairie
seemed too small to hold them, and the air too limited to
yield them space; to say they covered the coat of the
horse would be but to give a faint idea of their numbers;
they were literally six or eight deep upon his skin, and
with a single sweep of the hand one could crush myriads
from his neck." It is no unusual event during a wet
summer for oxen and horses to perish from the bites of
mosquitoes and buffalo gnats, and the venomous hard-
skinned little sand flies and bulldogs. So altogether, in the
insect tribe at least, the North-West can be considered

productive, for mosquitoes are abundant on the wet ground, sand flies on the dry, chinch bugs in the oakwoods, and stinging ants everywhere. An exposure of a few hours' duration sometimes is enough to cause death to domesticated animals. It is said that the Sioux were sometimes in the habit of killing their captives by exposing them at night to the attacks of mosquitoes. The farmers of that region usually build smokes or smudges in the evenings and mornings, and the cattle stand in the smoke to keep clear of the insects, and will refuse and leave their feed so as to get near to the fire. By day the udders of the kine and tender parts of horse and cattle are rubbed with a mixture of tar and coal oil, which, although relieving the cattle of the hair, still is of great benefit by keeping off and killing the insect pests,—so the inventor of a mosquito annihilator has yet a fortune awaiting its application. In journeying through the North-West each traveller should provide himself with a good rubber blanket, slit for about six inches and well bound in the centre, with buttons attached on the long side, with two elastic loops and straps at the short ends—thus rendering the article, at once, blanket, overcoat, tent or carpet bag; also a buffalo robe and good overcoat, trusty rifle, serviceable knife, and small barker for special service. The traveller can then go most anywhere, be unmolested, and hold his own.

The Province of Manitoba (pronounced Màn-it-o-bàh, signifying Demon Lake) is named from the Lake, which is similar in size to Lake Winnepegos, their length being about 130 miles, whilst their breadth is about thirty. The water of Manitoba is clear, whilst that of Winnepegos is muddy, and in most parts brackish. One of its peculiarities is that considerable quantities of salt is evaporated at

WINNIPEG RIVER, MANITOBA.

places, and in parts the saline influence is so great that the water hardly freezes in winter. Manitoba is something like 100 miles in length north to south, by 135 miles from east to west, and at present numbers about 114,000 in population. It is represented in the Dominion Parliament by two members in the Senate and five members in the House of Commons. It has also its local legislature, and a Lieutenant-Governor to whom is paid a salary of $9,000 per annum, but, unlike the Lieut.-Gov. of Quebec, he cannot increase it some $15,000 by putting on style, therefore he is the sole object of admiration for the Lieut.-Governor of the next Province, Keewatin, for that unfortunate individual but receives $1000 annually for the exercise of his vast powers. The Province contains an area of about 9,000,000 acres, of which the one-twentieth claimed by the Hudson's Bay Company and the school reserves amount to about 707,680 acres. The Province itself occupies nearly the actual centre of the North American continent. Lands can be bought at a reasonable figure, or, as a H. B. Co. official remarked, can be had for nothing at all. "Just go there and squat, and see nobody turns you out." But a settler needs at least £400 or $2,000 to start with, otherwise he will have a hard time for the first few years, and in the end will find that, after all, the few comforts obtained have been dearly purchased at the cost of family happiness and all that makes life enjoyable. To get along at all in comfort the settler *must* be the owner of the soil he tills and employ his labor, otherwise he will be but a servant of servants, and experience a harder time to actually live than the half-breeds themselves. The Pembina Branch Railroad is in active operation from Emerson on the U. S. boundary line, pass-

ing Winnipeg, to Selkirk, near the Delta of Lake Winnipeg, a distance of 81 miles, whilst the Canada Pacific R.R.
runs from Selkirk to Thunder Bay, a distance of 433 miles.
Extensive timber districts are to be met with in the vicinity of Rat Portage, where large saw mills have been
erected, which are expected to supply the lumber required
for buildings and fences in the Western country. In
portions considerable timber exists suitable for building
purposes and also for fuel, but is found chiefly on the
banks and bottom lands of the creeks and rivers of the
Province, whilst on the prairie there are small groves of
poplar and willow fit for nothing but a summer camp
fire. The timber of Manitoba consists chiefly of muskegs
(swamp) spruce, poplar, balsam poplar, being abundant
on the islands in the various lakes, but whilst the timber
is not large, still part of the Province and part of Keewatin
is thickly wooded with oak, spruce and tamarac. It is
predicted by enthusiasts that in the near future the Province will become a good wheat and cereal producing district, and from the following extracts, taken from "The
Trade Review" published at Winnipeg, will be seen the
statements upon which these hopes of success are based.
The subsoil of the region is a gravelly or sandy loam,
whilst the surface soil is a brown or black loam of from 8
inches to 30 inches in depth. A seemingly good farming
country obtains along the rivers for some distance, but an
extensive tract of country between the Province and the
Saskatchewan is utterly barren, desolate and unfit for
settlement. Being part of the great American desert, it is
sterile and uncultivable, a dreary expanse of wild sage
and saleratus; the surface is sandy, gravelly and pebbly,
cactus and aloes abound, and grass is found only in the

rare river bottoms, where the soils of the different strata are mixed, although as we progress westward the geological formation rapidly changes, the limestone deposits disappear and are succeeded by a variety of sandstones, some red and compact, others grey and coarse. Pudding stones abound, and many of the mountains are supposed to be mainly composed of this rock. However, the following testimony regarding the raising corn or maize is taken hap-hazard from the September (1881) number of that journal. G. V. Fitzgerald of Ridgeville says : "I have raised corn in the garden successfully." Mr. Simon Ballantyne of West Lynne says, " I have never raised corn, but it is successfully grown in sheltered places." George A. Tucker of Portage la Prairie is not quite so equivocal, and says : " I have raised some kinds of corn successfully." Gardner Granby of High Bluff states : "I have tried a little corn in the garden and it did well." Next Mr. James Davidson, also of High Bluff, avers that, " I have raised some corn this year which looks well." Whilst John A. Lee, also of High Bluff, does not commit himself when he says, " I raised some yellow corn last year, it grows very fast but it is short." All of which goes to prove that corn may be raised in the Province of Manitoba, but whether it can be made to pay the farmer is for the latter to find out. Testimony as to the supply of wood in the Province is conflicting, but reports from High Bluff, Portage la Prairie, West Lynne, Morris, Westbourne, St. Anne du Chene and Clear Springs state that "wood for fuel is abundant and at a low price," whilst R. Black, of Birds Hill, states, "wood is not readily obtained, but we have never been cold owing to the want of it." . Mr. George Taylor of Poplar Point says: " wood can be got, but not very conveniently, in Winnipeg;

the price ranges from \$7 to \$12 per cord, whilst coal commands \$20.00 per ton." The breaking up of the land
throughout the Province generally occurs in the latter
part of April, at which time the weather as a rule is dry
and pleasant, no rain of any consequence falling until June,
when sowing has been finished. The weather during the
latter part of August and throughout September is usually
clear, bracing and pleasant, so that harvesting is seldom
interfered with. Many of the resident farmers, such as D.
MacDougal of Meadow Lea, Nelson Brown of High Bluff,
John Sutherland (senator), Kildonan, Robt. Bell of Rock-
wood, F. W. Aylmer of St. Leon, and J. S. P. Casley of
Ridgeville, all testify to the country being a productive
one, and a good one for the farmer with small means. The
crops, such as turnips, carrots, mangel wurtzel, beets, onions,
potatoes, cabbage, tomatoes, melons, cucumbers, citrons,
beans and peas grow splendidly, but all agree that the
settler should in no case arrive earlier than the month of
May or he would be disheartened before commencing his
first season. Small fruits, such as strawberries, currants,
gooseberries and raspberries, bear in abundance, whilst
potatoes are said to surpass even those grown in Prince
Edward Island, Nova Scotia and New Brunswick. The
intending settler is also advised to bring cattle and good
medium-sized, close-made horses with him, and if he can
find, or bore for good water they will thrive. Flax, timothy,
white Dutch and alsike clover also grow well, and produce in
some instances from a ton and a half to two tons to the acre;
while, as an instance of rapid growth, the fact can be mentioned that oats sown on the 27th of April were ready to cut
on the 14th of July, whilst an acre of timothy produced over
a ton.

TEEPEE AND RED RIVER CARTS.

· The principal towns of the province are Emerson on the east side of Red River, at the boundary line, with a population of about 1,500 ; Pembina ; West Lynne, population 500—this town is a good wheat market, and situated close to the Mennonite Settlement, and is expected to become a town of some importance ; Portage la Prairie on the Assiniboine River, some sixty miles by road West from Winnipeg, with a population of about 1,000 ; Morris, on the Red River, twenty-five miles from Pembina, and near the branch R. R. ; St. Boniface, opposite Winnipeg, on Red River, has a population of over 1,000, and is the oldest town in the Province ; Selkirk, a rising town, near the delta of the Red River and on the borders of the reservation—the terminus of the C. P.R.R. during 1882 ; Rat Portage or (Ka-ka-be-kitchewan) the Steep Rock Fall, a lively little town of some 500 population, with a floating addition of railroaders, speculators, Indian traders, prospectors, etc., etc.,— the land on which the town is located belongs, of course, to the H. B. Co., and is situated at the head of the Lake of the Woods and mouth of the Winnipeg River, which river receives the surplus waters of Lake Winnipeg. The rapid influx of emigrants and settlers cause numerous clusters of tents and hamlets to dot the country, which are soon designated and named as towns, and a tax collector and officials duly appointed. In the various settlements around the old H. B. Co. posts on the Red River west, on the Assiniboine, and still further west in the "Fertile Belt," between the north and south branches of the Kissaskatchewan, the settlers are generally Half-breeds, or offsprings of marriages contracted by the Company's officers and servants with Indian women. There are two classes of Half-breeds in the country, the English and the French, the latter being descended from the pioneer hunters and traders, who came from Lower Canada. Many of them being retired servants of the Company, and accustomed to roving habits, it was some time before they could be persuaded to adopt the quiet life of a settler. Many did settle, but they were restless and hard to manage, and as soon as they began to be enlightened were continually rebelling against the authority of the Company, so arbitrary in its administration. In earlier times buffalo being in large numbers at no great distance from the settlements, and the Hudson Bay Co., in order to more rapidly accomplish their purpose of denuding the country, *purchased* (I like that word as applied to the transactions of the Hudson Bay Co., it looks so honest and business-like) from the Indians and Half-breeds both the skins and the surplus meat, thus bringing on a famine, and creating a starving scarcity amongst the residents, which produced a combined organization of the tribes, and a war, that resulted almost in extermination of the bison, was inaugurated; useless massacres of that noble animal were indulged in that shortly swept him from the face of the plain. Capt. Butler, from whose work several extracts have been made, speaking of the practice in vogue with the Crees, says: "The true home of the bison lay in the great region of prairie between the Rocky Mountains, the Mississippi, the Texan Forests and the Saskatchewan River; and within this immense region of not less than 1,000,000 of square miles in area the havoc worked by the European, the Indian and Half-breeds, has been terrible; and only a few years must elapse before this noble beast, hunted down in the last recesses of his breeding-grounds, will have taken his place in the long list of those extinct giants, which once dwelt in our world. When the trader pushed his way into the fur regions the vast herds of the plains experienced a change in their surroundings : the meat pounded down, and mixed with fat into "*pemmican*," was found to supply the wants of the fur traders. The Indians formerly hunted the buffalo with arrows, and wondrous tales are told of their accuracy with the bow. A good Sioux archer could discharge nine arrows upward, before the first had fallen to the ground. With such power could he transfix a bison as to drive the shaft clean through the beast, and find it on the ground on the other side. It is yet considered in the West no great feat to put an arrow into the ace of spades at a distance of forty yards: So expert, also, were the Indians in riding that they could draw an arrow from the flank of the beast before it fell. The bison is a dull, surly and stupid animal, timid and wary; fleeing in terror at the approach of the White Man but seemingly not afraid of the Red; but to bring one down it requires hard riding, with the risk of a collar-bone being broken by the chance of the horse stepping through the roof of a prairie-dog's house; but when headed, wounded or tired, the old bull rarely fails to charge, and makes a stubborn fight. So the Crees, not satisfied with the ordinary methods, devised a plan by which great multitudes of bison could be easily annihilated: This method of hunting consists in the erection of strong wooden enclosures into which the buffalo are guided by the supposed magic power of a medicine man. Sometimes for days the medicine man will live with the herd, which he half guides, half drives into the enclosures; sometimes he is on the right, again on the left, and sometimes in rear of the herd, but never to windward of them. At last they approach the pound, which is usually concealed in a thicket of wood. For many miles from the entrance to this pound two gradually diverging lines of tree stumps and heaps of snow lead out into the plains. Within these lines the buffalo are led by the medicine man; and, as the lines narrow towards the entrance, the herd, finding itself hemmed in on both sides, becomes more and more alarmed, until at length the great beasts plunge on into the pound itself, across the mouth of which ropes are quickly thrown and barriers raised. Then commences the slaughter. From the wooden fence around arrows and bullets are poured into the dense plunging mass of buffalo careering wildly round the ring, always going in one direction, with the sun. The poor beasts race on until not a living thing is left, then, when there is nothing more to kill, the cutting up commences and pemmican making begins. The manner in which this favorite food of the Indian and half-breed is prepared is this, although it can be made from the flesh of any animal, still it is nearly altogether composed of buffalo meat: the meat is first cut into slices, then dried either by fire or in the sun, and then pounded or beaten out into a thick flaky substance; in this state it is put into a large bag made from the hide of the animal, the dried pulp being soldered down into a hard solid mass by melted fat being poured over it in proportions four-fifths fat to the total weight of beat meat, the most high-toned and aristocratic being mixed like an Englishman's plum pudding with a quantity of *piah olillies, Sol-le mie, Sal-lal,* or service berry *(Amelauchier Racemosa),* that grow profusely near the feeding grounds. The shrub is small with a white flower, but the fruit is of great utility; the berries are abundantly produced and easily gathered; the fruit is dried

in the sun, and forms an important addition to the winter
stores of the natives, whilst the area of its growth is widely distributed throughout the Saskatchewan and even into
British Columbia.

The Indians and half-breeds relish and thrive upon it,
eating as much as four or five pounds of the composition
in a single day. The H. B. Co., some few years ago, are
said to have paid, or at least have been so charged by
their agents, to one plain party of hunters the sum of
£1200 for their surplus meat, which was more than the
agricultural class ever received for their surplus produce.
So it is no wonder that agriculture did not receive much
attention from the half-breeds and settlers of a few years
ago. On the prairie the price of a buffalo robe ranges
from $1.00 to $2.00 in kind—seven water grog command-
ing $4.00 per bottle,—and are prepared by the squaws,
who scrape the skin with an iron or bone scraper, and
then, by rubbing in quantities of brain or marrow, work
the skin with the hand until it is thoroughly soft and
pliable. If the hides are to be used for clothes, or tent
purposes, they are well smoked, and the hair is removed
by placing them in lye ashes; they then most effectually supply the place of canvas, which they resemble
in whiteness and facility of folding; their uses are mani-
fold, for clothing, tents, bedding, and in fact supply
the utmost wants of frontier life. The fancy robes painted
inside, and decorated with eyes and split porcupine quills,
dyed a gamboge yellow and covered with hieroglyphics,
being from $15 to $40 each.

From Winnipeg to Fort Ellice is about two hundred
and twenty miles, over an undulating and sparsely
wooded country, with soil of sandy loam, with here

and there ridges of sand dunes, which, although it
may afford a scant subsistence, will never be thickly
settled, the soil not being equal to ordinary prairie.
According to Lieut. Warren the tract called the Sand Hills
occupies an area north of the Platte River of not less than
20,000 square miles; the soil somewhat resembles that of
the county of Simcoe, Ontario, but the rivers are few and
the creeks small, water is said to be obtained at from four
to fifty feet below the surface. The lakes and pools on the
surface are generally saline and brackish, but the air on
these prairies and rolling grounds is healthy and exhilarat-
ing, generally fresh and breezy, even in the months of
July and August, whilst the nights are so cool that blankets
are welcome, but the route West on this parallel was
formerly much dreaded as involving semi-starvation, and
most likely a thorough plundering at the hands of the
natives, half-breeds and other residents whom the Hudson's Bay and other trading companies had despoiled, but
still we are on the prairie drinking in health with every
breath. Whilst galloping over its rolling, grass covered
surface, how the heart bounds, the pulse becomes elastic,
whilst the whole spirit joins in ecstasy at its freedom and
cries with joy, "Almighty power that gave, how we thank
thee. Oh that men would praise the Lord for his goodness
and his wonderful works to the children of men." Nothing in view; not a sound to be heard, the serene vault
of heaven o'erhead, and the grassy turf beneath our feet,
the feeling is one of complete content. What care we for
the bickerings and jealousies of civilization? What care
we for the trials, sufferings and privations of those cooped
up in crowded cities, whose daily life is one of toil and
anguish, and whose only aim is to secure enough to keep

life in their frames, and their bodies free from the meshes of the law? Freedom is found but here. Still closer and closer civilization creeps, but yet a little while, and these boundless wilds, when peopled, will find men in authority placed over them, the law of men supreme, the homage to the Creator traded on; but little reck we at the present what is yet to come before us. To keep their minds on daily life and the effort to survive is the policy now adopted; then and only then, when the fallacy of the cursed doctrines that teach the sacrifice of human life shall be exposed, will the terrible secret of existence be revealed.

Away still further to the north from here we come to the southern borders of the Hudson Bay, a country over which the H. B. Co. have still exclusive control, and for hundreds of miles up its western borders. This bay or sea was discovered by Henry Hudson in the year 1610, who also perished there during the year. It is about 900 miles in length by 600 at its greatest breadth, with a surrounding coast of some 3,000 miles. It lies between the parallels of 51° and 65° N. lat., being nearly six times as large as Lake Superior. The coasts are generally high, rocky, rugged, and sometimes precipitous. The bay is navigable for a few months in summer, but for the remainder of the year is filled up with fields of ice. The transitions of the thermometer in summer are from 10° to 40° in the space of 48 hours, and the range throughout the year is 140°, whilst the torrents of rain that fall are surprising. The sea is entered on the N. E. by Hudson's Strait, which is about 500 miles long, with a varying breadth and an intricate navigation obstructed by numerous islands. The principal bays and inlets on this great inland sea are James Bay on the S. E.—which is 240 miles long by 140 in width—Buttons

Bay, Port Nelson and Port Churchill on the Western
coast; and it is claimed by many that the establishment
of a port at Churchill in lat. 54°, 30′ N., 102°, 15′ long. W.
would open up a port in the interior of the continent at a
distance from Liverpool of 150 miles less than from that
port to Montreal, thus effecting a saving of near 1,100
miles in transit, should ever this portion of the country
become productive enough to require shipments. The
natural results of the opening up of such direct navigation;
in the case of the country being extensively settled, would
be that the Fertile Belt and the country west of the Rockies,
bordering on the Pacific, would become an independent
community and alienate themselves entirely from the
Eastern Provinces or at least east of Lakes Superior and
Huron.

From Fort Ellice, at the junction of the Assiniboine and
the Qu'Appelle, the view is fine, whilst the valley of the
Assiniboine is at least two miles in width, fringed
with willows and small timber. In this central country are stationed the North-west Mounted Police, whose
chief ambition, so far, seems to be monopolized in the effort
to keep themselves alive, and to inspire with terror the
Half-breeds and natives generally. At times even confiscat-
ing the accumulations of the settlers in order to impress upon
them the proper amount of respect due to authority; but
when indiscretions become too frequent the Indians have
a mode of retaliation by allowing every once in a while a
few of the noble emblem of authority to be reported
missing. The amount set apart as the cost for the main-
tenance of the police is some $344,823.77. The buffalo
having been driven off, other game being destroyed, and
domestic cattle not having arrived at times, these guardians

of the pub : peace have suffered considerable inconvenience in attending to the wants of the inner man, and, being somewhat æsthetic in their taste, have become Hippogramists. It is astonishing to note the rapidly-increased value attached to a pony when eaten by the police, as the bill is presented to the Government for settlement. Bigdogs, as they were formerly called, are valued from $2.50 to $5, but when used for food the Government is informed that the value of horse belonging to chief " Yellow Sky," killed and eaten by mounted police, was $65. Other items seemed to rise in proportion, for we find cab hire for comm__ioner at Toronto, on his way to present claims, $69 ; hire of dog train, $43 ; buying one dog, $12 ; cutting a prisoner's hair in these wilds cost $1 ; burying an Indian, $2 ; digging a grave for an Indian, $4 ; and repairing the Union Jack to wave over him cost the country $5. In British Columbia it costs more to plant an Indian, viz., $31, whilst the board of a sick Indian for fourteen weeks was counted at $10 per week amounting to $140,—good enough prices I should think for even an army contractor. There is set apart annually for Indians in Manitoba the sum of $57,572.43 ; how much the aborigines receive— but, no matter, an Injun will lie : they are treated with fatherly care and must not sass back.

From Fort Ellice, twenty-five miles to the southward, is the main line of the C. P. R., now in course of construction south of the Qu'Appelle to the Moose River, thence through Kicking-horse Pass into British Columbia, the northern pass by Leatherhead and Tete Jaune Cache having been abandoned on account, it is said, of their impracticability. Ten miles west from Fort Ellice, on the 101st parallel of west longitude, is the boundary line of the North-west territory, which extends a distance of some 600 miles west to longitude 114° W., centering on the divide between the M. W. and B. C., and extending from latitude 49° N., to Hudson's Bay and Wrangel Land.   Should any one wish to reside in those higher latitudes, it embraces a territory estimated at some 40,000 square miles.

From Fort Ellice to Fort Carleton, the present trading post of the fertile district of the Kissaskatchewan, is about 310 miles, over quite a variety of country: the trail commencing with a road winding between broad hillocks strewn with granite boulders, thence over a sandy and somewhat broken country ; over prairie covered with tufts of tall sedge grass and by rounded hillocks and ridges crowned with aspens.   Dr. 'Grant,' in his notes, gives the thermometer on the 9th of August as register-ing 34°, and the party suffering severely from cold,— a desirable locality for summer visitors, but, as my mate observes, a little out of the way, and in the country extend-ing north-west from Fort Ellice, frosts are usual in July and August.   It is thought that if forests are planted there would be a greater rainfall, less heavy dews, and probably fewer frosts ; however, in my opinion, this portion of the country will be about the last to become permanently settled, for vast treeless plains, with no water except in the marshes, are not attractive localities for intending settlers.   No game being found renders the district still less desirable.   No sound breaks the stillness except the chirp of the cricket, gopher or prairie-dog running to his hole in the ground.   The ridges are gravelly, the grass scant in summer, and only tall enough for hay in the depressions or marshy spots.   Further west, but near the branch of the Saskatchewan, the country becomes

SASKATCHEWAN RIVER, N. W. T.

better, and one begins to find the prairie hen, partridge and
teal ; but in the bush and bottoms mosquitoes are still
plenty during the summer months, when the face of the
prairie is covered with sedge, mosquito, bunch grass and
vetches. Travelling with a party, or when paid by Government, is a pleasure, the roads good, and the exercise delightful, healthy and invigorating ; the cattle and horses gaining
on the trip and arriving at their destination rolling fat and
in good spirits. The mode of conveyance during those months
being the Red River cart and horseback riding, but in the
winter, after the first fall of snow, this is all changed, and
dog teams are used to draw the sleighs, for the cold soon
reaches a limit that renders the saddle unsafe, and the
horses suffer so much in trying to paw away the snow to
get at the withered bunch and crab grass beneath that the
change is welcomed, besides being less trouble. In describing
the team Butler says " dogs in the territories of the North-
west have but one function—to haul. Pointer, setter,
lurcher, foxhound, greyhound, Indian mongrel, miserable
cur, or beautiful Esquimaux, all alike are destined to pull
a sled of some kind or another during the months of snow
and ice ; all are destined to howl under the driver's lash, to
tug wildly at the moose-skin collar, to drag until they can
drag no more, and then to die. The dogs haul in various
ways : the Esquimaux run their dogs abreast; the natives
of Labrador and along the shores of Hudson Bay harness
their dogs by many separate lines in a kind of band or
pack ; while in the Saskatchewan and Mackenzie River
territories the dogs are put one after the other in tandem
fashion. A complete train numbers four, but three, and
sometimes even two, are used. The train of dogs are har-
nessed to the cariole or sled by means of two long traces,

between which the dogs stand one after another, the head of one dog being about a foot behind the tail of the dog in front of him. They are attached to the traces by a long collar, which slips on over the head and ears and then lies close on the swell of the neck; this collar buckles on each side to the traces, which are kept from touching the ground by a back band of leather, buttoned under the dog's ribs. The back band and collar is generally covered with little brass bells and gaily colored ribbons. Great pride is taken by the Half-breed drivers in turning out a train of dogs in good style. The fact is patent that in hauling the dog is put to a work from which his whole nature revolts, with the single exception of the Esquimaux, and to haul with him is as natural as that of a pointer to point. The hauling dog's day is a long tissue of trial, for from the first streak of dawn to the close of day he is in harness and at hard labor, with but one meal a day of two pounds of pemmican or a frozen white fish or two, as the intense cold increases 'and the dogs tire out. The ice cuts their feet and the white surface is often speckled with the crimson icicles that fall from their wounded toes; the Half-breed drivers, too, are brutal fellows, and belabor their team without mercy at times. This inhuman thrashing, the frantic howling of dogs, the bitter and terrible cold, make up the mode of winter travel. From the first covering of snow the whole surface of the plain is one vast sheet of white, so bright and glistening as to render men blind, and sometimes crazy, by the continual glare. Not a sound is heard over this immense waste, save now and then at night the sharp bark of the coyote wolf,—not a speck or even a bird dots the deep blue vault of heaven, nothing but solemn stillness and intense cold, culminating about midwinter at from 40° to 44°

below zero or over 70° degrees of frost. The cold becomes piercing, and a bitter wind sweeps across its surface. In midwinter the snow falls every day, with a high westerly wind, veering towards the north, and thick with poudré, dry icy specula hard as gravel, and blizzards jump up all of a sudden in seemingly pleasant weather—commencing with a gale and increasing to a hurricane, the wind blowing at the rate of from forty to fifty miles an hour, whilst the thermometer registers from 35° to 40° below zero, which, with the clouds of snow dust, hard as bullets, the effect can well be imagined. Men are silent, their lips are blue, and refuse to utter the words they feel. Where the skin is exposed it becomes frost-bitten and afterwards rots away; eyes and nostrils are glued together, and icicles hang from the eyelids, to touch a knife with the hand would burn like a coal of fire. The hot tea freezes whilst it is being drunk, breath freezes instantaneously into solid lumps of ice, and 40° below zero means death, in a period whose duration would expire in the hours of a winter's daylight, if there was no fire or means of kindling one on the trail.

Such, then, is winter travelling in a land where conscientious agents of unscrupulous companies try to induce the *poor* whites of Great Britain and Continental Europe to go, settle and colonize, knowing full well that the rigors of the climate mean *disease* and *death* to the poor settler and his family, if he is not provided for by the Government, a wealthy company, or individual capitalists. Would it not be a wise policy on the part of the Dominion Government if, instead of spending some $250,000 annually for emigration purposes and for political hacks, party agents and appointees to absorb, both abroad and at home, in singing the praises of our broad Dominion, living them-

selves in clover and upholding a mock and petty dignity,
whilst their poor dupes were undergoing suffering and
bitter privation,—would it not be better if those agents were
retired, and their salaries appropriated to the erection of
homes and the furnishing of provisions for poor settlers
who are induced to locate in this region, at least enough to
tide them over until such crops as can be raised in this
latitude be gathered in.   Although Icelanders, Laplanders
and Esquimaux may thrive, still a poor white man will
die without material help and some substantial provision.

The soil from about 150 miles east of Fort Carlton is a
dark loam and prairie buckshot, that bears evidence of
fertility, and of producing timber such as poplar, black
Jack, and some few hard woods.   The region is known as
the Touchwood Hills, and around them are immense plains
of bare and scanty vegetation, which formerly was the
stamping ground of the buffalo, and at one time covered
with their trails, but at present is the home of the prairie
dog and the coyote, the ground owl and the snake.   The
Indian and the buffalo have for the most part both disappeared, and have cleared the way for the white speculator and the settler.   Soon lots will be advertised for sale
at low prices for cash, whilst a town site can be obtained
at ridiculously low figures.   To those settlers who
travel or seek their homes off from the line of railroad, it
is necessary to advise them to provide an outfit, and the
following can be obtained from about $350, or £70.0.0 :
two yoke steers, milch cows, waggon with double cover,
two ox yokes, ox chain and tar bucket, large canvas tent,
axes, spades, shovels, triangles for fire, etc., etc.   Three
barrels flour, 100 lbs. each of ham, bacon, crackers and
sugar; twenty-five lbs. of coffee, raisins, currants, rice,

dried apples, beans, peas, etc., small stove and buffalo robes. With an outfit as above you can not only travel and seek out a location, but, by starting and breaking up the land early, can squat until the gathering of the first crop, then, should you become dissatisfied with the surroundings, pack up and move on, for the war once waged upon these plains between man and the brute creation, is now a war of trade, civilization and speculation, and, though less disastrous in its ending, is waged by the Christian white against his brother man, and carried on by the representatives of the same companies whose chartered rights hastily given by a profligate king enabled them to denude the country of its products. At present, says Butler, "there is something unspeakably melancholy in the aspect of the plains: not a sound in the air or on the earth, all is silent and deserted, and the feeling on camping is one of utter loneliness, although at times, in summer, straggling remnants of herds of buffalo are sometimes seen, but their trail is soon found and followed by the Half-breeds and Indians who roam the country. The water found is brackish and undrinkable, but it is stated that good water can be procured by digging—the surface pools in summer time being only what is left of melted snow and spring and summer rains, tainted with decayed vegetable matter, strongly impregnated with sulphur and alkali and filled with animalculæ, in color like that of an abandoned cyprus swamp. Whiskey in this region is a necessity not only to disguise the bad taste of the water but to destroy the living organisms with which it abounds, for a traveller naturally objects to making an aquarium of his stomach, however tough and well-lined that organ may be.

It was over a portion of this territory that so many of

the old-time emigrants gave up disappointed, and laid down their lives in despair; even the anecdotes that survive carry a tinge of despondency with them.   A man meets with a broken-down waggon of emigrants on the prairie, and, accosting the wretched-looking boy who was engaged in the pleasant task of nursing a starving baby, says, "Wall, Sonny, what's up?"   "Wall now," replies the youth, "guess I'm kinder streakt: old dad's drunk, ole mam's in hy-sterics, brother Jim be playing poker with two gamboliers frum the trading post, sister Sal's down yonder a courtin with a entire stranger, this ere baby's got the diarée, the team's clean guv out, the waggon's broke down; it's twenty miles to the next water, and I don't give a dam if I never see the Rockies."

West of the Touchwood Hills, on the trail to Fort Carlton, remnants of the Salteaux and other tribes are occasionally met, the fort being the trading post.   Nearing the banks of the Saskatchewan there are evidences in summer, on every side, of a rich and fertile country, well wooded, abounding in lakelets, swelling into rolling prairie, and opening out into a wide and fair plain.   The soil to Fort Carlton is a dark loam and the vegetation good.   Right here I would say that if a company, with the welfare of the emigrant at heart, would purchase large tracts of land, cut it up into small farms, say forty to sixty acres, erect good substantial frame dwellings, furnish farming implement and household utensils—together with provisions for the first year—to the emigrant agricultural laborer, taking pay for his farm by a mortgage, and his obligation of indebtedness, the valley of the Saskatchewan could be made to "blossom as the rose," and vast numbers of the north of Europe's poor agriculturists become good producers, and bless the company who gave them a chance to earn their daily bread, their independence, and their own home and property at the same time. Such a scheme has already been mooted, and the idea well received; and when the capitalist can see a prospect of a fair return for his outlay no doubt the project will be carried through to a successful ending. The land is there rich and fertile, needing cultivation and labor, but for the poor laborer unaided to try to develop its resources would be to make it a hell to him; but with the assistance of capital the region would become the garden spot of the North-west. It is rich, fertile and fair to the eye, man lives long in this climate, and his children are healthy and strong; the cold of winter is excessive, and the strongest heat of summer is not intense. The Autumn days are bright, clear and beautiful, the frosts are early to come and late to go, and the snow is seldom deep and never sloshy. Root crops flourish, timber in spots is plentiful, in others scarce, prairie, bunch, sedge and musquito grass grows thick and rich. The lake shores are covered with verdure, whilst fish in the waters are abundant—lakelets and pools are everywhere; in fact, it is just the country where a man can " be out of society's reach to wander and roam all alone."

Fort Carlton is situated on the north branch of the Saskatchewan River, which is here about 400 yards in width, the banks being fully 200 feet in height, so that a June freshet is not so dreaded as on the banks of the lower Mississippi. The fort was also a trading-post of the H. B. Co., who acted as brokers for all obselete and condemned war material of Great Britain, at highest possible obtainable figures, to the Crees and Blackfeet, who were magnanimously instructed how to use them against each other as well as

against the buffalo, since which time they have occasionally allowed their patrons and teachers to acquire a
taste of the knowledge so gained.   Such was the quality
of the Brummagen guns supplied to the Indians, that,
getting bent, it was no uncommon thing to see a brave
straightening out his fifty-skin gun-barrel of Birmingham
make—first cost 7s. 6d.—between two saplings, or in a
crevasse in the rock.   Of late years there have been
frightful epidemics of small-pox raging in the camps around
the posts, and so fatal has been the ravages of the plague
occasionally fully three-fourths of the entire tribe were
swept away ; whilst in the camps and villages of the Crees
and the Blackfeet, the Stonies and the Prairie Indians, in
some instances sweeping the entire village out of existence,
in others leaving but a remnant of a once powerful tribe.
This disease was another of the civilizing effects of the
red man's contact with the white.   The much-abused and
thoroughly-swindled Indian may in time have full justice
done him, and his present seeming vindictiveness accounted
for.   The testimony of others as well as Columbus aver
" there is not a better people than these, more affectionate
and mild ; " but it is the same old story of the white man's
rapacity and greed : first he was the missionary, the welcome
guest, the honored visitor ; then the greedy hunter, the
death-dealing vendor of fire-water and poison ; then the
settler and exterminator, hating the red man for possessing
the spirit of independence and the love of freedom.   Many
efforts have been made by missionaries to christianize the
Indians, and they have succeeded in making many converts,
both among the Indians, Half-breeds and H. B. Co.'s
servants, and as a result have educated a formerly trusting,
truthful and honest people into being most consummate

LOTS FOR SALE.

hypocrites and thieves,—whilst as genuine unscrupulous liars they have few equals and no superiors; and the lies they tell for variety in some instances are but little worse than the *truth* they have been taught. How shocked would some of the pious ones in the Old Country be if, whilst drawing their dividends, the means of its acquisition were thoroughly and truthfully explained. A few miles from Carlton the road is sandy, gravelly and rugged, running for the most part through the sand-hills, unproductive and unfit for cultivation; the sole timber to be found is but a few scattering willows or aspens. The only reliance then for camp fires at night are buffalo chips, when you are lucky enough to find them, or sage brush,—the latter flares up, burns briskly and hot for a few moments, and then suddenly dies out, leaving a strong medicinal odor; the former is useful as fuel, and burns almost like turf, and steaks cooked by the fire require no pepper. It has been stated that no farms or gardens are cultivated at Carlton, for the reason that the Indians, who come to trade and see what they can get, would, without the slightest intention of stealing, use the fences for firewood, dig up the potatoes and turnips, and let their horses get into the grain fields, —so the nearest farms are located at the Prince Albert Mission, and are spoken of as being productive, although suffering occasionally from frosts and early droughts. From Fort Carlton to Fort Pitt, also situated on the north branch of the Saskatchewan River, is about 190 miles in a N. N. W. direction. The river itself makes a sweep first southerly as if it would join the southern branch, then northerly as far as Fort Pitt. The country is broken and hilly, a portion being called the Thickwood Hills; salt lakes and marshes abound, whilst the soil is not as good even as

that found east of Fort Carlton. Nearing Fort Pitt some of
the lakes abound with fish, so, should you be fortunate
enough to have the corn meal, the seasoning, and a good
camp kettle, a splendid chowder for a hungry man is not
long in being produced.   Proceeding westward the country
becomes more broken, until at length the region of the Red.
Deer hills is entered—a wild rugged tract of country to the
north of the Saskatchewan, the projected branch of the Canada Pacific Railway keeping well to the southward of the
river.

   In the bottoms and in the marshy spots wild gooseberries,
currants or service-berries, and choke-cherries that pucker
the lips like a green persimmon, are found in abundance,
but it is firmly believed that the Indians and Half-breeds
who inhabit these regions grow so thin on the fare they
obtain—like a poor white man in the Lower Provinces—
that they have to carry rocks in their pockets to keep from
being blown away by the frequent blizzards.   A large portion of this hill country still belongs to the Governor and.
Company of Adventurers of England.   The H. B. Co. have
at Fort Pitt a trading-post, although their cattle ranche and
garden is some ten miles distant.   The fort stands on the
north shore of the Saskatchewan River, which is here more
than four hundred yards wide.   On the south shore immense
bare bleak hills raise their wind-swept heads for hundreds of
feet above the river level.   No trace of wood is within sight
—nothing but a few grassy spots enliven this wild looking
scene, and travelling is heavy and laborious over the sandy
pine-covered ridges, which rise to the north-west of Fort
Pitt. Continuing on, creeks are numerous, but the country
not desirable, the course being across wide opens or up or
down a long bare slope.   Roads are bad and difficult to get

over, owing to the steep banks at the creeks, and boulders, deep ruts, wash-outs, mole and badger holes.

At Victoria, about forty miles from Fort Pitt, is a small Half-breed and Cree settlement, and from this place west the country becomes more hilly, but presents a pretty appearance, the hill sides covered with heavy wood; in the hollows are marshes or lakelets. Vegetation is luxuriant, but these productive stretches only extend a few miles at a time, and then comes a stretch of inferior ground, with little to show but scrub birch, like a portion of the northern part of New Brunswick, where the scrub pine flourishes; then as Edmonton is neared the country resembles as immense park, and for some eighty miles is certainly a rich and delightful tract. Edmonton, also one of the H. B. Co's. trading posts, is on the high level on the north bank of the Saskatchewan River, some 100 feet above the bed of the river, which at this place is a broad stream some 300 yards in width. Farming operations, boat building, flour milling and blacksmithing are actively engaged in, whilst on the opposite side of the river are the villages of both Crees and Blackfeet. In course of time, as the country becomes settled, this portion from the fort to the Rockies will become the favorite with stock raisers; whilst the intevening land contains seams of coal of varying thicknesses and other minerals in abundance. Both Edmonton and Fort Pitt are situated within the war country of the Crees and Blackfeet, and were the scenes of many a sanguinary conflict between these fierce and implacable foes; many are the legends extant that would fill the heart with horror at the recital of the cruelties.

Some eleven miles north-west of Edmonton is a French Half-breed settlement, situated on the shores of Grand Lac or St. Albert, which has several times been visited by the epidemic of small-pox. These settlements are generally started by the old servants of the fur companies, and afterwards kept together by the Church pioneer grabbers. Some religious prospectors have done good, even amongst the Indians, and no longer do the *elite* of the different tribes call for missionary roast underdone, or a baby on the half-shell, a Methodist stew, or similar delicacy, but now petitoon eagerly for a little more rum and a few more missionaries to render the district entirely civilized. As an American officer reported, a white man can go anywhere throughout the Indian territory without molestation—so it is not the Indian who causes much trouble; probably far more is suffered from the hands of the civilized conservators of the peace than from the savage and semi-savage inhabitant.

From Edmonton to the Rocky Mountains is some two hundred miles over varied country, good both for farming and stock-raising, although on the margin of the lakelets summer frosts nips often, and frequently destroys both the barley and wheat planted, still for root crops, small fruits and berries the land is good; fish are still plenty in the lakes, whilst duck, pelican and geese are plentiful in summer. Crossing the succession of wooded hills which divide the water system of the north from that of the south Saskatchewan, we again encounter the projected track of the C.P.R., which road on the prairie is now actively progressing, at a rate that may be considered prodigious, over three miles per day being laid by one contractor. The system of building a road over the prairie is one of the most simple : the plough runs a furrow on each side of the 4 feet 8 in. track, the upturned earth levelled off, the ties laid, the rails spiked, and lo, and behold ! the Government

FORT EDMONDTON, N. W. T.

has value received for the work performed on the central section at the rate of $10,000 per mile in cash; and 12,500 acres of land for each mile completed. Of course the road will be a success, but it will certainly have to be rebuilt before three years have elapsed after acceptance. The building of the central section, as it is called, being assumed at 1,350 miles, although in reality much shorter, will cost the people, in cash, $15,000,000, in land, 18,750,000 acres. It is on the lands in this vicinity, and to the base of the Rockies, that the various colonization companies and M. P's have selected for their ranches, and have " *leased* " from the Government for a period of twenty-one years all the land they required at the rate of $10.00 for 1000 acres. During the first two months after the contract was signed over seventy-eight applications were received from those in the ring, organizing companies, and the land applied for amounted to some 4,215,371 acres, about the only land worth having in the territory. Eight applications were granted, so whilst the poor emigrant, agriculturist and settler contributes his $2.50 per acre for possession he can console himself that the following parties obtained theirs at the rate of $10 per 1000 acres :

	No. of Acres.
Cochrane Ranche Co...................	100,000
D. Ford Jones, M.P	100,000
Allan Patrick...................	34,171
F. S. Stitson & Co....................	100,000
Capt. T. D. Milburne................	100,000
J. E. Chipman & Co..................	100,000
Gibbs & Morgan.....................	100,000
J. P. Wiser, M.P......	100,000

These are but a few of the number who could be quoted, but they are sufficient to convince any sensible man that, should he locate under their auspices, the system of slavery was not yet dead in the land, for no effort will be deemed impossible if it only has for its aim the establishment of oligarchial rule.   Passing the lonely shores of Gull Lake we soon come upon the abrupt line of the Three Medicine Hills, from whose gorges the first view of the Rocky Mountains is to be had.   The highest peaks arise near the McLeod River, and extend southwards some 200 miles to the head of the South Saskatchewan, and amongst whose fastnesses, in spite of the vigilance of the hunters, bears and wild sheep are yet to be found.   The first impressions of the sight of the Rocky Mountains are thus described by able writers : " Looking west the traveller beholds the great range in unclouded glory, rising their snow clad sierras in endless succession.   From the Medicine Hills an immense plain stretches to the mountains, like gazing from the table lands of Chihuahua, Mexico, a plain so vast that every object of hill and wood and lake lay dwarfed into one continuous level ; and at the back, beyond the pines, the lakes and river courses, rises the giant range, solid, impassible and silent, a mighty barrier rising in the midst of an immense land, standing sentinel over the measureless solitudes of this lone and depleted land.   The peaks in this region are the highest of the range, those to the southward decreasing in altitude as lower latitudes are reached, whose teeth or saw-like summits are covered with an eternal crust of snow, whose meltings in summer seek widely severed oceans.   The Mackenzie, the Columbia, Colorado and Saskatchewan (the affluents of the Colorado and Columbia carry off the greatest amount of drainage) spring from the

THE ROCKIES.

waters that trickle down those lofty peaks and seek their home in the far separated divisions of the Atlantic, Pacific and the Arctic. The H. B. Co. had also a trading-post at the foot of the mountains, in a level meadow, clear of trees, whilst at some little distance a dense forest lies round it. As settlements are effected both the export of lumber and coal will be one of the industries of this region, for over considerable portion of the prairie or grass region little is found but cotton-wood, aspen and slim copse of willow—neither serving the purpose of fuel for a settlement. From a late estimate, made by order of the United States Government, it was ascertained that the heat produced by 2,500 lbs. of Rocky Mountain coal and 2,500 lbs. of Coos Mountain coal was equal in intensity to that of a cord of oak wood, 8 feet in length, 4 feet in breadth and 4 feet in height. Over the plains and meadows at the base of the mountains but a few years ago roamed the Indians in vast numbers, but a policy of extermination had to be silently worked out to give to the whites the lands they coveted. So now by the aid of the white man's disease (*small-pox*), poisoned springs, fire-water, and corrosive sublimate, the work is well-nigh accomplished, and civilization will rejoice in the acquirements of the lands of its red brother. The Indians generally use pantomimic or sign language with the whites, and although it is a labor of years to thoroughly acquaint one's self with the system, still an interpreter who understands the various conventional and instinctive signs is preferred even by the whites to a good speaker. So reports come in of a man sent among the Cheyennes to qualify as an interpreter who returned within a week and proved his competence by going through a pantomime with a running accompaniment of grunts, which was amply

sufficient knowledge to pass him with the army officers
and Indian agents, for it has long been a matter of surmise
how an Indian agent, with a salary of but $2,000 per
annum, could build within the first two years a $40,000
house out of his income.   The broad lands which skirt the
base of the mountains are covered with a rich pasturage,
which highly adapts them for grazing, and will in the future
become a pastoral region, and numerous land companies are
being formed with all kinds of so-called advantages and
inducements offered.   It is worthy of note that Dukes,
Lords, Earls and others of the nobility who, whilst in Baath,
look with contempt upon anything savoring of trade, and
who affect to despise a tradesman, do not hesitate to lend their
names and assist in floating land companies that will eventually bring ruin and degradation to thousands of families,
leaving desolation in their wake; but even noblemen of the
present day are seized with a desire to obtain a portion at
whatever cost.

The Rockies are irregular in their ranging, and at
times comprise three sections, the center being the
Rocky Mountains proper, the others being known as the
Sierras, the Wasach Range, Wind Mountains, Snowy Range,
etc.   The curious formation of the mountains is most
noticeable, the ridges are formed of short but acute angular
cappings, and it often happens that after ascending two-
thirds from the base the upper parts become wall-like and
insurmountable.   It is this portion of the range that will
present the greatest obstruction to the skill of the engineers
in the construction of the C.P.R., although, if once surmounted, and snow sheds for the length of a few hundreds
of miles be built, the road will no doubt become an
accomplished fact and workable.   The lowest valleys are

4,000 feet above sea level, the mountains are from 6,000 to 11,650 feet in height, whilst some peaks tower thousands of feet above that altitude. These mountains des Roches are sometimes of black slatey rock, and are absolutely rock without admixture; sometimes found piled one above another like heaps of gigantic slates, but often they lay in a succession of rugged precipitous ridges.; others again differ, some being broken, presenting sharp edges; others ragged, like coarse white coral; others formed of thin layers of black looking stone, which crumbles in the hand like some of the ancient sandstone of Egypt, but between the McLeod on the North, and the Belly River south, the Rockies constitute several distinct ranges entirely separate from the central range. In these valleys thaw is seldom known, whilst the air is highly rarified by its altitude. Travellers, and even horses, suffer from a difficulty in breathing, and take months before they are climated'; pneumonias, coughs and lung diseases are the most prevalent at these altitudes, and no doubt, if population ever abides on its slopes, the graveyards will reap as good a harvest as those at Leadville or amongst the Black Hills generally. The rarified air of these mountains produces a great oppression on the lungs, which is accompanied with bleeding, so that a new arrival can always be told when seen going about holding a blood-stained handkerchief to his mouth. The Yellow Head Pass, now abandoned by the C. P. R., is stoney, a rough divide with cahots and pitch holes, with the twisted and knarled roots of the stunted black cedar protruding across the roadway, making travel dangerous, sometimes skirting, again climbing, then down in the valley, wheeling successively around three-quarters of the compass, now through a gorge, and again through a

kanyon. The rivers are shallow and rapid, but generally
clear, their banks being bordered with fir and spruce, but
the trees are small, being kept down by cold and frequent
avalanches of snow and stones. Amongst these mountains
the changes of temperature are very sudden : at noon one
hides from the burning sun and at night one trembles in the
icy blast : but in breaking through again we are mired axle
deep in the sloughs, or struggling desperately to reach small
mounds of earth tufted with greasewood for a firm footing.
This is the mode of crossing the mountains of the Setting
Sun.   Once over, past the divide where the rivulets and
mountain torrents rush down to assist in forming the Columbia (*Tacoutche Tasse*) River, which takes its proper
source from a series of lakes in lat. 50° 10′ N., long. 39°
22′ W. from Washington ; but after once forming as a river
takes immense sweeps around the ranges and rushes terribly through the kanyons on its way to the sea.   It is here
proper to remark that Messrs. Lewis and Clark were
amongst the first, whilst exploring the western coast of the
United States, to wander into the region of country that led
them to the head-waters of this noted river, and at places
found it over 300 feet wide.   The bed of the river has in
course of ages undergone great changes, the water having
cut channels through baysaltic and gneiss rock and, having
changed its course, has left most remarkable evidences of
its power.   The deserted channels are near the source of
the river, from whence, doubtless, in remote ages, glaciers
cut their way to the ocean.   The upper country of the Columbia is exceedingly barren, but westward of the rapids
the valley is beautiful and fertile, enormous trees growing
on it, whose height often exceed 300 feet, with a circumfe-
rence of forty-five feet. These streams also form the Fraser,

the Peace (although the Peace rises and runs in lat. 55° to 57°, N.), Mackenzie, Myette and Colorado rivers, and run their various courses to the Arctic, the Pacific and the Atlantic oceans, through the Yellowhead Pass, whose height is thought to be but 3,700 feet.

So, finally, after tripping over rocks, wearying the eye with constant gazing on range after range of dark, still, somber solemn piles of barrenness, blessing all creation, and yourself in particular, for ever having started on the trip, at last you feel that you have fairly entered the long-sought land, and the mind wanders back to the days and weeks spent in, coming, the wishes, longings, mixed with partial prayings, whilst east of the Rockies. " Oh to be in Columbia ! " But once on the western slope the demijohn is uncorked, and the remark is made "Hurrah, boys, here we are at last in the land of gold;" the difficulty is solved and our troubles most over, and now we are within the portals of the golden province. The Rocky Mountains form the eastern boundary of British Columbia, whilst between them and the Cascades is generally designated as the East Cascade region. If whilst east the mind was engaged in conjecture of what it would accomplish, when once west, it has settled down to business in reality, in wishing, longing and most earnestly praying to get out of the confounded country, for, from the summit of the Rockies to Tete Jaune's Cache is some seventy miles, over rocks, slatey and sharp, hog wallows and boulders. The banks of the Fraser River in this portion are rock-bound and unproductive, and the Cache is the head of even canoe navigation; it was first decided that the C.P.R. would take this route, but the utter barrenness of the region, the numerous ranges of hills and mountains render the pass

not at all desirable or even practicable,—so it is now
decided that the crossing will be made by Kicking Horse.
River, in lat. 51° 20′ N. and long. 116° 50′ W. from Green-

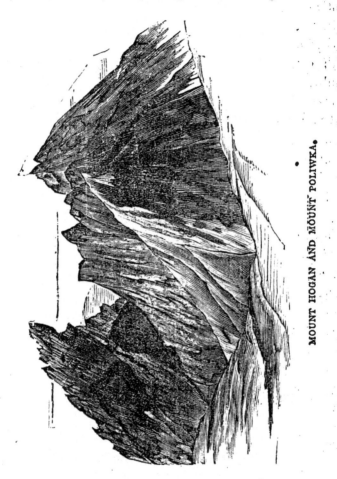

MOUNT HOGAN AND MOUNT POLIWKA.

wich and 39° 50′ W. from Washington, between Mount
Goodsit, Mount Lefroi and Mount Cramp, near the source
of the Kootenay River, some 120 miles to the southward
of Yellowhead and 125 miles north of the Kootenay Pass,

so near the boundary line of 49°, which route, no doubt, will be of far more advantage to the R. R., should it ever be completed. It may be at this point a man reviews the situation: he himself is toughened, but with boots worn out, clothes played out, grub most out, and altogether we feel in a h—l of a fix, but we still must go on: so the pony stumbles over loose rocks, falling over roots and knots, sticking in the mire and bog; the way is wearisome and hard-worked, until finally the Caché is reached by following the course of the Fraser River. Here you may possibly meet with a few strangers—tan-colored gentlemen, Indians, or, as they are familiarly called, Siwashes; even should you come across some poor prospector who had wandered so far out of his way, or even a wandering Chinaman, you would instantly recognize the fact that you were in an alien land, for the first question would be in a dialect introduced by the early traders amongst the Indians, " Waw Waw Boston spose mesika klatawa kopa kamloops pe Victoria," which, according to the latest revised, means, "Say, American, are you going to Kamloops or Victoria. If you answer, "Nika klatawa saghilie illahie pe Boston illahie lejaub klatawa hyak." —" I'm going to heaven or the U. S. P. D. Q." Then you are assailed with, " Boston kloshe iskum hyin muckamuck Siwashe, o-lo, o-lo chuck. Kloochman piah sick, siwashe sick. Hyas klohowyum nika, Boston potalch mucamuck Siwashe klap hyin pil chickamin—" American good, get plenty to eat ; Indian hungry and thirsty, wife sick, Indian sick and poor. If give something eat, Indian will show plenty, heap gold." But after eating and getting all possible Mr. Ingine generally skips out to call on his relatives around Moose Lake or between the high steep rocks that side the Fraser. From the Caché the southern trail leaves the river and turns south-east until it meets the north branch of the Thompson River, whilst another goes northward and westward to Alexandria, Barkerville and the Cariboo District, the trail to which, like that across the isthmus from Aspinwall to Panama, was marked by bleaching bones of early adventurers. Tales still extant are terrible, whilst localities are pointed out that were even marked by the practice of cannibalism itself.

Working northward, rounding the ranges, crossing the Thompson and Clearwater, between the kanyons, amidst the expanse of Quesnel and Horsefly lakes, passing creeks and lakelets, so runs the trail to Alexandria on the Fraser, along which trail, at intervals, are small spots of land, cultivatable for root crops and the hardest species of grain. Small tracts of pasturage are met with, but for the most part, as far as Alexandria, in lat. 52° 33′ 40″ N. and long. 122° 26′ 56″ W., the country is wooded. The altitudes of this district are from 2,100 to 3,054 feet respectively, and average a mean of 3,086 feet above the level of the sea. At the former height several varieties of grain and vegetables are raised yearly, thus showing a comparatively fertile soil, and that agricultural pursuits may be engaged in wherever a strip of promising ground is found and located. Wheat was raised at the H. B. post as early as 1845; other cereals and culinary vegetables flourish and produce good results for this portion of the country. The timber principally is balsam, pine, hemlock, and spruce fir; cyprus or yellow cedar extends almost to Alaska, and is most useful as piles for wharves and docks, as it resists to a greater extent than any other wood the attacks of the teredo or sea worm, which causes such havoc on wooden pilings in salt water. With a poor variety of yew and a small good close-grained

CARIBOO MINERS AND INDIANS.

birch the woods of this district may be said to be complete. From Alexandria upwards the country can only be regarded as a hunting or mining region. The H. B. Co. having so long had control, nothing of consequence is now left to hunt, for few animals that could be either of use or service to man were left to reproduce after the Company once located their post. Extermination of everything living seems to have been their aim and desire, and it is to the rapacity and greed of this and other companies that has turned a territory once teeming with life, and which would have afforded food for millions, into a desert and a solitary wilderness, although occasionally north of 57° north lat., reindeer, cariboo and big horn are sometimes met with yet.

Still following up the course of the Fraser River, almost due north along its rock-bound borders, we cross numerous creeks and tributaries, until arriving at the Quesnel in lat. 53° 17' N., long. 122° 27' W., thence we take a north-easterly course over an exceedingly rough and uninteresting country, over steep banks and around high benches, we cross the Cotton Wood at an altitude of 2,530 feet and the Van Winkle and Lightening creeks at altitudes of 3,654 feet above the level of the sea—in the kanyons of each of which creeks gold has been found in more or less quantities from the year 1861 ; but the expense of actual living and erecting stamp mills and other machinery for grinding quartz has been so great that wherever paying quantities have sought to be produced it has been too long a-coming to please the shareholders, for on a summing up it was found by the Costello Company that it taxed the Company some $33,852 in cash to take out $20,476 in gold ; however, several of the mines are in paying condition, and are

worked by the companies in control, with such labor—
whites, Chinamen and Indians—as may present itself. After
several years of comparison, from 1858 to 1876, it was computed that an average of 3,171 miners were employed, and
that each earned a wage of some $663 per year. This
region was rushed for a time, but soon toned down, and
the various alluvial diggings on the creeks rapidly became
exhausted, so that quartz-mining became the sole stand-bye
for prospectors ; but nominally the high benches, which
flank the course of the Fraser and other rivers and creeks
have as yet been practically unexplored, although numerous
localities give indications of containing gold deposits, but
an enormous amount of capital will have to be located in
the district before it can be peopled and thus thoroughly
explored.   From Yale, the head of river navigation on the
Fraser, to Barkerville there is a weekly line of stages,
whilst freight averages from $7\frac{1}{2}$ to 8 cents. per pound on
sugar, tea, salt, powder and shot alike, in the spring, whilst
in the fall the rate is some $12\frac{1}{2}$ to 15 cents. per pound.
Other districts nearer Victoria, and even south of the boundary in California, are naturally forming a greater attraction
to the miners, as better paying yields have been found in
the Cassiar fields, and on Thibets and Dease's Creeks,
again in the Gold Range, and the Upper Arrow River, in
lat. 50° 20″ N.

Returning back to Alexandria we follow the swift
running current of the Fraser, and thus come into the
central section, as it were, of British Columbia—this
second or central section extending from the latter town to
Yale, a distance of some 220 miles, in the upper portion
which covers from lat. 49° N, to lat. 53° N., nearly 240
miles from south to north. The town of Yale being

situated in lat. 49° 33′ 44″ N. and long. 121° 25′ 58″ W.
In the upper part of this district summer frosts interfere
materially with the growth of the less hardy cereals and
tender vegetables, but turnips, mangels and potatoes flourish
and generally produce well ; black and Norway oats thrive
also. Pasturage in sections throughout the district is very
extensive, and of an excellent character for fattening stock.
Along the Thompson and in the southern portions, bunch
grass, pea vine and rye grass herbage thickly covers the
ground, affording most excellent grazing and is unsurpassed
for fattening stock. In the intervals between the hills the
tracts are well watered by mountain streams, whilst in the
level depressions numerous lakes abound, with good timber
for shade or shelter. Numerous heads of cattle graze and
roam at large throughout the southern district, being
driven thither to fatten by settlers of the province and
Americans from the adjacent territories of Washington and
Oregon ; whilst from these districts large droves are regularly sent to the Victoria, New Westminster and Nanaimo
markets. In Texas and New Mexico, where immense herds
roam over the prairie, they become wild and unmanagable,
and numerous *raqueros* or cow boys, are employed to
"round them up," in order to mark and brand them ;
then after cutting out and turning loose all not wanted for
the "drive," those "boys" have to corral and watch the
kaviyard, all the way along the trail until a market is
secured. Here no such difficulty and expense is incurred,
for when the cattle are turned loose on arrival at the grazing
ground they wander and browse quietly during the night
off the pasturage and along the sides of the hills, but when
the sun is high there appears vast legions of old settlers,
in the shape of gad-flies, who with their shears or incisors

full a half inch long, and as sharp as razors, proceed at once to
prospect and register their claims on the hides of the unfor
tunate bovine.   This proceeding on the part of the 49-ers
render the cattle frantic and mad with joy or grief, and they
bellow, and paw, and gallop around, with their heads down
and their tails at half mast, whilst their Indian herders
quietly smoke their *peep pee kinootle,* and build up a
smoke or smudge fire, which, as soon as seen by one perse-
cuted animal,the news is telegraphed to the balance and they
come bulging and rushing home to stand in the smoke,
as if a tornado or an earthquake had stimulated them in
their exertions.   After once in the line of smoke the cattle
will stand all day and even refuse corn at $1.60 per
bushel until night comes on again, and the old settlers
have retired from the day's labor.   Sheep thrive in this
district, although the herds are not numerous.   The climate
itself is proverbially a healthy one.   It is not the fact of
having good health that is the detriment to emigration,
but how to live after you get there is the problem to be
solved, but probably that question will be settled to the
satisfaction of the politicians at least after a while, and the
glorious future of the province. will be heralded on paper,
and demonstrated at numerous dinners by a political pet
on a salary of $5,000 per annum with pickings.

Still down the Fraser various settlements of Indians,
miners, Half-breeds and Chinese are met with, such as Soda
Creek, Whiskey Creek, Dog Creek and Clinton,twenty miles
below Alexandria, a town of some 1,600 inhabitants, from
whence a little stern-wheeled steamer runs to Quesnel,
some sixty miles to the north, and located at an altitude
of 4,920 feet above the sea level ; and when water in the
Fraser is good the boat can proceed some twenty miles

still further up stream, at which point the river navigation may be said to end. The current of the Fraser is very swift, and numerous rapids occur; the rise and fall in the body of water during the freshets being something enormous, and causing in the lower Fraser, below Yale, and in the vicinity of Sumas immense damage, thus forming a grave detriment to the settlement of that portion of the country. Between Soda and Dog Creeks and Yale the mining is chiefly confined to Chinese and Indians, who make out but poorly, but the high benches which flank the course of the river give every indication that gold may be found.

Leaving the river at Clinton we strike across the Bonaparte River, meeting the Thompson at the foot of Kamloops Lake, a sheet of water some twenty-five miles in length by two to five miles in width, bordered by rolling prairie, open or slightly timbered, extending some 130 miles northward. At the head of the lake stands the old Fort, opposite the trading-posts of the H. B. Co., where the horses and brood mares of the Co. were wintered, and which now is the site of the town of Kamloops and the junction of the north and south branches of the Thompson River, which flow directly into and form the lake. So far this is the terminus of contracts awarded by the Government for the completion of the Pacific R. R., as the route from this point to the east of the Rockies, although having been decided upon, has yet to have considerable labor expended upon it. Of course since the advent of the workers on the R. R. new life and energy in the town itself has been evinced, and no doubt but it will become a distributing centre for the mineral, grazing and agricultural districts surrounding it, although for successful farming on the prairie irrigation has to be employed.   The district may in time render a fair day's wage as a mineral district, for the first gold found by the natives was in this section, and Chinamen and Indians semi-occasionally still make wages by prospecting on the Thompson.

Ashcroft, a small town some fifty-five miles from Kamloops, can either be reached by boat or road, over rolling prairie or slight hills that wear a grey and arid look, as if they longed for water, in fact, the continual cry all over the province a mile from the river is for irrigation; sand and clay, trap and basalt constitute the topography of the country to Ashcroft.   The town at present contains a promiscuous population of some 1,500; but from this town to Lytton, at the mouth of the Thompson, the river is too full, rapid and rocky for mining, and the best way to travel in this country, even with a light load, is to take a guide, an axe and a spade, and not object to working yourself, for affectation is not tolerated, and an Englishman, although he came from "Lunding," is quickly, tersely, and emphatically informed, in language more energetic than polite, that not "being a guverment officer, he isn't worth a dam," so that even in this district, style and government pay count, and a man can put on all the frills imaginable.   Lytton being at the junction of the Thompson with the Fraser is some forty-three miles below Lillooet, and fifty-seven miles above Yale, the town constitutes a good market for produce, and at present claims a population of near 600, a mixture of Roughs, Chinamen, Siwashes and Indians who reside in tumble down log shanties.   The town itself is situated upon a flat some 200 feet above the body of the river; there are several small farms and some mines in its neighborhood, mostly worked by Half-breeds and Chinese. The town was named in compliment to Lord Lytton, of whom the residents are seemingly proud. The hotel is built of big hewn logs, the chinks being filled with mud, whilst the roof is formed of barked young spruce, then a layer of hay, and an outer coating of mud about eight inches in thickness, the floors are roughly boarded or slabbed, the dining-room has a rough rock chimney in which logs are always kept burning. The sleeping apartment is divided off, by means of newspapers pasted on old sacks, and delapidated blankets into numerous small bedrooms, for the lodgment of those who put on style and wish to be private, but the odor is the same in each apartment. A room furnished with a stove, a rough pine counter, and numerous barrels all of one brand, and shelves stocked with a variety of bottles and glasses constitute the entire establishment. Meals four or six bits, drinks two bits, lodging two bits constitute the figures. The road from Ashcroft to Lytton was a part of the work undertaken on the discovery of gold in Carriboo, and although expense was great, and the difficulties in overcoming the kanyons of the Fraser and the Thompson were thought to be almost insurmountable at first, still the road is still kept in tolerable condition, the soil around is poor, sandy and arid, but less so than that further east. At Lytton the C. P. R. R. crosses the Fraser, and continues its way on the southern bank of the Thompson to Kamloops.

Following down the Fraser thirty-two miles bring us to Boston bar, at an altitude of 472 feet only above the Pacific—formerly a gold bearing bar—and then we begin to come into the, underbrush and cedars, the moss upon the trees becomes plentiful, and reminds us of old times in

Louisiana and our once happy home in Texas, but is also indicative here of a moist and rainy region. Rocks, hills and bluffs constitute the scenery, the benches or terraces show that the water in times long past ran in far greater depths than at present, which engenders solemn thought, that, when the edict went forth, "Let the dry land appear" of the vast and rushing torrent of water that swept and came tearing between these volcanic upheavals. With the exception of some small patches of open land along the river bottoms on 'which cultivation is continually attempted, and which attemps as often fails, then passing big Canyon, at the bar, we make our way some twenty-four miles to Yale, the head of steamboat navigation on the lower Fraser, and distant from Lytton fifty-six miles by road and 110 miles from New Westminster, at the mouth of the Fraser River. The town of Yale is a pretty and picturesque one, being situated on a bend of the river in a narrow gorge. A short distance below the town the Fraser "bars" at "Texas Bar" Emery Bar and American Bar, and as early as '58, gold was found in considerable quantity. At present, the town is supposed to contain some 5,000 inhabitants, it was named after one of the H. B. Co.'s officers, and is important as a forwarding point, large quantities of goods and merchandise being shipped by the semi-weekly line of steamers from New Westminster, which have to be transferred at this point to the backs of mules and mule teams for distribution in the different districts, the freight generally ranges in spring from 7½ to 10 cents per pound.

The streams in the vicinity yield good trout salmon, white fish (Talo yaz) ; little salmon, and other fish are also found in considerable quantities. Taking the steamer, a flat-

bottomed, stern-wheel boat, we find one good thing about the river, and that is if we are in a hurry to leave the country we certainly can, for the Fraser runs us down stream in one day more miles than the steamer can make going up in four. The scenery is fine along the banks : the hills rise in gradual wooded slopes for hundreds of feet, whilst bald and weather-sarred rocks loom up at intervals. Along the bottoms, to below Sumas and Chiliwack, several attempts have been made by the Siwashes and settlers at cultivation, but the terrible freshets and floods of the Fraser, have almost destroyed hope. Levees have been projected, and in part attempted by the Government, but so far but little of a permanent nature has been completed. The river here makes a bend in its course, and from almost due south runs S. W., and then westward, finally emptying into the Strait of Georgia. And just west of this point we enter into what is called the West Cascade region—a region mild in temperature rarely over 80° in the shade in summer, or 20° in the sun in winter, with a bright and clear atmosphere, with small amount of rain in summer, but heavy dews fall at night. In the fall thick fogs are of constant occurrence, but when they rise the weather continues bright and fine. In the break up the light frosts in the spring then comes on the rainy season. Altogether this region, with Vancouver Island, is the most suitable for settlers from Europe in British Columbia, besides having the great advantage of being *near the sea;* but in this humid climate very little except green crops come to perfection or thoroughly ripen. The Sumas prairie settlement contains some 25,000 acres, and has some sixty or seventy farms located ; whilst on the southern side of the river, between Chilliwack and Cheam, a distance of twelve miles, and from the river to the range

on the south, a distance of fifteen miles, is a fine stretch of
agricultural land, at present unoccupied, but subject to
overflow by the freshets of the Fraser.   Timber in plenty
for settlers' purposes, cedar, fir, pine and maple of great size,
are found on the land, but levees will have to be built
before the district becomes an attraction, for the water
rushing down, being fed by numerous streams and branches
of the different rivers which flow into the Fraser, on arriving at the lower lands or flats form immense basins, sometimes flooding an entire settlement of 31,340 acres ; and the
districts have been flooded more or less every year since the
first attempt at settlement.   Another difficulty experienced
is that of draining the district when once flooded, for the
effect of the ebb and flow of the tide in the Pacific makes
the obstacles to be surmounted in reclaiming these districts
to be still greater.   The flood of 1878 left but two houses out
of water, and those were built on the highest points of land.
The depth of water in the Sumas lake, that ordinarily is but
some four feet, rises at such times to the height of twenty-six
to twenty-eight feet.   The Indian and Half-breed settlers on
the Skow Kale have made several ineffectual attempts to
divert the calamity by erecting dykes or levees around their
farms, but, until specific action is taken by the Government,
settlers cannot be induced to locate towards the mouth of
the river, as they would naturally prefer.

Still sweeping westward, through a well wooded district,
we pass Langley, a small farming community, who supply
the markets of New Westminster and Victoria with their
produce.   The soil as we near the delta of the Fraser is
alluvial, black mould with clay bottom, something like the
Mississippi below New Orleans, or the Thames from Greenwich to Southend.   Dairy farms, stock farms and market

FORT MOODY PACIFIC TERMINUS C. P. R. R.

farms are well worked and productive. Yet passing the low tide lands and flats we soon finish the journey by landing at the wharf, in the town of New Westminster, in lat. 49° 12′47″ N., long., from Greenwich, 122° 53′ 19″.

Ten miles below, on Dease Island, is the Cooperville fishery, a canning establishment. The town, like those of delta towns generally, is but small, and at present contains some 3,000 inhabitants. The river, owing to shallow water, is not navigable for vessels over eight feet draught, so the nearest port available for shipments is at Burrard Inlet, on the other side of the spit of land that the town is located on. The saw mills generally are here situated, and the shipment of lumber is direct, the Moody Nelson Company, having agencies both in the United States and Great Britain. These mills employ on an average some ninety whites, fifty Chinese and thirty Indians, at a wage of from $1.25 to $2.25; the output of lumber from the inlet being some 30,000,000 feet with 2,000,000 feet of spars pine.

It is astonishing how naturally men take both to gambling and drinking on the coast : nothing is too small to bet on, and no anticipated pleasure so great as that of getting tight, an easy race to bet on is one prepared as follows, an Indian generally secures after a short but successful hunt two little animals called Enepoos. If he can get one with a cross on his back and the other an ordinary grey he is the more delighted ; one is christened cat-lick and the other Scotchie, a sheet of paper or piece of planed wood is secured ; two pieces of cork with pins through them make the starting and termination posts, and then the betting commences, and is carried on with enthusiasm until the race is won or lost, after which the paper is burned and a bet is made as to which animal will pop the loudest, and pay day in anticipation gives rise to the boast. " *Siwash heap patlum tomolla klip sun.*"

From the inlet to Victoria is some seventy-six miles or six hours by steamer across the Gulf of Georgia. This city is the capital of the Province, and situated on an inlet at the south-eastern extremity of Vancouver Island, in lat. 48° 25 20″ N. and long. 123° 22′ 24″ W., sixty-five miles distant from the Pacific Ocean and 750 north of San Francisco. The harbor being a shallow one, completely land-locked, vessels drawing over sixteen feet cannot enter, so the mail steamers, men-of-war and merchantmen make use of the excellent harbor of Esquimalt, three miles distant, at the north-west end of the inlet. The Town of Victoria is well laid out, and contains good streets, macadamized roads for short distances, with substantial public buildings and neat dwellings; good water is supplied the city from Elk Lake, some seven miles distant. Beacon Hill park, a pleasant ground for recreation, borders on the Straits of Fuca, and is one of the most enchanting and picturesque places on the Pacific coast. Gazing south over the straits the wild and broken Olympian range comes in view, whilst east Mount Baker raises his snow-capped head 10,700 feet skyward. Mountain ranges, islands and water stretches meet the view at every turn, whilst the healthfulness and salubrity of the climate has become known, and resulted in attracting numerous summer visitors for health or pleasure. The present population of Victoria, exclusive of Indians or Chinese, is 5,293. The harbor is well buoyed and easy of approach. Stationary harbor lights and floating lightship moored off the sands of the Fraser point the way for a night entrance. For the harbor of Esquimalt the lighthouse on Fisgard Island does duty. This light shows bright and clear to vessels approaching from the sea, but as the shores of Victoria are neared the lighthouse shows red. This harbor is a commodious one, the anchorage ground of blue clay is a good one for holding, and averages a depth of from six to eight fathoms. It is expected that as the harbor is so easy of approach that docks will be erected, and Esquimalt become the head-quarters of the Pacific squadron. The Province of British Columbia was admitted into the Dominion confederation in the year 1870, and, being comparatively out of debt, special terms had to be offered to induce her to come in, amongst which were the stipulations that Canada should be liable for all the debts of the province at the time, and was to receive by half-yearly payments in advance, interest at the rate of five per cent. on the difference per capita of debt between her and the provinces of Nova Scotia and New New Brunswick ; also that the Dominion Government grant, an annual subsidy of $35,000, and an annual grant equal to eighty cents per head of the population, then estimated at 60,000 (payable half hearly *in advance*), until that population reaches the number of 400,000 ; also to provide mail service fortnightly to San Francisco, and semi-weekly to Olympia, and also defray the salary of the Lieutenant Governor, $9,000. Administration of justice average $45,616, the revenue being $517,261.57, cost of collection $21,055.70; customs and revenue, postal and telegraphic service, lighthouses, quarantine and hospitals, geological survey and penitentiary, besides pensioning off old officials, building a graving dock, to cost $500,000 at Esquimalt, and guaranteeing interest at 5 per cent. per annum on the work—the total Dominion subsidy approximating $225,-029.09, whilst the total revenue considered necessary amounts to 603,543.00. To allow British Columbia

to be represented in the Dominion Senate at Ottawa
by three members and by six members in the House
of Commons, which representation will be increased, for
which privileges and emoluments, the Government of
British Columbia consented to join the Confederation
and give to the Dominion the public lands of the province
along the line of the C.P.R.R., not to exceed twenty
miles on each side ; and, in consideration of the land so to be
conveyed, to aid in the construction of the Railway the
Dominion Government must further pay to the province,
the sum of $100,000 per annum, in half-yearly payments,
in advance.   So, from appearances, B. C. was not so cheap
an addition after all.

The Island of Vancouver contains an area of nearly
12,000 square miles, its length is 282, breadth from
thirty to sixty-five miles, its surface is very mountainous and woody, whilst its sides are pierced by numerous estuaries, inlets, sounds and harbors available for
the deepest-draughted ships. The most mountainous region
is inland, whilst the highest peaks, Albert Edward (6958),
Alexander (6500), Crown Mounts (6082), Victoria (7484)
and Mt. Alston (6,500) are all situated towards the north
of the island   The surface of the west coast is covered
with good timber, fir, hemlock and cedar, whilst its ribs
are seamed with the best coal on the Pacific coast, and also
producing some of the finer metals, with agricultural lands of
sufficient area for 30,000 country people, whose labor would
produce sufficient to feed a population of a million.   The
islands adjacent in the strait of Georgia have capacity for
raising the finer grades of sheep.   The waters that lave its
shores abound with fish, from the sturgeon, peet, yaz, talo
yaz (little salmon), white fish, loche, carp, salmon,—which,

by the way, when they once enter the rivers of the mainland to spawn are never known to return to the sea, for after wearing out their tails, fins and scales in the ascent, look so dejected and forlorn that they quietly lay down and die in myriads in the pools and eddies of the rivers. Another valuable and prolific fish that abounds in these waters is the oolahan ; it appears in immense shoals and is caught both with the scoop net and the rake, like the bunker of the New England coast; it is very fat and oily, and esteemed good eating, but when dried it has other uses, for the natives put its head in a beer bottle and, lighting the tail end, they burn it for a candle. The halibut, cod, smelt, flounder and sardine are also found. The climate is unsurpassed for salubrity, being, like New Mexico, mild and genial. Tender plants are nurtured in the open air, whilst from the mountains rushes a water-power sufficient to drive the looms of the worlds. The following extract shows the available lands for cultivation : near Victoria, say 100,000 acres ; Saanich peninsula, 37 square miles, 64,000 acres ; Sooke, 3500 acres ; Cowichan, 100,000 acres ; Salt Spring Island contains an area of 90 square miles, of which some 5,750 acres are fit for settlement ; Nanaimo District has 45,000 acres cultivable land ; whilst Comas boasts of 50,000 acres, as good and as fertile as any in the Dominion. The Chinese in Victoria are many of them well established in business, as butchers, grocers, merchants, hotel and restaurant keepers, etc., and old residents, instead of, like Bill Nye, bewailing the fact, and asserting that " we're ruined by Chinese cheap labor," make the best of the disadvantages they labor under, and stand the heathen off for a month's fodder, and then withdraw their custom to patronize his rival, and by that means keep within the

breast of the heathen a spirit of humility, instead of arrogan e
and pride, for, when a Chinaman gets too ostentatious, he is
occasionally cleaned out entirely, but still that operation
occurs so seldom as really not to count.

British Columbia is represented in the Dominion Parliament by members in the Senate and members in the House
of Commons; is governed by her Lieut. Governor, who
receives a salary of $9000 per annum; and also has her
provincial or local legislature of members.

From Victoria the steamers Maude and Cariboo Fly
make fortnightly trips to Nanaimo, seventy-five miles distant, Comox, sixty miles from Nanaimo, and other ports on
the east coast of Vancouver Island, calling on the return at
landings on Texada and Salt Island. The fare to Nanaimo
is $4.00 single, and return $6.50; to Comox is $6.00
return $10.00; meals on board are : breakfast and tea 50c.,
dinner 75c., which is certainly within reason, whilst the
table set far exceeds that of the mail lines on the Eastern
lakes and St. Lawrence. Freight to all landings between
Victoria and Nanaimo is the same, viz., $3.00 per ton of
forty feet, to Comox $4.00 per ton; cattle being brought
from those points to market in Victoria are charged at the
rate of from $5.00 to $6.00 per head respectively. The
Town of Nanaimo was originally established by the development of the coal mines worked in the vicinity. The.
coal at this place and Newcastle Island is said to be the
best produced on the Pacific coast. The coal fields are composed of coarse grits, sandstones and shale. The seams of
coal by the association of the various fossils is claimed
to have been formed in the Cretaceous age. The coal yields
over 10,000 cubic feet per ton of 2,240 lbs, has an
illuminating power of sixteen candles, and produces

HAMOTHCO RIVER, B.C.

a good coke. An analysis gives its composition as follows : carbon sixty-eight, volatile matter twenty-two, ash ten, hydrogen 5.32, nitrogen 1.02, sulphur 2.20, oxygen 8.70. The same class coal is also produced in quantity across the harbor on Newcastle Island, whilst the free-stone quarry on the island is also successfully worked. The present population of Nanaimo is about 1200 adults and 400 to 500 Chinese.

The next landing, Comox, is the place of shipment for a small agricultural community: the village numbers about 100, which is in part supported by the Baynes Sound Coal Company, who own at Baynes Sound, some ten miles S. E. of Comox, over 5000 acres of excellent Coal lands. A new saw mill has lately been erected, in order to supply lumber, wharves, laborers, buildings, etc., etc., without necessitating the labor and expense of bringing it from the mainland. The trip down the Straits of Georgia is a pleasant and delightful one, the sky serene, the air clear and bracing, cool and invigorating, not too warm during the day, after the morning mists rises, and not too cool for exercise in the evening,--so we wend our way among the many islands that dot the Straits, either admiring the everlasting ranges and hills to be seen on either hand, or speculating as to the names of the numerous mountains that prominently stand taller than their fellows; and, when tired of constant gazing, take a quiet hand at poker, or imbibe a jigger of red-eye, at two bits a drink, or $1.00 for the hull crowd. Soon again we enter the narrow entrance to the harbor, and shortly afterwards land at the Stone Street wharf. There are several good hotels in Victoria, and the charges are very reasonable, which is more than can be said of some hotels in the Eastern Provinces. The Pacific Telegraph Hotel, by Andrew Astrico, and the

Temperance Hotel are about the best—the charges at either
not exceeding $7.00 per week ; whilst, should a good whole-
some, cléanly-served meal be desired, at the Eagle Restaurant is the place to obtain it; and its proprietors, Ah Poi
and Wung Pow, are the Celestials who will wait upon you
to your entire satisfaction.

Crossing the spit of land between Victoria and Esquimalt,
we reach the latter port in time to embark on the good steamer Vancouver, bound for the Golden Gate and San Francisco, some 760 miles away. And after a nearly three days
trip are landed in that beautiful and extravagant city, from
whence we are to endeavor to reach San Diego, the Lower
California terminus of the Southern or Texas Pacific Railway, a line which, throughout its entire route, runs through
a country smiled upon by everlasting spring.

FINISH.

Regarding the apparent future of the Dominion but few
words will suffice. This is but one Continent from the
" Pole to Panama," then why should not interests be mutual,
and the inhabitants brothers, let their residence be above the
Lake of the Woods or below the table lands of Mexico.
Whether Canada annexes the United States, or in time
becomes a part and parcel of the country where so many Canadians have found a welcome and a home, would make but
little difference to the people at large, and the amalgamation
of interests would but be opposed by the politicians, who
are, all over the Continent, each year losing more and more
of the feeble hold and sway they have over the minds of the
people, who are generally beginning to think and act inde-
pendently and in accordance with their own ideas, in the

interests of the whole country, instead of confining themselves to petty and sectional jealousies. But a short time since that despicable spirit was dominant, the Eastern Provinces would almost "Boycott" Quebec, whilst Ontario declared it her duty to form the friendship whereby she was most benefited, and opposed and hated Quebec, which hatred is generously returned; whilst Columbia declared that if she was too much governed by the East she would secede, and so leave the barren Eastern Provinces to their fate. These jealousies, although, as the North West settles up, each year will assume greater portions, and, from a mild murmur at first, will in time cause serious and bitter trouble all along the border, for the people will hardly have the meekness of the old-time Lowlander to allow the " Picts" and " Scots" to invade and despoil at their pleasure. The countries are one in land, but the people are the opposites in character. When the Canadian or European crosses the border he is made to feel that he is welcome, and urged to become a citizen, but when the stranger arrives in Canada he is literally frozen out, even the religious community joining in the belief that to assist the new comer to obtain a foot-hold would not be "business," for fear he would become independent both in thought and action.

It is somewhat remarkable to notice how closely in all respects the lands of the far North West resemble those of the far South on the Northern Continent of America, or the country bordering on the Arctic circle becomes a counterpart of that portion lying near the equator. The same barren stretches of everlasting sand; the tangled cypress under-growths and swamps, amid whose precincts frogs abound in myriads, and keep up a continuous concert; some emit sounds like hammering on thin tin, others seem to

mimic the hoot of the owl, others squeak, whilst, above all,
the hoarse basso-profundo of the genuine bull-frog makes
itself heard, and lets folks know " he's thar." They and the
wild fowl that frequent the locality in the spring and fall
with the squirrels, and seem to be the only denizens of these
vast tracts, the knotted everglades, the strips of fertile and
productive soil, with the salt marshes and salt springs that
at some future time will, no doubt, become a source of
revenue, and, with the assistance of Artesian wells (should
pure and drinkable water be found in their vicinity), may
become the means of attracting quite a little community of
settlers for the development of the industry of salt evapor-
ation and export.   The mountain ranges and broken ground
all have their fac-similes above lat. 50° N., and below lat.
34". N., therefore the commercial interests of both these
extreme sections are, to all intents and purposes, identical ;
the seasons in the southern portion being neither so severe,
nor yet so limited in duration, although more prone to
enervating fevers than those of the far North ; but, where
frost is seen almost every night in the year, and ice forms
in August, the constitution and frame must be one of iron
in order to withstand its rigors.   It will therefore become
a matter for deep and earnest thought and consideration to
the intendent citizen, whether he be from the provinces or
from the older countries, to fully determine how and where
to select his place of destination, for a mistake at the start
to a man of family may be fatal to the energies of a life-
time ; therefore very little heed should be paid to the agents
of large corporations, who for the most part have little
interest in promoting the welfare of the new-comer, and whose
chief aims are to get settlers located on the lands represented by themselves, and to receive their salary and com-

mission, sometimes earning it at the expense of the lifetime happiness of those whom they have induce to come. That the older countries and Canada are to attempt a governmental organized system of emigration, in order to colonize the far west with permanent settlers, seems to be a conceded fact; but after offering, perhaps, superior inducements for a while, whether the Bureau will not degenerate into a mere political machine, yet remains to be seen. It is therefore probably far the best course to pursue in determining a location, to obtain and act upon advice from parties directly residing in the district desired, and to rely more thoroughly on the statements of extensive property owners, who at once become neighbors, and who represent the interests of the whole community. Should the citizens of the Upper and Lower Provinces become more liberal in their views on the encouragement, and welcome the new arrival to a home in their respective provinces, no doubt it would not only redound to the benefit of the community, but assist materially in adding to the wealth of the province itself; whilst, on the other hand, citizens leaving the older portions for the West would at once be climated, and with a knowledge of the obstacles to be met and overcome. In many portions of New Brunswick, Quebec, along the banks of the St. Lawrence and the Ottawa rivers, and in the province of Ontario are opportunities offered to the settler and investor which in many respects are unrivaled, but a spirit of pride in being an American will have to be first evinced, and a spirit of jealousy and sectionalism obliterated, before any great influx of either capital or labor can be induced to, assist in building up the prosperity of a section, or in working altogether in the interest of the country.

The most Homelike and Comfortable Hotel

AT THE SEAT OF GOVERNMENT IS

THE WINDSOR,

OTTAWA, Ont.

E. DANIELS, Proprietor.

For Merchants, Travellers, Tourists and Business Men, this Hotel
is most admirably situated, being [in close proximity to the Parliament House,
Banks, and Business
Offices.

RATES, $2 PER DAY.

Strictly moderate for a first-class House,

Its rooms are cool, airy and comfortable, whilst its appointments
are in every respect first-class.

SPECIAL ARRANGEMENTS FOR VISITORS REMAINING BY THE MONTH.

Good Drives,
Fine Scenery
and Pleasant Boating

EXCURSIONS CAN BE INDULGED IN.

THE OLD HAT.

I had a hat it was not all a hat—part of the rim was gone, yet still I wore it on, and people wondered as I passed; some turned to gaze, others just cast an eye and soon withdrew it, as 'twere in contempt, but still my 'hat, although so fashionless, in complement extreme had that within surpassing show. My head continued warm —being sheltered from the weather—spite of all the want (as has been said before of brim.

A change came o'er the color of my hat—that which was black grew brown, and then men stared with both their eyes (they stared with one before); the wonder now was twofold, and it seemed strange that a thing so torn and old should still be worn by one who might— but let that pass, I had my reasons, which might be revealed but for some counter reasons, far more strong, which tied my tongue to silence. Time passed: green spring, and flowery summer, autumn and frosty winter came, and went, and came again, but still, through the seasons of two years, in park, in city, yea at routs and balls, the hat was worn and borne. Then folks grew wild with curiosity, and whispers rose, and questions passed about—how one so trim in coats, boots, pumps, gloves, trousers, could ensconce his caput in a covering so vile.

A change came o'er the nature of my hat—grease spots appeared, but still in silence on I wore it; and then family and friends glared madly at each other. There was one who said— but, hold, no matter what he said,—a time may come when I— Away, away, not till the season's ripe can I reveal thoughts that lie too deep for common minds, —till then the world shall not pluck out the heart of this my mystery. When I will I will!'

The hat was now greasy, and old, and torn; but torn, old, greasy, still I wore it on. A change came o'er the business of this hat—women and men and children scowled on me; my company was shunned. I was alone; none would associate with such a hat. Friendship itself proved faithless for a hat. She that I loved, within whose gentle breast I treasured up my heart, looked cold as death. Love's fires went out, extinguished by a hat. Of those who knew me best, some turned aside, and scooted down dark lanes; one man did place his finger on his nose's side and smiled. Others in horrid mockery laughed outright. Yea, dogs, deceived by instinct's dubious ray, fixing their owlet glare upon my ragged hat, mistook me for a beggar, and they barked. Thus, women, men, friends, strangers, lovers dogs—one thought pervaded all : it was my hat!

A change, it was the last, came o'er this hat, For, lo! at length the circling months went, the period was accomplished; and one day this tattered, brown, old, greasy coverture, (time had endeared its vileness) was transferred to the possession of a wandering son of Israel's fated race, and friends once more greeted my digits with the wonted squeeze. Once more I went my way alone along, and plucked no wondering gaze the hand of scorn with it, annoying finger; men and dogs once more grew pointless jokeless, laughless, growlless, and at last, not least of rescued blessings love—love smiled on me again, when I assumed a bran new beaver of famed Samuel's mould, and then the laugh was mine, for then outcame the secret of this strangeness—'twas a bet.

THE ST. LAWRENCE HALL,

ST. LAWRENCE HALL.

HENRY HOGAN, Proprietor,
St. James St., Montreal, P. Q., Canada.

For the past thirty years this hotel familiarly known as the "St. Lawrence," has been a "household word" to all travellers on the continent of North America, and has been patronized by all the Royal and noble personages who have visited the City of Montreal.

This Hotel, including the entire block, has recently been acquired by MR. HENRY HOGAN, the former proprietor, who has handsomely and appropriately decorated and renovated the interior, and completely refitted the whole of the apartments with new furniture, comprising 100 new rooms, making the present number of apartments 250 ; a new and elegant passenger elevator has also been added, whilst the halls and public rooms are illuminated by the Electric and in-candescent lights, making it the most attractively lighted hotel in the Dominion.

The Hotel is admirably situated, being in the very heart of the city, and con-tiguous to the General Post Office, the principal Banks, Public Buildings, Law Courts, Commercial Exchanges, Railway and Telegraph Offices.

The Hotel will be managed by MR. SAMUEL MONTGOMERY, under the immediate personal supervision of Mr. Hogan, than whom no one is better qualified to conduct an hostelry of such magnitude as the St. Lawrence Hall, and than whom no one has gained a better reputation as an obliging, generous and con-siderate host.

TERMS MODERATE.

LAND REGULATIONS

OF THE

Canadian Pacific Railway Co.

The Company offer lands in the Fertile Belt of Manitoba and the North-West Territory, for sale, on certain conditions as to cultivation, at the price of $2.50 (10s. stg.) per acre, one-sixth payable in cash, and the balance in five annual instalments, with interest at six per cent. a rebate of fifty per cent., for actual cultivation being made as hereinafter described.

The ordinary conditions of sale are :—

1. That all improvements placed upon land purchased shall remain thereon until final payment for the land has been made.

2. That all taxes and assessments lawfully imposed upon the land or improvements shall be paid by the purchaser.

3. The Company reserve from selection at the above price, all mineral, coal, or woodlands, stone, slate, and marble quarries, lands with water power thereon, and tracts for town sites and railway purposes ; and, as regards lands having some standing wood, but not hereby excluded from selection, the purchaser will only be permitted to cut a sufficient quantity for fuel, fencing, and for the erection of buildings on his land until he shall have received the final conveyance thereof.

4. The mineral and coal lands and quarries, and the lands controlling water power, will be disposed of on very liberal terms to persons giving satisfactory evidence of their intention to utilize them.

5. The purchaser will be required, within four years from the date of the contract for the purchase of the land, to bring under cultivation, and sow and reap, a crop on one-half of the said land, except when otherwise expressly agreed and declared in the contract by reason of any special obstacle to such cultivation. Dairy farming, or mixed grain and dairy farming, to an extent to be agreed upon, will be accepted as the equivalent of cultivation, entitling the settler to the rebate.

6. A credit of $1.25 (5s stg.) per acre will be allowed for all land so cultivated during four years.

7. A reservation of 100 feet in width for right of way, or other railroad purposes, will be made in all cases.

8. If the purchaser of a section, or part of a section, being a *bona fide* settler resident upon the land purchased, or upon an adjoining section, fails to carry out in their entirety the conditions of his contract with respect to cultivation and cropping, within the specified time, the Company reserve the right, in their own option, to diminish the quantity to be conveyed to him, under his contract, to such extent that he shall not be entitled to demand a conveyance of more than double the quantity cultivated and cropped, the quantity which he may so demand not to exceed one-half of the quantity mentioned in his contract, and, if not exceeding 160 acres, to be taken in the quarter section in which the greater part of such cultivation and cropping has been done ; or, if in excess of 160 acres, then such excess to be taken from an adjoining quarter section ; and as to the portion of the land contracted for, which the Company shall decide not to convey to such purchaser, his claim to the same shall be forfeited, ands uch portion shall not be conveyed to him by the Company ; and thereupon the price shall be adjusted as if the contract of sale had originally been made for the portion actually conveyed to the purchaser.

The object of the foregoing clause is to prevent the Company's lands from falling into the hands of speculators to the disadvantage of the actual settler ; but as respects *bona fide* settlers, the purpose and aim of the Company is to afford them every possible consideration and facility.

9. Special contracts will be made for tracts exceeding one section, for settlement purposes or for cattle raising.

10. Liberal rates for settlers and their effects will be granted by the Company over its railway.

11. The land grant bonds of the Company will be received at 10 per cent. premium on their par value with accrued interest, in payment for lands, thus further reducing the price of the land to the purchaser.

For further information, apply at the office of the Company, Bartholomew Place, London, England ; to John H. McTavish, Land Commissioner, Winnipeg, Manitoba, or to the Secretary of the Company, at Montreal, Canada.

GEORGE STEPHEN, President.

CHARLES DRINKWATER, Secretary.

W. S. WALKER, B.C.L.,

Barrister, Advocate, &c.

COMMISSIONER FOR

Ontario,

Quebec,

New Brunswick,

Nova Scotia

& Manitoba.

Member of the United States Law Association.

Issuer of Marriage Licenses for the Province of Quebec.

OFFICE: 59 ST. FRANCOIS XAVIER ST.,

ALLAN RUTHERFORD,

(LATE 3d AUDITOR U. S. TREASURY,)

Attorney and Counsellor at Law,

Corcoran Building, 15th and F Streets, Room No. 99,

(OPPOSITE TREASURY DEPARTMENT.)

WASHINGTON, D. C.

Will practice before the Supreme Court of the United States, Court of Claims, Claims Commissions, and the different Committees of Congress. Being thoroughly familiar with the course of business before the Executive Departments, will give special attention to all matters before the Patent Office, General Land Office, Treasury, War, Interior and other Departments.

REFERS TO

Hon. JOHN C. NEW, Assistant Secretary U. S. Treasury,
Washington, D. C.

Hon. JAS. GILFILLAN, Treasurer of the U. S., Washington, D. C.

Hon. HENRY C. JOHNSON, Commissioner of Customs,
Washington, D. C.

Hon. O. FERRIS, 2d Auditor U. S. Treasury, Washington, D. C.

Hon. E. W. KEIGHTLEY, 3d Auditor U. S. Treasury,
Washington, D. C.

Hon. JACOB H. ELA, 6th Auditor U. S. Treasury, Washington, D.C.

Hon. SAMUEL F. PHILLIPS, Solicitor-General, U. S.,
Washington, D. C.

THE .RUSSELL,

OTTAWA, Ont.

THE SEAT OF GOVERNMENT.

Travellers, Tourists, and Canadians generally, should remember that since the additions and alterations have been completed "The Russell" is admitted to be one of the most.

Recherche Houses of the Dominion,

and has a capacity for over 400 guests. It is now fitted with every improvement that Art or Science can suggest, making it at once the most desirable and the most comfortable in Canada, and is the favorite with the members and officials generally.

Cool, Neat and Comfortable Rooms.

Cuisine the best the Country afford .

Whilst all its appointments are strictly first class.

A GENIAL HOST WHO ANTICIPATES THE WANTS OF HIS GUESTS.

In close proximity to the houses of Parliament, and business centres of the city.

Lovely Drives, Fine Scenery and good g·ounds for recreation, near at hand.

An excellent Livery in connection with the Hotel.

J. A. GOUIN,
Proprietor.

INTERNATIONAL POSTAL CARDS RECEIVE PROMPT ATTENTION.

LIST OF WATERS
ON EXHIBIT.

CHARLES GURD & CO.
BELFAST GINGER ALE.
SUPER CARBONATED SODA WATER
SARSAPARILLA   LEMONADE.
LEMON SODA   CHAMPAGNE CIDER
MINERAL   WATERS.
SELTZER WATER   ESSENCE WATER
VICHY,   POTASH.
CHALYBEATE,   LITHIA.
CARLSBAD SPRUDEL.

GOD BLESS OUR DOMINION
THE CELE   MINERAL

TWO
FIRST PRIZES
AWARDED
1880.

GOLD
MEDAL
AWARDED
1881.

CHARLES GURD & CO.

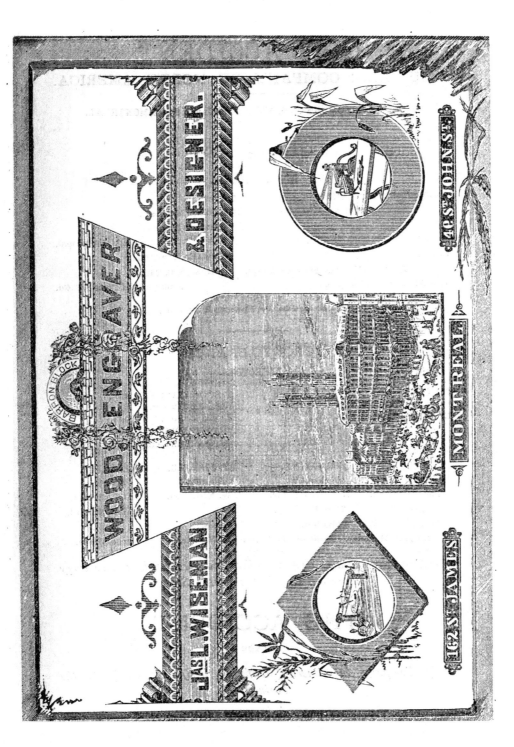

JAS. L. WISEMAN

WOOD ENGRAVER & DESIGNER.

BARRON BLOCK

MONTREAL

40 ST. JOHN ST.

162 ST. JAMES

THE ACCIDENT
INSURANCE COMPANY OF NORTH AMERICA.

HEAD OFFICE OF THE COMPANY, 260 St. James Street, MONTREAL.

DIRECTORS.

MONTREAL.

President.—SIR ALEXANDER T. GALT, G.C.M.G.,

Vice-President.—JOHN RANKIN, ESQ., Merchant.

	EDWARD MACKAY,
HON. JAMES FERRIER, Senator.	Director Bank of Montreal.
D. L. MacDOUGALL,	EDWARD RAWLINGS.
President Montreal Stock Exchange.	WM. MOORE, Quebec,
WM. ALEXANDER, Toronto.	Manager Gulf Ports S. S. Co.

Managing Director, EDWARD RAWLINGS.

TORONTO BRANCH.
DIRECTORS.

Col. C. S. GZOWSKI,	T. SUTHERLAND STAYNER.
Vice-President, Ontario Bank.	WM. ALEXANDER.
Hon. D. L. MACPHERSON,	JAMES MICHIE,
President of the Senate.	Director Canadian Bank of Commerce.

Agents.—GZOWSKI & BUCHAN, Corner Toronto and King Streets.

QUEBEC.	HALIFAX, N.S.	ST. JOHN, N.B.	HAMILTON.
Directors.	*Directors.*	*Director.*	*Directors.*
Pierre Garneau.	Hon W. J. Stairs.	J. W. Nicholson.	A. G. Ramsay.
Jas. G. Ross.	Thos. E. Kenny.		W. E. Sanford.
Wm. Moore.	Adam Burns.	*Agent.*	*Agent.*
Agent.—T. H. Mahoney.	*Agent.*—G. M. Greer.	E. W. Gale.	Seneca Jones.

The Company has also Branch Offices and Agencies in nearly every important City in the United States.

THE ACCIDENT

IS THE

Only Company in America confining itself exclusively to the business of

INSURANCE AGAINST ACCIDENTS.

CPSIA information can be obtained
at www.ICGtesting.com
Printed in the USA
LVOW01*0224121216
516869LV00008B/65/P